UNSPEAKABLE SUBJ

Pgs 5/6
Pg1dd
Pg 168

UNSPEAKABLE SUBJECTS

FEMINIST ESSAYS IN LEGAL AND SOCIAL THEORY

NICOLA LACEY

·HART·
PUBLISHING

OXFORD

1998

Hart Publishing
Oxford
UK

Distributed in the United States by
Northwestern University Press
625 Colfax, Evanston
Illinois 60208–4210 USA

Distributed in Australia and New Zealand by
Federation Press
PO Box 45, Annandale
NSW 203 Australia

Distributed in the Netherlands, Belgium and Luxembourg by
Intersentia, Churchillaan 108
B2900 Choten, Antwerp
Belgium

Hart Publishing is a specialist legal publisher based in Oxford, England.
To order further copies of this book or to request a list of other publications
please write to:

Hart Publishing, 19 Whitehouse Road, Oxford, OX1 4PA
Telephone: +44 (0)1865 434459 or Fax: +44 (0)1865 794882
e-mail: hartpub@janep.demon.co.uk

British Library Cataloguing in Publication Data
Data Available
ISBN 1–901362–33–7 (cloth)
1–901362–34–5 (paper)

Typeset in 12pt Bembo
by SetAll, Abingdon
Printed in Great Britain on acid-free paper
by Biddles Ltd., Guildford and King's Lynn

Acknowledgments

The author and publishers thank the following for their permission to reproduce copyright material:

Mansell Publishers, for "From Individual to Group?", from B.A. Hepple and E. Szyszczak, *Discrimination: The Limits of Law* (1992) pp. 99–124; Sage Publications, for "Theories of Justice and the Welfare State", from (1992) 1 *Social and Legal Studies* pp. 323–44 and for "Normative Reconstruction in Socio-Legal Theory", from (1996) 5 *Social and Legal Studies* pp. 131–57; Blackwell Publishers for "Theory into Practice: Pornography and the Public/Private Dichotomy", from (1993) 20 *Journal of Law and Society* pp. 93–113; JAI Press Inc. for "Community in Legal Theory: Idea, Ideal or Ideology?", from (1996) 15 *Studies in Law, Politics and Society* pp. 105–46; The Faculty of Law of the University of Western Ontario, for "Unspeakable Subjects, Impossible Rights", from (1998) *Canadian Journal of Law and Jurisprudence*; Edinburgh University Press, for "Closure and Critique in Feminist Jurisprudence", from Alan Norrie (ed.), *Closure or Critique: New Directions in Legal Theory* (1993) pp. 194–213; and Oxford University Press, for "Feminist Legal Theory Beyond Neutrality", from (1995) 48 *Current Legal Problems* pp. 1–38.

Contents

Acknowledgments   v
Preface   ix

Introduction to the Essays   1

PART I: FEMINIST CRITIQUE OF INDIVIDUALISM IN LEGAL
AND POLITICAL THOUGHT

1. From Individual to Group? A Feminist Analysis of
   the Limits of Anti-Discrimination Legislation   19
2. Theories of Justice and the Welfare State: A Feminist
   Critique   46
3. Theory into Practice? Pornography and the
   Public/Private Dichotomy   71
4. Unspeakable Subjects, Impossible Rights: Sexuality,
   Integrity and Criminal Law   98
5. Community in Legal Theory: Idea, Ideal or
   Ideology?   125

PART II: QUESTIONS OF METHOD IN FEMINIST LEGAL
THEORY: WITHIN OR BEYOND CRITIQUE?

6. Closure and Critique in Feminist Jurisprudence:
   Transcending the Dichotomy or a Foot in Both
   Camps?   167
7. Feminist Legal Theory Beyond Neutrality   188
8. Normative Reconstruction in Socio-Legal Theory   221

Bibliography   251
Index   267

Preface

The essays which appear (in modified form) in this book were written during the last seven years, and develop ideas which have been forming over a longer period. During this time I have incurred far more debts of intellectual gratitude than I can possibly acknowledge here. I do, however, want to mention a number of people and institutions whose influence on my work in feminist theory have been of particular importance.

My interest in issues of law and gender was first prompted by workshops run by the Women Law Teachers Group in the early 1980s, and further stimulated by discussions at the conference "Feminist Perspectives on Law" organised by the Women's Caucus of the European Critical Legal Conference in 1986 and by seminars run by the Oxford University Women's Studies Committee between 1984 and 1990. Perhaps (optimistically) because the impetus for their existence has been diluted by the diffusion of lively pockets of feminist endeavour in a number of law schools and conferences around the country and in the journal *Feminist Legal Studies*, or (pessimistically) because of the increasingly pressured academic environment, the first two of these groups have since disbanded. They have, however, had a lasting influence on my work, and several former members remain among my closest colleagues. My editorial involvement with the proceedings of the 1986 conference led to my becoming an associate editor of the *International Journal of the Sociology of Law* and then, in 1992, of *Social and Legal Studies*. The editorial boards of these two journals have been a constant source of both personal support and intellectual exchange about feminist ideas. My two and a half years in the Law Department at Birkbeck College provided me, for the first time, with a working environment which not only tolerated but positively encouraged the incorporation of feminist analysis in legal education, and with a wonderful group of colleagues who shared many of my intellectual concerns. My criminal law and jurisprudence students at Birkbeck, as well as the students at Oxford University who attended Mary Stokes' and my feminist legal theory seminars, and my students at the Australian National University in

1992 and at the Humboldt University in Berlin in 1996, gave me lots of ideas and reassured me that the effort to introduce feminist issues to the law curriculum was worthwhile. As several of the essays in this collection argue, the capacities of any individual depend upon her social environment, and I feel very lucky to have been associated with each of these institutions.

Another set of feminist themes which find expression in this collection have to do with the connections between private and public, personal and political, affective and rational dimensions of human life. It is therefore a particular pleasure to be able to acknowledge the importance of a number of friendships for the work represented in this book. I should like to thank Susanne Baer, Elizabeth Frazer, Sandra Fredman, Ngaire Naffine, Katherine O'Donovan, Frances Olsen, Renata Salecl, Suzanne Shale, Carol Smart, Mary Stokes, Celia Wells and Lucia Zedner, not only for their generosity in commenting on papers and debating ideas over the years, but also for leavening the academic world with that most indispensable intellectual resource: a sense of humour. Richard Hart has been an exemplary editor, combining efficiency, support and genuine intellectual engagement on a scale rarely encountered in the world of academic publishing. Finally, but principally, David Soskice discussed many of the ideas in this book with me, allowing me to convince him (well, *most* of the time . . .) of the importance of feminist social theory, and convincing me in turn (well, *most* of the time . . .) that men can be good feminists. Along the way, among other things, he cooked me wonderful dinners and made me laugh a great deal. This book is dedicated, with my love, to him.

NICOLA LACEY

London, 1997

An introduction to the essays

Let me begin with an admission. If somebody had told me, when I graduated from University College London in 1979, that a decade later I would regard feminist legal theory as an important part of my work, I should have been quite baffled. While, like many of my contemporaries, I found it natural to describe myself as a feminist, the idea that feminism might be of relevance to the content of my legal education had simply not occurred to me. When I returned to UCL as a lecturer in 1981, after two years as a graduate student in Oxford— an experience which had done nothing to change my consciousness on the matter—I heard that a group of women legal scholars were meeting regularly under the aegis of the Women Law Teachers Group. I had, of course, noticed with irritation that I was one of only five women law teachers at UCL. (The students had noticed it, too, and large numbers were soon beating a path to my door, looking for a sympathetic ear to a variety of problems, notably the legal profession's continuing resistance to genuine equal opportunities a mere six years after the enactment of the Sex Discrimination Act . . .) So I went along to a meeting of the Group, looking forward to extending my network of female colleagues and to exchanging experiences of life as a woman in the academy. What I encountered was something very different, and a great deal more disturbing. Certainly, the Group provided a supportive network which was, and remains, of great personal importance to me. What I was not prepared for was that it introduced me to a set of intellectual debates which would gradually, over the next few years, lead me to question a number of the most basic assumptions upon which my legal education—and my own teaching—had been founded.

The essays which form this collection themselves tell the story of this intellectual journey, and I do not propose to summarise either the essays or the direction of the route in this introduction. I do, however, want the introduction to achieve two things. The first is to give a sense of why this journey seemed necessary to me, in the hope of convincing the reader that it will be worth accompanying me in the pages which follow. The second is to identify some broad themes which run through the essays, in the hope of helping the reader to maintain a sense of continuous direction notwithstanding the varied practical terrain occupied by the different chapters. By providing at this stage a broad definition of what I mean by feminist legal theory, and by identifying how I take feminist legal theory to relate to various other forms of legal and social thought, I also hope to give the reader a sense of what distinguishes my own approach from that of other writers in what is now—happily—a fertile and variegated field of legal scholarship.[1]

Characterising feminist legal theory

I need, then, to begin by saying something about what I mean by "feminist legal theory". There are two questions here. First, what do I mean by "feminist *legal theory*" as opposed to "feminist criticism of particular laws"? The two are, of course, rather different. When I went to my first meeting of the Women Law Teachers Group, I certainly did not need to be convinced that, for example, the law of rape operated in deeply objectionable ways from even the most moderately feminist point of view. The idea of feminist legal theory, however, goes much further, in that it suggests that there is something not merely about particular laws or sets of laws, but rather, and more generally, about the very structure or method of modern law, which is hierarchically gendered. To most lawyers this is a far more counterintuitive claim than that of feminist bias in particular laws. It is, however, absolutely central to any strong feminist theory of law. All of the essays in this collection, therefore, engage at some level with the question of whether there are things of a *general* nature to be said about what we might call the sex or gender of law.[2]

But this is to say only something very vague about what makes a "legal theory" *feminist*. It is crucial to acknowledge from the outset

[1] See for example Bottomley (ed.) (1996); Bottomley and Conaghan (eds.) (1993); Cornell (1991), (1995); O'Donovan (1985); Naffine (1990); Naffine and Owens (eds.) (1997); Olsen (ed.) (1995); Smart (1989), (1995).

[2] In this introduction, I shall use the terms "sex" and "gender" interchangeably. In early feminist scholarship, it was usual to draw a strong distinction between the two, with "sex" referring to bodily or biological characteristics and "gender" to the social roles and meanings attached to particular sexed bodies. "Sex" was taken as given, and "gender", understood as a social construct, was the primary analytic tool of feminist thought. As time has gone on, however, feminist theory has questioned the sex/gender distinction, and has been increasingly inclined to view sex as much as gender as socially constructed. These developments are discussed in detail in Chapters 4 and 7: see further MacKinnon (1989); Lacey (1997).

that to refer to "feminist legal theory" is to gather together a set of heterogeneous approaches, many of which make appearances in the chapters of this book. In this introduction, I shall not be concerned with these important differences. I shall simply set out from an inclusive conception of feminist legal theory as proceeding from two foundational claims and as characterised by a particular methodological orientation. First, at an analytic and indeed sociological level, and on the basis of a wide range of research in a number of disciplines, feminist legal theorists take sex/gender to be one important social structure or discourse. Feminists hence claim that sex/gender characterises the shape of law as one important social institution. Analytically, therefore, feminist legal theory aspires to provide a more sophisticated conception of law than can theories which ignore the influence of sex/gender. Secondly, at a normative or political level, feminist legal theorists claim that the ways in which sex/gender has shaped the legal realm are presumptively politically and ethically problematic, in that sex/gender is an axis not merely of differentiation but also of discrimination, domination or oppression. Normatively, therefore, feminist legal theory aspires to produce both a reasoned critique of current legal arrangements and—in some versions—a positive conception or vision of how law might be constructed in ways which move towards ideals of sex equality or gender justice. Though not all feminist legal theorists endorse a utopian project, the critical reconstruction of ideas of equality, justice and rights has been one of the most persistent preoccupations of feminist legal thought.[3] Finally, at a methodological level, feminist legal theorists are almost universally committed to a social constructionist stance: in other words to the idea that the power and meaning of sex/gender is a product not of nature but of culture. Feminist legal theorists are hence of the view that gender relations are open to revision through the modification of powerful social institutions such as law.

Within this broad conception, it is worth distinguishing two main schools of feminist legal thought. The first, which might be called liberal feminism, is committed, as is mainstream legal theory, to the ideals of gender neutrality and equality before the law. Its focus is primarily instrumental, seeing law as a tool of feminist strategy, and the impact of law as a basis for feminist critique. By contrast the second approach, which I shall label difference feminism, is sceptical about the possibility of neutrality; it has an implicit commitment to a more

---

[3] For further discussion, see Chapter 8.

complex idea of equality which accommodates and values, whilst not fixing, women's specificity "as women"; and it has a focus on the symbolic and dynamic aspects of law and not just on its instrumental aspects.[4] Looking back, I would say that in 1981 I was already—like most of my colleagues—a liberal feminist, albeit not a very thoughtful one. What I found disturbing about the scholarship to which I was introduced was the way in which it required me to amend or even to think beyond certain aspects of the liberal framework which had informed my legal education. In what follows, I shall therefore concentrate on the implications of this more radical approach to feminist legal theory—difference feminism—for the tenets of conventional legal scholarship and theory, so as to show how my intellectual journey began. In doing so, I do not mean to imply that I find all aspects of difference feminism persuasive: indeed, the essays in this collection question or reinterpret some of its central claims. What I do maintain is that difference feminism poses a challenge to the framework of conventional legal scholarship which is of sufficient intellectual power to demand a meticulous and reasoned response. A rigorous formulation of the most powerful arguments of difference feminism is therefore of central importance to contemporary legal theory.

The feminist challenge to conventional legal scholarship

Over the last fifteen years, a number of important intellectual movements such as "law in context", "socio-legal studies" and "critical legal studies" have begun to reshape the approach of legal education. Notwithstanding their influence, the orientation of most courses in law remains a broadly positivist one. By this I mean simply that legal education assumes the existence of a relatively discrete social phenomenon—law—and sees itself as imparting both knowledge of particular laws and techniques through which students can broaden and use this knowledge in intellectual and practical contexts. Furthermore, in so far as law courses reach beyond the description and analysis of law, they tend to do so by contextualising that analysis within a set of broadly liberal ideas which are thought to inform legal arrangements in modern societies such as Britain. I therefore want to single out a number of assumptions common to positivistic and liberal legal scholarship which are the target of feminist critique

---

[4] For more detailed discussion, see Chapters 6 and 7.

of the gender bias of law and legal method. These various points are closely interwoven, but I think that it is useful to separate them out to get a sense of the range of arguments which have been influential in the development of feminist legal thought.

The neutral framework of legal reasoning

A central tenet of both positivist scholarship and the liberal ideal of the rule of law is that laws set up standards which are applied in a neutral manner to formally equal parties. The questions of inequality and power which may affect the capacity of those parties to engage effectively in legal reasoning have featured little in either mainstream legal theory or legal education. These questions have, on the other hand, always been central to critical legal theory, and they find an important place within feminist legal thought. In particular, the work of social psychologist Carol Gilligan[5] on varying ways of constructing moral problems, and the relationship of these variations to gender, has opened up a striking argument about the possible "masculinity" of the very process of legal reasoning.

As is widely known, Gilligan's research was motivated by the finding of psychological research that men reach, on average, a "higher" level of moral development than do women. Gilligan set out to investigate the neutrality of the tests being applied: she also engaged in empirical research designed to illuminate the ways in which different people construct moral problems. Her research elicited two main approaches to moral reasoning. The first, which Gilligan calls the ethic of rights, proceeds in an essentially legalistic way: it formulates rules structuring the values at issue in a hierarchical way, and then applies those rules to the facts. The second, which Gilligan calls the ethic of care or responsibility, takes a more holistic approach to moral problems, exploring the context and relationships, as well as the values, involved, and producing a more complex, but less conclusive, analysis. The tests on which assessments of moral development have conventionally been made by psychologists were based on the ethic of rights: analyses proceeding from the ethic of care were hence adjudged morally under-developed. It was therefore significant that Gilligan's fieldwork suggested that these two types were gender-related, in that girls tended to adopt the care perspective, whilst boys more often adopted the rights approach.

[5] See Gilligan (1982).

Gilligan's assertion of the relationship between the two models and gender is a controversial one. Nonetheless, her analytical distinction between the two ethics is of great potential significance for feminist legal theory. The idea that the distinctive structure of legal reasoning may systematically silence the voices of those who speak the language of relationships is a potentially important one for all critical legal theory. The rights model is, as I have already observed, reminiscent of law: it works from a clear hierarchy of sources which are reasoned through in a formally logical way. The more contextual, care or relationship-oriented model would, by contrast, be harder to capture by legal frameworks, within which holistic or relationally-oriented reasoning tends to sound "woolly" or legally incompetent, or to be rendered legally irrelevant by substantive and evidential rules. Most law students will be familiar with the way in which intuitive judgements are marginalised or disqualified in legal education, which proceeds precisely by imbuing the student with a sense of the exclusive relevance of formal legal sources and technical modes of reasoning.

There are, however, several important pitfalls for feminist legal theory in some of the arguments deriving from Gilligan's research.[6] One way of reading the implications for law of Gilligan's approach is that legal issues, indeed the conceptualisation of legal subjects themselves, should be recast in less formal and abstract terms. But such a strategy of recontextualisation may obscure the (sometimes damaging) ways in which legal subjects are already contextualised.[7] In the sentencing of offenders, or in the assumptions on which victims and defendants are treated in rape cases, for example, we have some clear examples of effective contextualisation which cuts in several political directions—not all of them appealing to feminists. In certain areas, it may be that legal reasoning is already "relational" in the sense espoused by many feminists, but that it privileges certain kinds of relationships: such as proprietary, object relations.[8] A general call for "contextualisation" may also be making naive assumptions about the power of such a strategy to generate real change given surrounding power relations: as the case of rape trials shows all too clearly, the framework of legal doctrine is not the only formative context shaping the legal process. The important project, then, is that of recontextualisation understood not as reformist strategy but rather as

---

[6] For a useful discussion, see Frug (1992) Ch. 3.
[7] See further Chapter 7.
[8] For further discussion see Nedelsky (1993); Irigaray (1992); see also Chapters 4 and 8.

critique: in other words, the development of a critical analysis which unearths the logic, the substantive assumptions, underlying law's current contextualisation of its subjects, and which can hence illuminate the interests and relationships which these arrangements privilege.

Law's autonomy and discreteness

Another standard assumption of mainstream legal scholarship is that law is a relatively autonomous social practice, discrete from politics, ethics, religion. An extreme expression of this assumption is found in Hans Kelsen's "pure" theory of law,[9] but weaker versions inform the entire positivist tradition. Indeed, this is what sets up one of positivism's recurring problems—that is, the question of foundations, of the boundaries between the legal and the non-legal; of the source of legal authority, and the relation between law and justice.[10]

This mainstream assumption, like the idea that legal method is discrete or distinctive, is challenged by feminist legal theory. Feminist theory seeks to reveal the ways in which law reflects, reproduces, expresses, constructs and reinforces power relations along sexually-patterned lines. In doing so, it questions law's claims to autonomy and represents it as a practice which is continuous with deeper social, political and economic forces which constantly seep through its supposed boundaries. Hence the ideals of the rule of law call for modification and reinterpretation. There are obvious, and strong, continuities here between the feminist and the marxist traditions in legal thought.[11]

Law's neutrality and objectivity

As I have already mentioned, difference feminism has developed a critique of the very idea of gender neutrality, of gender equality before the law, in a sexually-patterned world. Feminist legal theory deconstructs law's claims to be enunciating truths, its pretension to neutral or objective judgement, and its constitution of a field of discrete and hence unassailable knowledge.

This argument takes a number of forms in contemporary feminist legal theory. One derives from the Foucaultian critique of feminist writers such as Carol Smart.[12] The argument is that law, by policing

---

[9] See Kelsen (1967).
[10] For an extended analysis of this problem, see Davies (1996).
[11] See Collins (1982).
[12] See Smart (1989), drawing on Foucault (1972); (1977).

its own boundaries via its substantive rules and rules of evidence, constitutes itself as self-contained, as a self-reproducing system.[13] There is, hence, a certain "truth" to this aspect of law. But by standing back so as to cast light on the point of view from which law's truth is being constructed, we can undermine law's claims to objectivity. Another, rather different, example is Catharine MacKinnon's well known epistemological argument.[14] In MacKinnon's view, law constructs knowledge which claims objectivity, but "objectivity" in fact expresses a male point of view. Hence "objective" standards in civil and criminal law—the "reasonable person"—in fact represent a position which is specific in not only gender but also class, ethnic and other terms. The epistemological assertion of "knowledge" or "objectivity" disguises this process of construction, and writes sexually specific bodies out of the text of law. The project of feminism is to replace them. The difficult trick is to do so without fixing their shape and identity within received categories of masculine and feminine. Hence not all feminists endorse the idea of abandoning "reasonableness" tests or the appeal to otherwise universal standards.[15]

Law's centrality

In stark contrast to not only a great deal of positivist legal scholarship but also much "law and society" work, feminist writers have often questioned law's importance or centrality to the constitution of social relations and the struggle to change those relations. Clearly feminist views diverge here. Catharine MacKinnon, for example, is optimistic about using law for radical purposes; but many other feminists— notably British feminist Carol Smart—have questioned the wisdom of placing great reliance on law and of putting law too much at the centre of our critical analysis. Perhaps this is partly a cultural difference: the British women's movement has typically been relatively anti-institutional and oppositional. Yet even in the USA, where there is a stronger tradition of reformist legal activism, feminists associated with critical legal studies have been notably cautious about claims advanced in some critical legal scholarship[16] about law's central role in constituting social relations. Feminists have thus tended further towards a classical marxist orientation on this question than have their

[13] Cf. the arguments of autopoietic theory: see Teubner (1993).
[14] See MacKinnon (1989).
[15] See for example Cornell (1995) Ch. 1; for further discussion, see Chapters 4–7.
[16] See for example Unger (1983).

non-feminist critical counterparts. In terms of analytic focus, however, this has led feminists to address a range of social institutions—the family, sexuality, the political realm, bureaucracies—well beyond the marxist terrain of political economy. Feminists writers continue to be ambivalent about whether and how law ought to be deployed as a tool of feminist action, practice and strategy.[17] To the extent that feminist critique identifies law as implicated in the construction of existing gender relations, how far can it really be used to change them, and do strategic attempts to use law risk reaffirming law's power?

Law as a system of enacted norms or rules

Typically, feminist legal theory reaches beyond a conception of law as a system of norms or rules—statutes, constitutions, cases—and beyond "standard" legal officials, such as judges, to encompass other practices which are legally relevant or "quasi-legal". For example, the Oslo School of Women's Law had its main focus on administrative and regulatory bodies such as social welfare agencies, the medical system and the family.[18] This reorientation is born of a very basic socio-legal insight: that the power and social meaning of law are determined not only at its legislative, doctrinal and judicial levels but also by a myriad non-legal or partially legal decisions about its interpretation and enforcement.

This institutional refocusing is also connected with post-structuralist ideas, and notably with Michel Foucault's reconceptualisation of power—a reconceptualisation which has important implications for law.[19] Foucault distinguished between sovereignty power—power as a property or possession; juridical power; and disciplinary power—the relational power which inheres in particular practices and which flows unseen throughout the "social body". His argument was that the later modern world was gradually seeing the growth of subtle, intangible, disciplinary power, at the expense of both the old sovereignty and modern juridical power. Foucault was therefore inclined to think that law was waning in importance as a form of social governance. Smart, however, uses his argument about power in a different way in relation to law: she points out that law itself embodies disciplinary power. For one of the distinguishing features

---

[17] See in particular Smart (1989) Ch. 1; Bottomley and Conaghan (eds.) (1993).
[18] Stang Dahl (1986).
[19] See Foucault (1972), (1977); Smart (1989); for further discussion, see Chapters 3 and 5.

of disciplinary power is its subtly normalising effect, and as soon as we look beyond a narrow stereotype of law as a system of rules backed up by sanctions, we begin to see that one of law's functions is precisely to distribute its subjects with disciplinary precision around a mean or norm.

For example, the way in which legal rules distribute social welfare benefits or allocate custody of children (on divorce or via adoption) reflects judgements about the right way to live; it expresses assumptions about "normality". A yet more spectacular example is that of the construction of gay and straight sexualities in criminal laws and in family and social welfare legislation. These "normalising" assumptions have a pervasive power which also structures the administration of laws (e.g. of social welfare benefits and policing policies) at the bureaucratic level, generating phenomena such as reluctance to prosecute in "domestic violence" cases, the oppressive policing of gay sexuality, and the discriminatory administration of welfare benefits. Feminist (like other critical) analyses are interested here not just in legal doctrine but also in legal discourse, i.e. how differently sexed legal subjects are constituted by and inserted within legal categories via the mediation of judicial, police or lawyers' discourse. The feminist approach therefore mounts a fundamental challenge to the standard ways of conceptualising law and the legal, and moves to a broader understanding of legally relevant spheres of practice.[20]

Law's unity and coherence

Readers of both student texts and legal cases will be familiar with the very high importance attached by lawyers and legal commentators to the idea (or ideal) of law as a unitary and a coherent system of rules or norms. It is an idea which informs legal theory in a number of ways. Once again, Kelsen provides a spectacular example: his Grundnorm had to be hypothesised precisely because otherwise it would have been impossible to interpret law as a coherent, non-contradictory normative field of meaning. As a law student, one of the first things one is taught to do is to hone in on contradictory or inconsistent arguments. The idea of coherence as the idea(l) which lies at the heart of law finds its fullest expression in Ronald Dworkin's idea of "law as integrity",[21] but it is also voiced in procedurally-

[20] See further Chapter 8.
[21] Dworkin (1986).

oriented ethical and political theories, notably in critical theory of the Frankfurt School.[22]

Feminist scholarship, like much other critical legal theory, is concerned to question this belief in law's coherence and to reconstruct the pretension to coherence as part of the ideology of both law and jurisprudence: as part of what helps to represent law as authoritative, adjudication as democratically legitimate and so on. The critical analysis of contradictions, and the unearthing of what have been called "dangerous supplements" and hidden agendas, takes place both at the level of doctrine and at that of discourse.[23]

To take some specific examples, the assertion within legal doctrine of particular questions or issues as within public or private spheres is contradictory, question-begging, under-determined: sexuality, for example, is public for some purposes and private for others.[24] The idea of the legal subject as rational and as abstracted from its social context is undermined by exceptions such as defences in criminal law, shifts of time-frame in the casting of legal questions, and an arbitrary division of issues pertaining to conviction and those pertaining to sentence.[25] In contract law, one could cite shifts between a freedom of contract model and a model which views contract as a long-term relationship within which, for example, loss occasioned by the parties' general reliance upon the contractual relationship can be recognised and compensated.[26] Nor are these incoherencies confined to the doctrinal framework: they mark also the discourse through which human subjects are inserted into that structure. For example, the rational and controlled male of legal subjectivity is also the rape defendant who is vulnerable to feminine wiles and who is, on occasion, incapable of distinguishing "yes" from "no". The unearthing of such contradictions is not just a matter of "trashing": it forms part of an intellectual and political strategy—of exposing law's indeterminacy, of emphasising its contingency, and of finding resources for its reconstruction in those doctrinal principles and discursive images which are less dominant yet which fracture and complicate the seamless web imagined by orthodox legal scholarship.

---

[22] Habermas (1992).
[23] Fitzpatrick (ed.) (1991); see further Chapters 4, 5, 7 and 8.
[24] See Olsen (1983) and Chapters 3 and 5.
[25] See Kelman (1981) and Chapter 7.
[26] See Collins (1997).

Law's rationality

Perhaps most fundamentally of all, it is argued that contradictions and
indeterminacy in legal doctrine undermine law's supposed grounding
in reason, just as the smuggling in of contextual and affective factors
undermines law's apparent construction of the subject as a rational,
self-interested actor. Furthermore, in so far as law is successful in
maintaining its self-image as a rational enterprise, this is because the
emotional and affective aspects of legal practice are systematically
repressed in orthodox representations. Once one reads cases and
other legal texts not only for their formal meaning but also as
rhetoric, one sees how values and techniques which are not acknowledged on the surface of legal doctrine are in fact crucial to the way
in which cases are decided.[27]

These, then, are the principal ways in which feminist legal theory
has challenged the tenets of conventional jurisprudence and legal
education, and it was my (then very vague) apprehension of these
sorts of arguments which prompted me to start thinking seriously
about feminist legal theory in the early 1980s. As I hope this brief
account reveals, feminist theory engages with some highly complex
questions: it is not surprising, therefore, that it is a rapidly moving
field which constantly throws up new questions just as old ones
appear to be nearing resolution. It is—like all intellectually challenging approaches—marked by vigorous contestation. A more concrete
analysis of key feminist controversies appears in the chapters of this
book. What I hope to have achieved in this preliminary characterisation is to have communicated a sense of the intellectual vitality and
ambition of feminist thought. I hope also to have suggested the
extent to which feminist legal scholarship has to swim against a very
strong current of intellectual convention—something which, for
feminist scholars as well as students, is occasionally both exhausting
and disorienting.

*Feminist and "critical" legal theories: methodological and political
heteronomy*

It is implicit in what I have already said that the approach which I
shall be pursuing in this book is one which sets its face firmly against
the idea that feminist legal theory is itself—either politically or

[27] See for example Frug (1992).

methodologically—an autonomous intellectual field.[28] Feminist method, in my view, shares certain conceptual tools with other critical approaches, including marxist theory, critical legal theory, critical race theory and queer theory. Each of these approaches is concerned, along a certain dimension, to dig beneath the surface of legal and social arrangements so as to illuminate their deeper logics. In doing so, such approaches draw upon the intellectual resources of a number of disciplines, including history, economics, sociology, psychoanalysis, pscyhology, philosophy and political science. None of these "critical" legal theories sees legal theory as autonomous in the way in which, for example, analytical jurisprudence regards itself as being. This is a matter both of method—willingness to draw on a variety of disciplines—and of subject matter: the vision of the boundaries between legal and social theory as porous is informed by an interpretation of the legal world as inextricably linked with the political, social, economic and cultural worlds. Hence many of the chapters of this book engage primarily with what would generally be thought of as political or social theory rather than as jurisprudence.

There is a second, somewhat different, sense in which the essays in this collection refuse the idea of feminist legal theory as autonomous—a sense which might lead some feminists to decline to describe my approach as feminist at all. In my view—as reflected in the definition of feminist legal theory given earlier in this introduction—the question of both the practical significance and (hence) the relative political importance of sex/gender in any particular realm of social life is one which has to be carefully analysed in the light of other critical analyses and their interaction with the social construction of gender. In other words, though feminism must (and does by definition) start out from the assumption that sex/gender has a general significance across a range of social fields, it must maintain an open mind on the interaction between sex/gender and other important axes of social differentiation (and oppression) such as race, socioeconomic class, age, sexual orientation in any particular instance. A feminist political and legal theory could never, in other words, be the only legal or political theory which one needed. Moreover, I believe that a number of feminist issues in legal and social theory can best be identified by beginning one's analytic journey in an ostensibly

---

[28] This is a controversial issue among feminist scholars. It is also one which might be thought to have discrete institutional implications for the organisation of legal education, for example in terms of whether feminist questions should be integrated in the existing curriculum or dealt with in special courses such as "Law and Gender".

non-feminist location,[29] just as, conversely, an analysis of feminist issues can often illuminate more general problems in social thought.[30]

One could, of course, define this question about the relationship between feminist and other forms of critical social theory out of existence by arguing that an adequate feminist theory would always have taken account of other relevant social axes such as class and race. Certainly, as I argue in almost all of the chapters of this book, an adequate feminist legal theory needs to avoid essentialising either "woman" or "the feminine", recognising the ways in which such categories are inevitably mediated through and transformed by these other factors. I do, however, resist the idea of a complete or overarching feminist theory, which seems to me to encounter the intellectual objection that it inevitably suggests a certain political or empirical priority for sex/gender.[31] Hence these essays are informed by a preference to think in terms of a plurality of critical social theories contributing to an overall debate. Their project is to contribute to a feminism which recognises the problematic status of the category "woman" without making her disappear: which engages with the feminine as a construct, yet as a construct which has enormous social power.

The organisation of the collection

The reader should now be reasonably well equipped to embark upon the journey represented by the chapters which follow. In the expectation that at least some readers may work their way through the whole collection, I have arranged the essays in two groups which develop two main themes. The first group of essays are critical engagements with liberal individualism and its implications for law. These essays address liberal individualism in two different ways. First, they analyse the conceptual framework of legal systems and legal reasoning. For example, Chapters 1, 4 and 5 consider the sense in which the paradigm subject of law is constituted as an individual with particular characteristics—characteristics which turn out to be strongly gendered in a masculine direction. Secondly, these essays address the individualism of the ideals and values embedded in liberal legal ideology. For example, Chapters 2 and 5 analyse the way in which

---

[29] As in Chapters 2 and 5.
[30] See for example Chapters 1 and 8.
[31] See Chapters 6 and 8.

liberal conceptions of justice predispose liberal legal systems to the recognition of certain kinds of social arrangements and inhibit their recognition of others. Chapters 1, 3 and 5 also consider the relationship between these two forms of individualism in legal thought. A particular pre-occupation is the communitarian tradition in social theory, and the first part of the book gradually develops a view both of certain continuities between feminist and communitarian thought and of the ways in which communitarian claims require us to modify the individualist framework of conventional legal scholarship.[32] However, these chapters also build up a critique of communitarianism which suggests that significant aspects of communitarian thought are every bit as unsatisfactory, from a feminist point of view, as their liberal counterparts.

While some of these themes reappear in the Chapters 6, 7 and 8, with Chapter 5 in particular consituting a bridge between the two sections, the main preoccupation of the second group of essays is methodological. They engage with the question of what kinds of project feminist legal theory should attempt, tracing the relationship between feminist legal theory and other influential theoretical traditions in and beyond the legal. In particular, they identify a close relationship between feminism and interpretivism in social theory—an approach which the earlier chapters identified as one of the most persuasive aspects of communitarian thought. Thus Chapters 6 and 8 consider the relationship between analytic, empirical, critical, reformist and utopian projects in feminist legal theory, whilst Chapter 7 attempts a critical assessment of the contribution of two extra-legal disciplinary resources—psychoanalysis and rhetorical politics—to the development of feminist legal thought. An underlying concern of each of these chapters is the location of feminist thought within the (supposed) dichotomy between modernist and post-modernist approaches, and the capacity of interpretive method to undermine this dichotomy.

Though all of the essays have been modified to some extent so as to avoid overlap, they remain self-standing. Many readers may therefore wish to design their own routes through the collection, planning their own journeys and, very possibly, reaching different destinations from the author.

---

[32] For an analogous argument about political theory, see Frazer and Lacey (1993).

PART I

FEMINIST CRITIQUE
OF INDIVIDUALISM IN LEGAL AND
POLITICAL THOUGHT

From Individual to Group? A Feminist Analysis of the Limits of Anti-Discrimination Legislation

Over the last few years a plentiful and challenging literature has developed in which feminist writers have constructed an illuminating critique of legal approaches to dismantling sexism and sex discrimination.[1] Much of this literature makes passing or more substantial reference to questions of racism, generally in the context of an acknowledgement of the specificity of the oppression of black women. However, most of it[2] does not address directly the question of what use the critical tools and insights of feminist social theory might contribute to a more thoroughgoing analysis of laws designed to combat racism. This silence is born partly of a recognition and respect for the specificity and complexity of racism and its relationship to law; a (proper) inhibition from too easily regarding racism and sexism as simply analogous social institutions; and an understandable concentration on the question of women's oppression and its legal constitution, stretching beyond anti-discrimination legislation, which is the central focus of feminism.

However, I think it is true to say that many of us who are concerned with this general field of inquiry are uncomfortable with the fact that, with some notable exceptions,[3] there has been a relative lack in British law journals of critical analysis specifically focused on race discrimination law. There is no real British equivalent to American "critical race theory"; nor has the problem of the "intersection of race and gender", identified by Crenshaw, claimed serious attention among British scholars.[4] This is not to say, of course, that

---

[1] See for example O'Donovan and Szyszczak (1988); MacKinnon (1989), Chapter 12; Smart (1989).

[2] Including my own contribution: see Lacey (1987).

[3] See Fitzpatrick (1987); Lustgarten (1980), (1986).

[4] See Crenshaw (1988), (1989); for an exception in relation to Britain, see Fredman, Stanley and Szyszczak (1992). For examples of American "critical race" scholarship, see Bell (1987), (1992); Williams (1991), (1995); Harris (1990); Kennedy (1989); Lawrence (1987);

the question of racism is not canvassed in legal literature. Particularly in the criminal justice area, the racist practices and attitudes of public institutions such as the prison system and the police are debated regularly in specialist and general press.[5] However, it would be fair to say that in terms of analysis and critique of the potential positive role of law in combatting racism, there has been less published debate than in the area of gender. Given the under-representation of many ethnic minority groups[6] on the staff of law schools (and indeed in the higher education system generally) this is perhaps (depressingly) predictable. Whilst the contributions of members of non-oppressed groups to the struggle to understand and opppose racism in the legal sphere is to be welcomed,[7] both the prominence of ideas about the relevance of direct experience and particularity of perspective in much modern social theory and straightforward arguments of social justice identify this under-representation as a major cause for concern and activity. Whilst working for significant improvements on this front, it is obviously important for us to familiarise ourselves with developments in other countries, such as the USA, where black people have found a significant voice in the legal academy. However, it also seems worthwhile to ask what contribution feminist ideas, which are beginning to have some impact on the law school agenda in this country, could make to a critical understanding of race discrimination law. This is the underlying project which informs this chapter.[8]

Delgado (1987), (1995). On the dynamics of race in Britain, see Gilroy (1987) and, with specific reference to law, Fitzpatrick (1992a).

    [5] See for example Institute of Race Relations (1979); Gordon (1988).

    [6] The question of the proper language to be used in referring to ethnic minority groups is a difficult one, and most of the possibilities have some drawbacks. In response to the powerful arguments of Tariq Modood (1988), I shall refer in the British context to "Afro-Carribean and Asian people" in preference to the more usual "black people". This has the benefit of marking the fact that racial prejudice is not merely colour prejudice, but is also based on culture. The drawback with this usage is that it excludes other groups which are protected by the Race Relations Act 1976. I shall therefore also occasionally refer to "ethnic minority groups". Of course, members of majority groups are also protected by the Act, but I hope that the view of the social functions of anti-discrimination legislation which emerges from this article justifies the focus on "minorities".

    [7] For an interesting discussion of this point, see Kennedy (1989).

    [8] I should like to note at the outset my sense of discomfort both at the possibility of being seen to pre-empt or deny the distinctive perspectives of people from ethnic minority groups by generalising a white feminist perspective to their position, and, conversely, of being dismissed as one "marginal" approach talking to another. Certainly, there will be aspects of the issues which I am discussing to which my position as a middle class white woman will have made me insensitive. My conviction that racism, like sexism, cannot and must not be regarded as *exclusively* the problem of its victims, and that the intellectual as much as the political challenge posed by feminist and anti-racist analyses of law must be met by all lawyers, prompts me to continue with the project nonetheless.

My argument will fall into two main sections. In the first place, I shall explore the relevance of feminist critiques of sex discrimination law for race discrimination law. This will involve some discussion of the relationship between feminist and anti-racist approaches to law, and a more general account of the questions of social theory raised by feminism. Secondly, I shall move on from the feminist critique of anti-discrimination law to ask one specific question about possible reform: how far could we improve the symbolic and instrumental value of anti-discrimination law by employing the notion of collective or group-based rights? What legal and political questions are raised by this kind of approach? Finally, I shall try to draw some general conclusions about the usefulness of and dangers inherent in anti-discrimination legislation and make some tentative suggestions about where we might go from here. I shall in particular address the question of how reformist lawyers ought to respond to feminist and anti-racist scepticism about the gains to be had from law and legal processes.

FEMINIST PERSPECTIVES ON ANTI-DISCRIMINATION LAW

There is now a wide consensus, among lawyers with very different political points of view, about certain intractable problems thrown up by British sex discrimination legislation. Problems of proof; the hopeless inadequacy of the available remedies; the unsatisfactory nature of the resource basis and structure of the enforcement agencies; the inexpert nature of the tribunals hearing discrimination cases; the lack of legal aid for tribunal cases: all these are widely acknowledged to hamper the potential effectiveness of the legislation. All of these technical problems, and more, apply equally to the operation of the Race Relations Act 1976, and have been analysed and criticised by the Commission for Racial Equality in its proposals for reform.[9] The general message delivered by these and similar proposals is that, with some fairly substantial modification, but without any major change of direction or underlying principle, anti-discrimination law could be made to work tolerably well. Several rather different kinds of problem are, however, suggested by a feminist critique, and these seem to call into question the very structure and basis of anti-discrimination

[9] See Commission for Racial Equality (1983), (1985); for wide-ranging critical discussion of legislation against racial discrimination, see the essays in Hepple and Szyszczak (eds.) (1992).

law. I shall now sketch out some of these feminist questions, and consider their relevance for race discrimination law.

The underlying notion of equality of opportunity

It is widely recognised that a legal commitment to formal equality is insufficient to guarantee the fair treatment of groups which have suffered a history of prejudice and discrimination. This is reflected in the Sex Discrimination and Race Relations Acts' commitment to "equality of opportunity", and in their instantiation of the concept of indirect discrimination. However, this fundamentally liberal notion, the precise delineation of which is in any case by no means clear, poses problems for and puts limitations on the achievements to be made by anti-discrimination law. For example, indirect discrimination effectively uses an unequal outcome as a *prima facie* test for inequality of opportunity: a racially or sexually patterned result may be unlawful unless it can be justified irrespective or race or sex. However, the ultimate willingness of the tribunal to interpret an unequal outcome as an instance of unjust, illegal inequality is modified by the underlying ideology of equality of opportunity, which invites the tribunal to be receptive to the idea that unequal results may be explained in terms of the free, autonomous choices of individuals. For example, if the sexual segregation of the labour force, the concentration of women in low paid and part-time work, and the under-representation of women in highly paid and prestigious jobs are seen as flowing from autonomous individual choices which flow in turn from women's and men's legitimately different lives, the tribunal will be more sympathetic to arguments of justification and less persuaded by the plaintiff's argument that the result represents a legally recognised injustice. In other words, the tribunal's response to the evidence may be affected by the very stereotypes which many of us hoped that the legislation would serve to attack. Exactly comparable problems arise here in respect of race: although the hold of "naturalistic" or "biologistic" ideas about the appropriate place, role and characteristics of people from ethnic minority groups is perhaps now less tenacious than is the case with sex, the influence of stereotypes about what, for example, Afro-Carribean or Asian people are like can be directly relevant in race discrimination cases. This is because they affect both the plausibility of certain kinds of arguments about justification and the tribunal's reading of whether or not the unequal outcome is something which should be regarded with suspicion, or rather as merely the "natural" outcome of people's choices. The powerful hold of racist stereotypes in areas such as police practice and the treatment of prisoners[10] can hardly be doubted in most areas covered by the current Race Relations Act, and many more which are not.

The implication of the individual complaint

Following on from these difficulties with the liberal ideology of equality of opportunity, there are further limitations in the capacity of indirect discrimination to bite against structural sexism or racism which are inherent in the nature of the liberal legal form. Indirect discrimination seeks to address practices which have discriminatory effects, but it works by means of individual lawsuits which, it is hoped, will have wider knock-on effects. This has indeed happened in some instances, but the relative infrequency of successful cases is, as we have already noted, often deplored. One problem with the current legal approach is that a basic structural implication of any lawsuit is the idea that what is complained against is *abnormal*. This implication, once again, affects the tribunal's reading of both law and fact, and it constitutes a psychological and hence material barrier to success in indirect discrimination cases for a very simple reason. This is that in many areas of social life, institutional sexism and racism *are the norm*: they cannot be regarded as abnormal. Descriptive and prescriptive conceptions of "the norm" shade into one another, generating a reluctance to conceive the statistically normal as legally proscribed: descriptive normality confers legitimacy. Doubtless this speaks volumes on the general problem of laws which seek to legislate in advance of social practice and consensus. But it can hardly be doubted to pose a special problem for Afro-Carribean, Asian and female defendants who are addressing their complaints about heavily entrenched and rarely questioned social practices to a white male dominated legal forum. The statutory construction of (certain very limited kinds of) racism and sexism as abnormal has proved to be relatively impotent in the face of the broader social construction of them as normal. This seems likely to mark a significant difference in the experience of male plaintiffs under the Sex Discrimination Acts

---

[10] See for example Genders and Player (1989) Chs. 3–5; Gordon (1988).

and white plaintiffs under the Race Relations Act, whose complaints will often call into question practices (such as affirmative action) which are not so universally and unquestioningly endorsed. An interesting example of a "majority" plaintiff who *did* meet with little sympathy from the courts arose in the *Peake* case,[11] in which the practice complained of was assimilated with chivalry—precisely the kind of widely accepted sexist institution to criticisms of which the courts are likely to be resistant. The *Peake* decision, happily, no longer stands, but its history is of continuing interest.

Problems of comparison with the white male norm

A further problem in the operation of the Sex Discrimination Acts is a function of their definition of discrimination in comparative terms: both direct and indirect discrimination depend on a comparison of the plaintiff's treatment or position with what would have been the treatment of, or what is the impact of the practice upon, a person of the opposite sex. The major problem here is that the standard of treatment or the outcome which represents the point of comparison and hence the Act's conception of what is normal or legitimate is necessarily a norm set for (and generally by) men. This poses particular problems in areas such as pregnancy where a discrimination claim is either ruled out in an exercise of blinkered logic[12] or allowed on the basis of an inappropriate comparison between a pregnant woman and a sick man.[13] It also illustrates rather clearly the blunt critical edges of the legislation, which cannot provide any platform for litigants to criticise the formulation of the "normal" standard: they must content themselves with arguing for assimilation to it. Complaint about formal difference rather than substantive critique is the name of the game. Are similar problems posed for Afro-Carribean and Asian people by the comparative aspect of anti-discrimination law? Certainly, assimilation to a white-defined standard is seen as an eminently unsatisfactory goal by most anti-racist writers, and the desire to raise more radical questions about social justice has infused not only critical social theory but also popular culture and political movements. However, as in the case of gender,

[11] *Peake v. Automotive Products* [1978] QB 233.
[12] *Turley v. Allders Department Stores Ltd* [1980] ICR 66.
[13] *Hayes v. Malleable Working Men's Club* [1985] ICR 703; *Webb v. EMO Air Cargo UK* [1990] IRLR 124.

appeals to specific needs, interests, ways of life or sensibilities are inherently dangerous and double-edged in the context of a legal system informed by the formally egalitarian ideology of the rule of law, just as basic challenges to the conventional construction of standards and values are quite literally ruled out of court.[14]

Problems of symmetry

As Cotterrell has noted,[15] at a formal level, anti-discrimination legislation operates by means of decategorisation rather than categorisation. In other words, it picks out certain features or categories only in order to prohibit their operating as reasons for certain kinds of decisions. This reflects the liberal notion that all have *the same right* not to be discriminated against. It opens up the possibility of litigation by white men, because any recognition of race or gender difference is legally vulnerable, however important such recognition may be in addressing the disadvantage of women or certain ethnic groups.[16] The legislation is framed in terms of difference rather than disadvantage: it constructs the problem to be tackled as race and sex discrimination, rather than as discrimination against and disadvantage of women and certain ethnic groups. Quite apart from the fact that this seriously misrepresents the social problems to which the legislation purports to respond, it means that any kind of protective or remedial measure addressing disadvantage is suspect. In particular, it rules out affirmative action, even of a moderate kind, as objectionable in principle. It thus represents a serious limitation on the legal and political possibilities for tackling women's and ethnic minority people's oppression and social disadvantage.

The implicit validation of sexism and racism in the "private" sphere

Related to the comments I have made about the need for individual litigants to convince the tribunal that what happened to them was "abnormal", the converse, and equally damaging, implication of the legislation must be that less favourable treatment on grounds of sex

[14] One potential exception here in the gender area is the law on equal pay for work of equal value: see O'Donovan and Szyszczak (1988) Ch. 5.

[15] Cotterrell (1981).

[16] For critical discussion, see Fudge (1989); Smart (1989) Ch. 7.

or race or unjustified differential impact are legitimate where they fall
outside the limited ambit of the Acts. As Fitzpatrick has suggested,[17]
in the context of a society where racism is endemic, it is in principle
impossible to have "innocent" law: any legislation which attempts a
partial attack on race discrimination implies that only that racism covered by the legislation is of sufficient importance to merit political
intervention or to raise serious questions of social justice. This implication becomes less damaging the more thoroughgoing the legislation is, and as arguments about the relative ineffectiveness of legal
intervention become correspondingly stronger. Yet in a racist and
sexist society, it is impossible completely to escape the implication of
limited anti-discrimination legislation that discrimination not
addressed by it fails to raise questions of injustice calling for political
redress.

Empowering disadvantaged groups?

I hope that these brief comments will have been sufficient to demonstrate that the problems from a feminist perspective with respect to
the operation of the Sex Discrimination Acts raise comparable and
similarly intractable problems for race discrimination law. At every
turn the critical hold offered by the legislation is severely limited, and
becomes more so when applied by judges and others whose political
perspective encourages them to a restrictive view of its role. At the
point of deciding what constitutes less favourable treatment, sexist
and racist stereotypes can creep in; in deciding what is justified, the
view of anti-discrimination law as essentially concerned with dismantling restrictive practices and opening up a genuine market of
equal opportunity presdisposes tribunals to be sympathetic to economic arguments and discourages any clear appeal to the intrinsic
value of a more egalitarian world. If we want to get at the real structures of racism and sexism, individual lawsuits on this kind of model
are unlikely to be an effective vehicle.

FEMINIST SOCIAL THEORY AND CRITIQUES OF RACISM

We now need to explore how these specific criticisms of the anti-
discrimination legislation relate to more general themes in critical

---

[17] Fitzpatrick (1987).

social theory, and to consider how far these alternative critical analyses suggest ways of overcoming the problems inherent in the political framework of the present legislation. The points I have made are directly informed by the insights of feminist and critical legal theory. Several of the points turn on what has become known as the critique of liberal legalism—a cluster of ideas among which the ideal of the rule of law and the separation of the world into public and private spheres are two of the most important. The liberal legal world is one in which legal rules are applied and enforced in a politically neutral and formally equal way; the legal sphere is seen as relatively autonomous from the political sphere; all are equally subject to law and formally equal before it. There are stringent limits on the proper ambit of state intervention by means of law, which is seen positively as protecting individual rights and interests against political encroachment, and negatively as respecting a sphere of private life in which public regulation is inappropriate and indeed oppressive. The place in which the line between public and private is seen as falling has shifted over time, as has the content of the rights perceived as the objects of legal protection. Nonetheless, the public/private framework has exercised an enduring hold over legal practice, imagination and ideology.[18]

Several features of this framework have been the object of critique. Feminists have criticised the ahistorical, presocial view of human nature which underlies liberal rights theory and legal individualism, and have pointed out the ways in which the need to frame legal arguments in terms of individual claims systematically obstructs the project of revealing and dismantling structures and institutions which disadvantage women. These arguments have developed into a more general critique of the discourse of rights, which are seen as not only inherently individualistic, but also as essentially competitive and hence anti-socialistic. They are also seen as being tied in with the notion of formal equality—hence the need to ascribe equal rights to all and the inevitable obscuring of real social problems and disadvantages. In a world in which white, male and middle class people both have more effective access to legal fora and meet a more sympathetic response when they get there, the ascription of formally equal rights will in effect entrench the competitively asserted rights of these privileged people.[19] Far from dismantling the disadvantage of women, people from ethnic minorities and socio-economically underprivileged

[18] See further Chapter 3.
[19] For more detailed discussion, see Chapter 8.

groups, it may even have the opposite effect. In pursuing this potentially radical critique of liberal law, feminists have also been under-
standably preoccupied with questions of strategy: to what extent
should we try to exploit legal forms despite our doubts about principle
and practice, given that they are undeniably one of the socially salient
forms of public argument and power? I shall return to these questions
of strategy below.

Secondly, and related to this first point, feminist and other forms
of critical legal theory aspire to deconstruct the asserted neutrality and
objectivity of liberal legal forms, and to expose their substantive pre-
conceptions and the ways in which they in fact favour systematically
certain kinds of interest. An integral part of this deconstruction is the
denial of the possibility of making a separation between questions of
procedure and those of substance, and between substantive law and
its enforcement. Feminism is therefore necessarily committed to a
socio-legal and political analysis. One specific object of deconstruction, of particular interest in the anti-discrimination area, is that of the
legal subject. Feminists claim that far from being a neutral, genderless, classless and raceless abstract individual, the legal subject (as
unwittingly revealed in legal language) is in fact a white, middle class,
man. Hence the views and assumptions built into legal forms, rules
and principles, as well as the values and goods recognised by legal
arrangements, express the experiences and viewpoints not of the
abstract individual (itself an incoherent idea) but of the privileged
white male.

Furthermore, it has been argued that the nature of law as a closed
system of reasoning, administered by a high-status profession and cast
in exclusive and often obfuscating language, necessarily disadvantages
the less powerful in their attempts to use the legal system for reformist
purposes. Those whose interests are already reflected in legal rules
and arrangements have no difficulty in participating in the closed system of reasoning. In contrast, those whose interests and perspectives
are marginalised or ignored will often find that arguments which they
wish to introduce and see as relevant to a legal issue are regarded as
irrelevant and inadmissible. A notorious example is that of the fre-
quent experience of female witnesses in rape trials of being silenced
and of having their account excluded from the legal process.[20] This
can also be a function of the individualisation of legal disputes, and

---

[20] See further Chapter 4. See also Chambers and Millar (1987); Smart (1989) Ch. 2;
Temkin (1987) pp. 1–8.

here anti-discrimination law is once again an important example. The individual litigant in a race or sex discrimination case may well find that evidence about her employer's practices and attitudes in different spheres or towards different people and on different occasions which have formed an important part of her recognition of her own treatment as discriminatory are not admissible in proving her individual complaint.

One possible strategy, of course, is for feminists and anti-racists to attempt to intervene in the legal forum, reworking legal concepts and definitions so as to reflect Afro-Carribean, Asian, female, and other perspectives. A notable example of such a strategy is law defining and making actionable sexual harassment—a concept which reconstructs, from a feminist perspective, behaviour conventionally regarded as acceptable and even favourable to women as unacceptable, oppressive and illegal. This kind of social and legal reconstruction is one of the most important potential contributions of critical social theory, and in the anti-discrimination area it raises a number of possibilities for reform. One example might be the recognition of groups' rather than individuals' claims, combatting the notion of the legal subject as an abstract individual and putting the position and experience of an oppressed group explicitly on the legal agenda—a possibility which will be canvassed later in this chapter.

Thirdly, feminists have demonstrated the ideological power yet the disingenousness and indeed analytic incoherence of the public/private distinction. On the one hand, the liberal argument is that there are certain areas of life (paradigmatically, the family, but also, and of relevance to anti-discrimination law, certain kinds of market relations) in which legal intervention and regulation is inappropriate or should be severely restricted. This argument is used by liberals as a justification for law's keeping out: the assertion of "privacy" is then hived off from the preceding argument, presented as a matter of description, and the legal policy of non-intervention constructed as an absence or omission. Yet this stance of omission as politically innocent is disingenuous, for law in fact keeps out only where it is satisfied to leave in place the social arrangements and power relations which characterise the unregulated situation. Where law has the capacity to intervene, the decision not to do so is itself a political decision: omission, feminists argue, calls for justification as much as does intervention, for it effectively legitimises the *status quo*.[21]

---

[21] For further discussion, see Chapter 3.

On the other hand, the alleged distinction between public and private, although ideologically powerful, in fact collapses under just the kind of analytic scrutiny which liberal legalism prizes so highly. In the late twentieth century at least, even discounting the argument that omission is the political equivalent of intervention, it is quite simply impossible to find areas of social life which are legally constructed as entirely private. Even the family, to take a central example, is hedged around with legal regulation at practically every turn. The public/private distinction is intellectually vacuous in that it is question-begging, yet this analytic weakness serves rather than undermines its political power. A good example of this apparent contradiction is represented by arguments purporting to justify the limited scope of anti-discrimination law by simply asserting the existence of a private sphere not suitable for legal regulation without articulating just why such regulation is inappropriate. The feminist analysis sketched in this paragraph underpins the argument noted above that non-regulated areas may be seen as areas in which the legal system implicitly legitimises sexism and racism, given the social facts of their existence.

Fourthly, many feminists have called for a move away from analysis in terms of inequality *understood in the sense of difference from the position of or treatment normally accorded to men*.[22] This is not to say that the powerful notion of equality is abandoned: rather, it is recast in terms of the dismantling of oppressive and exploitative power relations and of a thoroughgoing challenge to the very construction of norms and values which have conventional status and which are argued to reflect the partial judgements of men or other dominant groups. Such a reconstruction of equality is clearly of direct relevance to anti-discrimination law, for in introducing a more radical egalitarianism one might hope to address the problem already canvassed about the limitations inherent in the notion of comparison with and equalisation to a white male-defined norm. However, it also introduces one of the major problems for feminism or indeed any other critical social theory whose analysis depends heavily on the specificity of the oppression of a particular group. I want to dwell on this problem because it is of direct relevance to my further question about the potential gains to be had in terms of a move to legal recognition of group-based claims.

---

[22] On the reconstruction of equality, see Chapter 8; for critical discussion see Littleton (1987); MacKinnon (1989) Ch. 12; O'Donovan and Szyszczak (1988); Smart (1989) Chs. 4 and 7.

I shall try to illustrate the problem using feminism as my example. Feminism, put very crudely, attempts to understand women's subordination and to struggle against women's oppression. As such, it is implicit in the feminist project that some features of that subordination are common to all women in a particular society, at least at some level—although the forms and nature of women's oppression are recognised to be historically and culturally specific. As we have already seen, feminist critique draws heavily on notions such as "women's" and indeed "men's" point of view or experience; this specificity of viewpoint is generally held to flow from the common experience of gender oppression or domination. What makes this kind of feminist claim highly complex is, of course, the fact—increasingly recognised and pondered upon in feminist thought—that not all women's oppression, even in one society, is just the same. The subordination experienced by Afro-Carribean women, Asian women, working class women, lesbian women and women who are single mothers may well be qualitatively different. Hence feminists must claim that gender is always *one factor* in constituting the social position and experience of all women and men, whilst acknowledging that gender is overlaid with many other factors, most notably in our society, by race, by class and by sexual orientation. Exactly the same points can be made, of course, about the experience of racial or religious oppression: the experience of Afro-Carribean and Asian women and men is not the same, nor indeed is that of different ethnic groups, as is clearly illustrated by recent research on the prison system which shows stark contrasts in the forms of prejudice encountered by different ethnic groups in prison.[23]

This recognition of the differentiated nature of social oppression is leading critical social theorists steadily away from attractively simple, monolithic theories such as marxism, in which everything is reduced to one explanatory concept, towards a more complex and pluralistic approach.[24] This is certainly to be welcomed, but it has to be acknowledged that so far it has raised more questions than it has answered. For it takes us into crucially important and intractable issues such as the status of assertions about oppression generated by different individuals and groups and the role, if any, to be accorded to their claims to "truth" and "knowledge";[25] the relationship between the different points of view generated within particular

[23] See Genders and Player (1989).
[24] See for example Connell (1987).
[25] For contrasting positions in this debate, see Kennedy (1989) and Williams (1991).

people according to their experience of different forms and combinations of prejudice and subordination; the extent to which oppression has to be understood in cultural as well as (or as opposed to) material (economic) terms; and political questions about how to move towards a society in which these different perspectives and experiences can be heard and recognised in the attempt to begin to dismantle oppressive power relations and to reconstruct human relations along non-oppressive lines. These important questions of social and political theory will be addressed in several of the later chapters of this book. For the purposes of this chapter, it need merely be noted that the fragmentation and diversity of the experience of oppression in society is of great significance for any group-based approach to reform of anti-discrimination law.

RACE, GENDER AND CRITICAL SOCIAL THEORY

I hope that enough has been said in the last section to show both that the methodological tools of a critical feminism are powerful in analysing a variety of social issues including those of race and ethnicity, and that this approach may be suggestive not only of critical points but also of positive future directions for anti-discrimination law. However, it must be re-emphasised that the argument is at the level of critical method, and does not imply any simplistic assumption about analogies between racial or gender oppression in this or any other society. The project so far has been to extend a certain kind of critical analysis, which in Britain has hitherto been applied to sex discrimination law, to anti-discrimination law more generally. However, the analogies and points of contact between sexism and racism must occupy our attention, because they raise intensely difficult and crucially important problems of principle and practice. For example, Asian women who have organised against domestic violence have often met with particularly strong police reluctance to intervene.[26] The police argue that this resistance is justified on the basis of the value of the extended Asian family and the need to allow that institution to settle its own disputes (hence avoiding awkward cultural conflicts). These women point out that this denial of support is not only sexist but also racist, in that it is based on stereotypes about

[26] An eloquent and incisive account of just such a situation was given by members of the Southall Black Sisters at a seminar held by the Oxford University Women's Studies Committee in its series on "Race, Class and Gender" held in autumn 1985.

the way in which Asian people live. There could hardly be a starker example of the denial of respect implicit in the marginalisation of an experience these women had struggled and sacrificed an enormous amount to express. It also represents the kind of doubly oppressive situation which is liable to arise from the fragmentation of human identity. These women were ignored by the white state power to which they appealed at the same time as being subject to censure in the community from which they came; in putting the issue in the public domain, they also inevitably risked the propagation of stereotypes of the authoritarian role of men in Asian families by media and police.

As social institutions, racism and sexism clearly exhibit certain important differences. The centrality of naturalistic and biologistic arguments in constituting and maintaining them, at least in Britain, is arguably different; membership of particular racial groups is heavily correlated with social class and with poverty, as conventionally understood, in a way which is not so obviously true of gender. The experience of racial oppression is arguably more diverse than that of sexism given the variety of stereotypes about different racial groups. Furthermore, the need to understand oppression in cultural terms is more contested, and the meaning of "cultural discrimination" less clear cut, in the case of women than in the case of ethnic minority groups. Even in the case of racial discrimination there has been a reductive tendency towards a focus on discrimination as colour prejudice as opposed to the devaluation of a particular set of values and way of life.[27]

However, much also connects racism and sexism. Both are strongly associated with a variety of forms of political and social disadvantage—educational, economic, in the arena of criminal justice—and both rely to a significant extent on stereotyped views about what is normal to, appropriate for or to be expected of members of that group simply by virtue of that membership. Perhaps most importantly, both have been recognised as social institutions—parts of the structure and patterning of social relations—rather than merely cumulations of individual prejudices, actions and decisions. This move from the recognition of discrimination to the naming of and struggle against sexism and racism is a crucial one, and opens up the possibility of and need for the common critical methodology outlined above. Finally, and more contingently, Afro-Carribean and

[27] On this point, see Modood (1992).

Asian people and feminists who have come to this kind of consciousness of racism and sexism tend to share a deep scepticism about
how far their situation is likely to be improved by resort to a white
male-dominated legal process which relies on individual assertions of
right. Can the legal process respond positively to this scepticism? Can
legal forms be de-individualised and politicised so as to reflect and
tackle racism and sexism understood in this way?

FROM INDIVIDUAL TO GROUP?

There are many ways in which the legal process might try to respond
to the scepticism of women, Afro-Carribean and Asian people. In
this chapter, I shall canvass only one: the move from an exclusive
reliance on individual enforcement in the discrimination area to
include a focus on the rights, interests and claims of groups.[28] This
kind of reconstruction seems to be well worth considering given the
powerful criticisms of the limitations inherent in individual enforcement and the accompanying representation of the paradigm legal
subject as an abstract individual which, it has been argued, is implic-
ity white and male. Could a move to the recognition of group rights
and/or collective remedies help to overcome the problems of legal
individualism or to deconstruct the notion of the abstract legal subject in acknowledging as subjects entities recognised precisely
because of their substantive social position? I shall discuss this question on the assumption that such a reform would not replace but be
combined with either the existing legislation, or a reformed statutory
framework of individual enforcement which might move away from
the liberal symmetry of the current legislation.

    Group rights may be understood in a variety of different ways,
several of which might be worth considering in reforming anti-
discrimination law. For the purposes of this discussion, I shall distin-

---

[28] This is not a novel suggestion. In his early work on the British Race Relations legislation, *Legal Control of Racial Discrimination* (1980), Lustgarten canvassed the idea of a "collective remedial concept of discrimination" (pp. 31–7). The disadvantage-based, remedial rights
which I suggest have much in common with Lustgarten's ideas, and his discussion is illuminating in defending the practicality of the notion and illustrating its continuity with current
approaches to anti-discrimination law in the USA. Interestingly, his original suggestion
attracted little comment or response. This may have been because of its relatively brief treatment in the context of a longer work, but it is probably also attributable to most commentators' unquestioning acceptance of the individual model at the time at which Lustgarten was
writing.

guish between just two senses of group rights. The first I shall call
"cultural" or "protective" rights. These may be adopted to protect
and express respect for the distinctive ways of life of peoples from
specific ethnic, racial or religious groups. An example would be the
rights of a Sikh to wear the dress appropriate to his or her religious
beliefs, or the right of a Muslim worker to observe traditional religious holidays or hours of prayer. This kind of right is already recognised to some extent in British law, both indirectly via the Race
Relations Act[29] and directly in legislation such as the Road Traffic Act
1988, section 16(2) (which exempts Sikh motorcyclists from the
requirement to wear a crash helmet provided that they are wearing a
turban). Such cultural rights are not so much group rights as rights
pertaining to a person by reason of his or her membership of a particular group, although one can certainly imagine occasions on which
it would be useful to allow the group itself to take legal steps through
its representative or authoritative body to ensure that such rights
were met. The development of these kinds of legal rights as one
means of ensuring tolerance of and promoting respect for cultural
diversity is something which calls for serious and continued consideration. Such rights do, however, raise some very difficult issues,
notably in terms of their potential for "essentialising" or "reifying"
particular cultural identities and for fixing particular individuals
within those identities.[30]

In this chapter, however, I want to assess the potential of a second
conception of group rights, which I shall call "remedial" rights.
These "remedial" rights focus on socio-economic disadvantage and
the distribution of basic goods rather than on cultural discrimination
and the value of cultural pluralism. These rights would apply to
groups which were suffering disadvantage as a result either of present
oppression or the present effects of past oppression, in areas of life in
which this was the case.[31] The essence of the right would be that

---

[29] See for example *Mandla v. Dowell Lee* [1983] 2 AC 548.

[30] See further Chapter 5. For an excellent discussion of the problem of "cultural essentialism", see Volpp (1994); on rights to cultural membership, see Kymlicka (1989).

[31] A link between the two senses of group-based rights is suggested by Charles
Lawrence's argument that in interpreting anti-discrimination law (and hence in ascribing any
"remedial" rights), the decision-making tribunal might be directed to consider whether the
"cultural meaning" of the existing disadvantage was a racial or religious one ("The Id, the
Ego and Equal Protection" (1987)). Whilst I find Lawrence's arguments about the importance of unconscious racism totally persuasive, my feeling is that, even if it would work in
the USA, in the British context a "cultural meaning" test would turn out to be highly
restrictive. The lack of a recent history of overt and blanket legislative exclusion of ethnic
minority groups from certain goods, along with the persistence of racist attitudes, would

positive and effective steps be taken to combat and overcome that disadvantage within a reasonable period of time. This would mean that the holders of such rights would typically be members of minority ethnic and religious groups and women, rather than white men, and that the very instantiation of the rights would therefore express the perceived social problem to which they purport to respond. The enforcement of these group rights would need to be supported by adequately resourced public agencies which would offer counselling, legal advice and representation, and which would monitor the effectiveness of remedies over a substantial period of time. The assertion of group rights would be met with remedies not only of the traditional legal kind—i.e. damages or injunctions distributed so as to have an impact upon assignable individuals who are members of the group—but also a wide range of radically different remedies which would not necessarily be susceptible of such distribution. This feature would be crucial in breaking the conceptual link between loss and remedy which characterises the individual legal form.[32] Hence contract compliance, quota systems and other affirmative action programmes, urban development programmes, educational reforms and money to set up community projects of various kinds would be possible responses to the legal assertion of the violation of a group right.

Should such rights be instantiated as legal rights, or must they rather be conceptualised as political rights? Would courts and tribunals as currently constituted be capable, politically or professionally, of administering legal actions asserting such claims? I would argue that it would be possible to legislate for such group rights in certain areas. For example, this might be done by allowing a group defined in terms of the Race Relations Act and Sex Discrimination Act categories (which it is to be hoped might be extended to include religion and sexual orientation) whose representation in an area of employment fell below its numbers in the general pool by a certain margin, or a group whose share of valuable educational resources was disproportionately low, to bring a claim for appropriate remedial action. As such, the action would have much in common with the procedural notion of a class action, but would have the additional feature of de-individualising the legal subject and opening the way for

mean that tribunals and juries would be reluctant to ascribe a "racial meaning" to *de facto* disparities. This judgment is reinforced by what we know of tribunals' interpretation of the "justification" test in indirect discrimination cases such as *Ojutiku v. Manpower Services Commission* [1982] IRLR 418.

[32] On this point, see Freeman (1978).

more wide-ranging remedies which are not tied to specific legally recognised harms. The essence of the action would be seen not so much as an assertion of the existence of widespread individual acts of discrimination against members of the group, but of an unjust disadvantage suffered by the group, the ultimate source of which would not be the subject of technical legal proof. This arrangement would overcome some of the main problems of legal proof and would be informed by an ideal of a substantive equality of outcome which goes well beyond the commitment of the present legislation. And although the structure of such actions would inevitably be complex, many of the technical problems which would arise have already been encountered and at least partially resolved in indirect discrimination cases under the 1975 and 1976 Acts.

What would be the main advantages of such an approach? First of all, such a notion of group rights would entail a form of class action which, as has been widely argued[33] and as is reflected in American experience, has a number of procedural advantages as compared with individual litigation. The encouragement, solidarity and consciousness produced by a class action; the wider relevance of individual pieces of evidence which can add enormously to the persuasiveness of the case; the possibility of interpreting discrimination as a patterned structure rather than as isolated individual act; progress in widening access to legal redress and moving away from a situation in which rights are in practice the preserve of the relatively privileged few among the underprivileged group; the possibility of spreading the costs of litigation: all these constitute major advantages of the class action approach. Obviously, the possibility of class actions exists without resort to the notion of group rights, but it is a natural concomitant of that notion and as such can fairly be regarded as one of its advantages.

Secondly, the recognition of collective rights would mean the direct and overt legal recognition of the specificity of the objects of racial and sexual discrimination. In other words, group rights would empower groups of people who experience a common socio-economic or educational disadvantage which is structured along racial, ethnic, gender or religious lines to assert themselves and the patterned nature of their disadvantage. Rather than stopping at giving all citizens *the same right* not to be discriminated against—a strategy which, as I have argued, obscures the nature of the real political

---

[33] See for example Gregory (1987) pp. 34–6; Chayes (1976); Pannick (1986) pp. 282–302.

problem—the collective approach would make those problems visible in the legal and political arena. For it would move beyond the exclusive reliance on a symmetrical approach, with the implication that the legal sphere might become a more symbolically as well as a more instrumentally powerful forum in which to assert and voice the disadvantages and injustices suffered by certain oppressed groups in our society. This would help to overcome the problem raised by the symmetrical individual enforcement model's implication that discrimination is something unusual, pathological, abnormal, and would put institutional discrimination centre stage. It would represent a significant step away from the notion of the abstract, gender and race-neutral individual legal subject who is equal with all other subjects before the law, and towards a legal recognition that sexism and racism mean that all subjects are *not* equal before the law, and that compensatory legal recognition and remedy is called for to combat the unfair disadvantage suffered by some legal subjects. It introduces into the courtroom the historical realities of racism and sexism, which could no longer be marginalised on the legal agenda by being divided up into individual pathological acts of discrimination of no general political significance. Litigation might become a forum in which an oppressed group actually advanced its cause and further developed its sense of solidarity and resistance to its race and gender-related disadvantage. Arguably, in other words, the notion of collective rights might help to politicise the legal process in a positive way.

Conversely, certain disadvantages and potential dangers are also inherent in the notion of collective rights. First of all, if we were to add a system of group rights to an otherwise unmodified structure of individual enforcement (and indeed to an essentially individualist liberal legal system), might the very starkness of the contrast itself serve further to marginalise racism and sexism as legal issues? Could the legal institutionalisation of a specific group paradoxically undermine the struggle against racism and sexism either by calling forth political hostility or by becoming a "specialist" or marginal area of legal practice? The first problem is met by the fact that such a change would not occur without some measure of political will and hence a change in the political climate, but the inhospitability of the legal system even to the limited models of agency enforcement introduced by current anti-discrimination legislation suggests that we should not merely dismiss the marginalisation point as a non-problem.

Secondly, important questions can be raised about whether the move from individual to group rights really overcomes feminist and other objections to the notion of legal rights, particularly if the structure of individual rights is left in place. In liberal political theory, the notion of collective rights has had the dubious honour of being both marginal and controversial, with purists tending to argue for the essentially individual nature of rights. Those liberals who are willing to countenance the notion of group rights tend to do so by analogy with individual rights, thus playing down their specificity.[34] This means that liberal notions of group rights tend to share many of the features of individual rights to which feminists, socialists and others object: their reliance on coercive enforcement and their oppositional and potentially divisive nature. If the liberal world of competitive assertions of conflicting rights by atomistic individuals is simply to be replaced or supplemented by a similar competition between self-interested groups, is this genuinely a political gain? Tom Campbell has argued persuasively for a conception of rights understood in terms of values and goods in which individuals or groups may legitimately have an interest (this could include the non-oppressive political treatment of both themselves and others).[35] He asserts that this conception escapes the disadvantages of the liberal model of competitive and coercive individual rights. As we have already seen, this kind of argument has not laid to rest feminist scepticism about the usefulness of rights discourse. But some of the most important of the relevant feminist and socialist arguments are addressed to a symmetrical liberal notion of rights, which the approach to disadvantage-based, remedial group rights which I have suggested would move beyond.

A third possible objection to the notion of group rights also flows from a scepticism about rights and their legal entrenchment. This is manifested, for example, in the arguments of Unger,[36] who asserts that the liberal legal project of fixing categories and boundaries in the concrete form of legal rules, and in particular in the form of entrenched constitutional rights, is retrogressive. In his view, the radical liberationist political project consists in precisely the opposite strategy—that of pulling down boundaries, questioning assumptions about how things have been organised traditionally, and making possible a wide variety of different kinds of social, personal and political arrangement. Unger's vision has itself been dubbed a kind of "super-liberalism", but in the version described it suffers from a naively utopian character which arguably disqualifies it as a serious

[34] See for example Raz (1986) pp. 198–203.
[35] Campbell (1983).
[36] Unger (1983), (1987).

argument against practical reforms which seek to intervene in the actual legal world experienced by relatively powerless, disadvantaged groups. His argument is connected, I think, with a certain kind of scepticism about the legal process which supposes that people always have a choice about whether to use legal forms or not, whereas in the present world, such a choice often doesn't exist. I shall return to this point in the concluding section of this chapter. Meanwhile it seems apposite to note that Unger's objection to the objectification and concretisation of particular categories and arrangements may not in any case bite against the kind of group rights which I am envisaging, which are contingent on the present existence of disadvantage and which would disappear with its dismantling.

Fourthly, a more serious problem for the notion of group rights seems to be the fact of fragmentation and diversity of individual and group identity noted in the last section. People in any social world are members of a number of different communities and groups, and suffer or enjoy a number of overlapping and interacting identities, advantages and disadvantages as a result. Those who are oppressed or advantaged for one purpose or in one sphere are not necessarily so in others. Hence we certainly cannot assume any kind of identity of interest among members of a group just because of one shared oppression, nor can we assume that, for example, racial oppression will have had the same kind of impact on the experiences, consciousness and life chances of all members of that group. A recognition of this kind of diversity, and a commitment to recognition of a plurality of oppressions, experiences and interests, seems to bring with it a nightmarish vision of the potential explosion of overlapping groups defined along different lines all competing with each other (and, implicitly, with parts of themselves) for the resources or changes necessary to dismantle their specific disadvantages. This vision bears some resemblance to the liberal, competitive notion of rights from which we are trying to move away. The practical and conceptual difficulties raised by the diversity of social oppression and the consequent fragmentation of group identity should therefore not be underestimated.

Conversely, we have to ask ourselves whether the legal constitution of *certain* groups identified in terms of specific forms of disadvantage as the bearers of special claims has its own dangers, given that they would be likely to be limited in number if only for practical reasons. For example, by apparently reducing the complexities of social oppression to two or three discrete, irreducible and separate axes, such a legal constitution of groups could be said to resonate with the reductionist mistakes of monolithic social theory which were criticised above. Furthermore, it can be argued (as indeed it frequently has been in discussion of reverse discrimination programmes) that the identification of women or a racial group as the object of a speficic policy of this kind serves to consolidate the very suspect categories which it is necessary to dismantle, and to reinforce the notion that race and sex can be legitimate reasons for action. This argument, which evokes Unger's critique, is, however, open to challenge. For it identifies the basis for reverse discrimination (or group rights) as the shared fact of race or gender rather than as the shared fact *of race- or gender-related disadvantage*.[37] The concentration on the latter rather than the former is crucially important, not least because it escapes the inference of reliance upon a more full-blooded identity of interest or indeed on any notion of the shared culture or values which may or may not characterise particular disadvantaged groups. Shared culture, values and ways of life can form the basis for, and indeed arise out of, discrimination and oppression, but this is not necessarily the case. Whilst, as we have already seen, there is a case for instantiating protective cultural rights to underpin respect for pluralism in certain areas, not all attempts to dismantle oppression need to cast in legislation the specificities of any particular self-identified group or culture. To this extent I am in sympathy with the direction of Unger's argument outlined above. I also take very seriously the lessons which we can learn about the difficulties of compensatory group-based rights from other countries such as India and Malaysia.[38] However, very significant differences exist between the Indian and Malaysian schemes and the more fluid approach which I have been considering, in which the legal structure would attempt to facilitate the self-identification of local disadvantaged groups within the broad categories of proscribed grounds of discrimination enacted in the Race Relations and Sex Discrimination Acts.[39]

Arguments are likely to be raised about the impact of the kinds of remedies which I have suggested. These are arguments often

[37] See Volpp (1994) for an application of this important distinction to the question of "cultural defences" in criminal law.

[38] See the essays by Menski and Phillips in Hepple and Szyszczak (eds.) (1992).

[39] Of course, one has only to look at the way in which the notion of a group and indeed of group rights has been used in political debate in apartheid countries such as South Africa to see that a reliance on the notion of culturally identified groups can carry with it serious political dangers. This is why the delineation of relevant groups in terms of (contingent) disadvantage as opposed to cultural identity is so important to my argument.

rehearsed in critiques of reverse discrimination, and they suggest that the individuals who benefit from such programmes are generally the relatively privileged among the disadvantaged groups. It follows that such strategies both miss their real targets and tend unjustly to disadvantage relatively underprivileged members of advantaged groups for the benefit of relatively privileged members of disadvantaged groups. This criticism is not wholly misplaced in its assertion that the effects of such programmes can fall in an unfortunately patterned way, but the *basis* for their criticism is misplaced. For it depends on the move from a group-based remedy to an individual-based objection. If we regard reverse discrimination as a genuinely group-based remedy, we are not called on to look in every case at questions of distribution between individuals, although distributive patterns over time will certainly be important. This argumentative move from group to individual is understandable because such objections are usually placed in the context of liberal discussions of reverse discrimination which attempt to defend it on the basis of individualistic theories of equal opportunity. Sophisticated liberal arguments for reverse discrimination have been put forward, but they are ultimately vulnerable.[40] This is because they have little to say about just why an egalitarian end-state as between particular groups is seen as desirable, or why an unequal outcome is seen as problematic in the absence of clear proof that a particular individual has suffered from the unjust inequality of opportunity suffered by at least some members of her group. Hence the liberal reply to the conservative objection that only the relatively privileged benefit from reverse discrimination programmes is not entirely satisfactory. Once again, I would argue that a satisfactory account can only be given on the basis of a more radical and thoroughgoing commitment to equality and to the elimination of social disadvantage.

GROUPS, LAWS AND POLITICS

I hope that I have now said enough to justify the tentative conclusion that it is worth the while of those of us committed to further political legal and action to combat racism and sexism to consider the symbolic and instrumental benefits to be gained by the constitution of collective remedial rights based on present social disadvantage. I have tried to show what kinds of questions critical social theory

---

[40] See for example Dworkin (1977) Ch. 9, and criticisms by Sandel (1982) p. 145 and Frazer and Lacey (1993) pp. 65, 87–8.

would raise about such group rights, and how these questions might be addressed. These questions are extremely complex and require a much more detailed analysis than I have been able to give them in this chapter. However, in conclusion, I should like to draw out one or two underlying questions for further comment.

The approach to group rights which I have sketched sits right on the traditionally constructed boundary between law and politics. This boundary is an artificial one, but given the conventional understanding of the specificity of legal and political processes, it is important to acknowledge that the kinds of remedies I have envisaged for breaches of group rights might well be seen as calling for political action and decision-making rather than for legal (judicial) determination. A more overtly politically significant constitutional court might well, in my view, be able to tackle such decision-making, but I would only hold to this view on the assumption that there would be radical changes in the training, selection, tenure and accountability of judges—changes which seem far from the political agenda in this country at the moment. On the present construction of the boundary between law and politics, remedial decisions with the significant resource implications likely to be effective in tackling racial and sexual disadvantage could only come from governmental institutions. As things stand at the moment, therefore, I suspect that effective recognition of group-based remedial rights would have to be at a political rather than a legal level. One compromise would be that courts should make a finding that a group right had been violated—probably on the same kind of basis as findings of *prima facie* indirect discrimination—and then refer the issue to a governmental or quasi-governmental agency with effective enforcement powers for remedial action, perhaps with a system of reference back to the court within a certain period of time.

A further feature of my arguments about group rights is that they apply in principle more widely than to the social institutions of racism and sexism. The specific implication of a commitment to disadvantage-based group rights is entirely socially contingent, but in a society such as ours it would certainly bite in principle against class oppression and socio-economic disadvantage in a variety of spheres including, significantly, education. In pointing out this kind of implication I am revealing just how radically egalitarian such an approach might be, were it to be pursued beyond the confines of the 'Sex Discrimination and Race Relations Acts' categories. Doubtless not everyone will accept the political attractions of egalitarian pluralism, and in this chapter I have not been concerned to defend it in a thorough way. I have been concerned rather to point out how a commitment to it can overcome some of the limitations widely recognised to characterise the current equality of opportunity approach. Hence I would suggest that its attractions are implicitly recognised by many who would baulk at its radical implications, in that it underlies the move towards recognition of racism and sexism as structural and as expressive of institutionalised power relations rather than as explicable as products of individual decision and action.

Finally, I should like to draw together some threads around the issue of left-wing scepticism about using the legal process to advance radical change on behalf of Afro-Carribean and Asian people, women and others. Feminist discussions of this issue (on which there is a wide range of opinion) are sometimes reminiscent of marxist arguments about the irreducibly oppressive nature of law, which become translated into something like a claim about its irreducible maleness. The marxist claim has always seemed to me to mark an unusual failure of imagination in marxist thought, and I feel the same about the feminist analogue. The claim that law under capitalism and law under patriarchy exhibit most of those oppressive features of those social systems seems to me both true and unsurprising. But we should beware both of reductionism and of a despairing and unrealistic surrender to the idea that the nature of law, unlike that of other social institutions, cannot be gradually transformed through political struggle and action. Even the fiercest critics of the Race Relations and Sex Discrimination Acts would, after all, be loath to see them repealed . . . Given its social power, we simply cannot afford to abandon the legal process as a site for political action. And we must not do so for a further reason, already touched upon: disadvantaged people do not always have a choice about whether or not to defend or advance their needs and interests by legal means. Sometimes they have to do so because legal action is initiated by other parties, and on other occasions they have to because no other avenue of redress is available or remains to be explored. We must try to alter law so as to make it more receptive to the arguments of the powerless, so as to stop it silencing their voices: we should not completely discount law as an arena for consciousness raising as well as material political advance.[41]

[41] For subtle and ambivalent assessments of the role of rights, see Herman (1994) and Crenshaw (1988). Crenshaw recognises the potential of legal rights both in combatting the "otherness" of black people in America yet also, conversely, in risking legitimation and co-optation. In the legal arena, winning and losing are, as she puts it, "part of the same experience". For further discussion of rights and feminist strategy, see Chapters 3, 4 and 8.

Group-based rights, then, just might be a step in the right direction, particularly if their recognition of disadvantage spilled over into
wider legal recognition at the level of defence to civil and even criminal actions, for example. This would be radical change indeed, but
if we are not prepared to think in this imaginative and speculative
way about law, we abandon it to its current status and our sceptical
stance becomes a self-fulfilling prophecy. I hope to have said enough
in this chapter to justify the conclusion that although the gains to be
had from law are at the moment quite limited, we must not abandon
the reformist project, just as we must not confine ourselves to a focus
on anti-discrimination law. Changing law must remain one modest
but important part of the radical political enterprise.

2

Theories of Justice and the Welfare State: A Feminist Critique

The topic of this chapter is one of considerable breadth. I shall, there-fore, adopt the time-honoured strategy of carving out a small portion of the relevant matter for particular attention. I intend to focus on three main issues. In the first place, I shall examine certain familiar criticisms of liberal theories of justice. These are the criticisms often voiced by communitarian, feminist and socialist writers, and my main interest in them here will be their bearing on the adequacy with which social democratic versions of liberal theory can accommodate the welfare state. Secondly, I want to subject the notion of the wel-fare state itself to some critical scrutiny. In particular, I want to ask how far conventional forms and interpretations of the ideal of the welfare state seem to realise the commitments which motivate them when we interrogate them from the perspective of a feminist cri-tique. In developing this argument, I am not meaning to claim any exclusivity for feminist critique; rather, it seems to me that the criti-cal methodology employed by feminism here is continuous with crit-ical perspectives which may be (and have been) used to reveal major deficiencies in the welfare state's response to questions of class and race, to name but two other important political issues. Finally, I shall consider in more detail one recent feminist critique of political the-ory, Susan Moller Okin's *Justice, Gender and the Family* (1989). This book both raises crucial methodological issues about modern politi-cal theory and explicitly addresses the question of the potentialities of social democratic liberalism for the just resolution of issues relevant to the scope and structure of the welfare state.

Before I reach these central questions, however, I need briefly to set this discussion in the context of its intellectual and political history, and to examine the two central concepts around which the chapter is organised. This will be the task of the first two sections. I shall then move on to discuss certain communitarian and feminist critiques of liberal theories of justice. Next I shall consider the feminist critique of the conception of the welfare state which has emerged in social democratic political theory, before turning finally to Moller Okin's critique of the liberal construction of the bounds of social justice and to some general conclusions about the implications of my analysis for legal and political theory.

THEORIES OF JUSTICE

The idea of justice has preoccupied moral, legal and, particularly, political philosophers ever since these activities were invented, with predictable results in terms of variety in both conception and methodology. In the face of this diversity, it is necessary to be selective, and I shall concentrate on two of the most influential late twentieth century conceptions of justice and their critics. In *A Theory of Justice* (1971) John Rawls famously elaborates and defends the notion of "justice as fairness", defined in terms of the principles of equal basic liberties for all citizens, fair equality of opportunity in the public sphere, and equality of wealth except in so far as inequalities are justified by their contribution to the well-being of the worst off. Debates about the meaning of these principles, the priority Rawls assigns to them, and the manner of their derivation have abounded since the publication of this extraordinarily influential work. For Rawls, justice is "the first virtue of social institutions": our constitution, public bodies and political practice alike must respect the principles of justice if they are to claim legitimacy. Justice represents the fair terms on which social cooperation may be mediated politically. Citizens are conceived as choosing the principles of justice behind a "veil of ignorance" about their own social position and conceptions of the good. Arguably,[1] Rawls' basic intuitions about the conditions for just decision-making are already embedded in his design of the "original position". As critics have noted,[2] this muddies the methodological role of the original position in Rawls' theory. It does not, however, in itself undermine the plausibility of the emerging principles, if they are found to be attractive on other grounds.

---

[1] And as Rawls himself has acknowledged in later work: Rawls (1980); (1985), both reprinted in Rawls (1993).

[2] See for example Nagel (1975); R. Dworkin (1975); Frazer and Lacey (1995).

The other recent liberal theory of justice to which I shall give special mention is that of Ronald Dworkin.[3] Whilst Rawls' conception
is of justice as fairness, Dworkin's might be termed "justice as equality and respect for individual rights". The basic tenet on which his
political philosophy rests is the existence of a right in all citizens to
equal concern and respect from government. In particular, he has
elaborated this idea in terms of a theory of equality of resources.
Whilst his theory, too, has methodological underpinnings which
resonate with social contract ideology, Dworkin's grounding theoretical device is an auction in which, unlike Rawls' original position,
the parties do know all about their society and conception of the
good.[4] The auction begins with each of the parties in possession of
an equal number of bargaining chips, and continues until no party
can improve her position by any further bargained exchange: given
their tastes and preferences, conceptions of the good and resources
available, nobody would swap their bundle of resources for anyone
else's. Like Rawls' original position, the design of Dworkin's auction
is itself informed by the evaluative premises which it supposedly
establishes. Once again, this should not be thought to rob the vision
of equality of resources combined with respect for individual rights
which forms the core of Dworkin's theory of justice of whatever
independent attractions it has.

Apart from the methodological similarities between these two
authors, they share a number of distinctively liberal preoccupations.
Notable among these are a hostility to perfectionism and a concomitant commitment to the idea that government's business is to facilitate citizens' living of their own lives according to their own
conceptions of the good. Justice, then, is about providing a framework within which individual freedom can be exercised in a social
context: the role of government is not to attempt to realise any conception of the good itself, but rather to ensure the justice of the social
context in which citizens live their own lives. These views explain
both Rawls' and Dworkin's hostility to utilitarianism and Rawls'
insistence on the "priority of the right over the good".[5]

The persuasiveness of these two modern liberal theories of
justice is amply attested to by the influence each has had in modern
political philosophy. My own reason for selecting them is that they

[3] See R. Dworkin (1977); (1981); (1986).
[4] See R. Dworkin (1981).
[5] On which, see Sandel (1982); for a critique of Sandel's position, see Kymlicka (1989)
Ch. 3.

represent the fullest development of liberal political theory in what we might call a social democratic or egalitarian direction. It is clear even from the very brief characterisation which I have given that each of them could properly be called a theory of *social justice*: in other words, that it has implications for the distribution of goods between citizens. Hence both Rawls and Dworkin envisage a substantial degree of positive state action, as well as an institutional framework to ensure the achievement and maintenance of just distributions between citizens. These theories of justice are therefore consistent with and indeed require some kind of welfare state.

In case it seems just obvious that this is what any theory of justice would do, we need to remind ourselves that both conservative and libertarian critics of social democratic liberal theories have rejected the idea that the scope of justice should be so broad. Hayek, for example, maintains that justice should be conceived in strictly formal terms as equality before the law, and that any positive redistributive role for government should be ruled out: indeed, he explicitly attacks the very idea of "social justice".[6] And Nozick has argued against all "patterned" theories of justice—those which seek to realise a certain "end state" or maintain a particular pattern or distribution.[7] Nozick maintains that a commitment to this kind of justice would require a constantly and oppressively interventionist stance on the part of government which would be inconsistent with the basic liberal value of individual freedom. He prefers to conceive justice historically in terms of (notoriously underdeveloped) principles of justice in acquisition and transfer, along with a principle of just compensation, which would be consistent with a minimal role for the state.

I shall not dwell on this debate, for whilst I accept that the libertarian concern with autonomy must be taken seriously, it seems to me that the debate between the advocates of social justice and the minimalists is either over or beside the point, in the sense that the minimalists have clearly lost the argument. The minimal state is one which literally does not exist in the relatively wealthy nations of the modern world, and even governments which are sympathetic to conservative or libertarian ideologies engage in redistributive politics.[8] The real debate for political theory must therefore be about the proper scope of and justification for political practices which seek to

---

[6] See Hayek (1960), (1976).

[7] See Nozick (1974).

[8] As Esping-Andersen (1990) has argued, the nature of the distributive orientation of particular welfare states also depends on their distinctive histories and institutional structures.

realise social justice, and the appropriate institutional framework for generating sufficient wealth to support the welfare state. It is hard to imagine any relatively developed state which did not in effect engage in redistributive activity. It is worth noting, however, that although from some libertarian perspectives theories of social justice like those of Rawls and Dworkin presuppose an unacceptably broad scope for government intervention, it is nonetheless the case that these theories envisage a restricted scope for the operation of principles of justice. For they basically have to do with political action, conceived as action by government and public bodies *in the public sphere*. Again, this is an issue to which we shall have to return.

THE WELFARE STATE

Theories of justice have increasingly implied or expressed rationales for and defences of the welfare state: conversely, most of us see the welfare state as being precisely about social justice. In Britain, the emergence of the welfare state in its fully developed form is usually traced back to the implementation of the Beveridge Report soon after the Second World War. However, the origins of a wider commitment to social provision can be traced to a much earlier period, notably to the idea of workmen's (sic) compensation in the late nineteenth century. The growth of state involvement in public provision of various kinds—health, education, poor relief and so on—has a long history, albeit one which accelerates markedly in Europe in the late nineteenth and twentieth centuries. It is also worth reminding ourselves that although modern welfare states are historically specific phenomena, the idea of public and collective provision is hardly a modern one. The ancient Greeks and Romans as well as many other early civilisations provided a wide range of public facilities which, whilst they differed markedly from some of the kinds of provision we now think of as central to the welfare state, reveal every bit as strongly a commitment to the idea that citizenship requires the provision of public facilities for its realisation.[9]

Ideas about the meaning of citizenship have been central to the development of welfare states, whether they have been expressed explicitly—in a constitution, for example—or left implicit in social and political arrangements. Conversely, particular welfare states

[9] See Walzer (1983) Ch. 3.

themselves generate conceptions of citizenship. Arguably, however, one particular idea has dominated the development of welfare states. This is the idea of need, and the recognition that citizens are entitled that the meeting of certain needs be guaranteed by communal provision as one of the fundamental rights pertaining to membership of a political community. Hand in hand with this is the idea that certain kinds of risk—such as those attaching to disability, illness, poverty, each of which relates directly to need—should be socialised. The idea of need has been controversial both philosophically and politically. Should needs be defined subjectively or objectively: are they relative or absolute?[10] Where a political consensus can be built around the idea of certain things as legitimate needs, to what extent should they be fulfilled: does a need for education include nursery and higher education: should the need for basic resources be satisfied by money or goods: should we recognise a right to subsistence or more; is the public provision for the meeting of needs inconsistent with private option to buy fuller provision? How can we generate the wealth needed to support an increasingly expensive welfare state to support ageing populations, and how are social democratic governments to sustain electoral support in the face of the rising tax levels needed to maintain existing levels of social provision under these circumstances?

These are just a few of the issues which have become the stuff of modern politics in the wealthy nations which can afford the luxury of debate about the relative merits of different degrees of social provision. Whatever the complexities of philosophical debates about the idea of need or the justification for state intervention by means of taxation, expropriation or prohibition, the articulated political debate is indeed about degrees. It is about what the extent of the welfare state should be, not about whether or not there should be one. In neither Thatcher's Britain nor Reagan's USA did any politician seriously suggest the total abolition of welfare benefits; the debate was rather about setting these at a level where their effect on individual incentives to independent economic activity was minimised. This is not to deny, however, that some of the "reforms" effected in the USA and Britain over the last two decades come perilously close to the effective dismantling of the welfare state in certain areas, nor that, even in the Nordic countries where the commitment to welfare provision

[10] See Barry (1965) Ch. III.3–5; Campbell (1983) Ch. 7; Fraser (1989) Ch. 8; Miller (1976) Ch. IV; Plant et al (1980) Chs. 2–4.

has been particularly strong, the welfare state is coming under increasing pressure as its demands on the economy expand.[11]

Inevitably, the extent to which provision for the needs of some conflicts with the freedom of others is a controverial issue. Those who make this kind of argument usually have economic freedom in mind, although issues of political freedom also arise. It is an important commitment, however, of supporters of the welfare state, that freedom has to be seen in terms which are not entirely negative, or at least not negative in a narrow sense.[12] This is both a political and a philosophical commitment. The idea is that freedom in a meaningful sense cannot be secured merely by ensuring the absence of external constraint in terms of coercion by some other agent. Real freedom also depends on the positive provision of certain facilities, the meeting of needs and so on, which allow us to live a free life in the sense that we can be said genuinely to be the authors of our own decisions.[13] Put in terms of an acceptable conception of negative freedom, this would mean recognising that external constraints which threaten freedom include factors such as economic need and ill health. Put positively, it means that we cannot be free unless we are provided with certain positive resources which allow us to develop ourselves and exercise our freedom effectively. A commitment to this broader idea of freedom entails that what may be argued to be the key political values of the modern state, welfare and autonomy,[14] are not in any simple relation of opposition with one another. Rather, they are linked in an intimate and complex way. This is not to say, of course, that the realisation of one person's freedom may not affect another's welfare: conflicts clearly can and do arise, and form the stuff of politics. But anyone committed to the ideal of the redistributive welfare state must be committed, I think, to the insight that the political value of autonomy depends in a very real sense on the meeting of welfare needs. It depends also, arguably, on the lack of very great inequalities of provision among members of one polity—inequalities which inevitably feed into people's conceptions of their own worth and dignity.

The idea of the *welfare* state therefore is that certain needs and interests of citizens are of such fundamental importance that society

[11] See Offe (1984); Esping-Andersen (1990).

[12] See Miller (1990), Ch. 1; Taylor (1985) Ch. 8.

[13] For further discussion of the idea of freedom and its implications for feminist theory see Chapters 3–5.

[14] See Lacey (1988) Chs. 5 and 8.

itself must guarantee their fulfilment. This conception of need or welfare is an objective one, in the sense that it refers to a social judgement rather than directly to the preferences of individual citizens. However, the distinction between objective and subjective is not absolute, because social conceptions of need will themselves be informed by decision-makers' ideas about standard preferences and feelings: about the subjective conditions as well as the objective conditions of human life—what people care about as well as what they have. Collective provision may be arranged in one of two ways. It may be available as a safety net: i.e. the assumption and hope is that citizens will provide, individually or collectively, a certain good or resource for themselves, but if they fail to do so, the state will step in to do so. The obvious example here is that of social security or welfare payments to people who are unemployed or whose employment provides insufficient funds for their maintenance at what that society regards as either a subsistence level or some more generous standard such as what is required for a decent or fulfilling life. Alternatively, provision may be intended to apply generally, often with the possibility of some degree of option out for those who wish to provide for themselves privately. Obvious examples here would be health, education and public facilities in areas such as sports and culture.

For the purposes of this discussion, I shall adopt David Miller's definition of the welfare state as "an institution with the following three features: first, it provides benefits (goods and services) to everyone in a particular society, regardless of whether they have contributed to the cost of providing them. Second, it provides *specific* benefits which are seen as meeting needs, rather than sums of money which can be used as the recipient pleases. Third, the institution is funded by mandatory taxation, with tax schedules having no deliberate connection with the benefits that various classes of people are expected to receive. In short the institution is potentially redistributive, specific in its aims, and compulsory".[15] I shall work with Miller's vision of the welfare state as committed to the elimination of poverty, provision for those with special needs, and the reduction of inequality.[16] We should note, however, that the majority of welfare states also operate a two tier—contributory and non-contributory—system in areas such as unemployment insurance. I shall advert to these areas of partially contributory provision despite the fact that they fall outside

[15] Miller (1990) pp. 99–100.
[16] Miller (1990) p. 8.

Miller's definition, as they raise some of the most important feminist questions about the welfare state.

THE LIMITS OF LIBERALISM?

As we have seen, modern liberal theories of justice, even in their anti-perfectionist form, have moved in a social democratic direction, and not only allow for but positively envisage the existence of a welfare state. Nor are Rawls and Dworkin unusual in this: in the late twentieth century, liberal orthodoxy *is* welfarist.[17] Raz's work in particular develops an illuminating argument about the ways in which a realisation of autonomy presupposes and depends upon the provision of public goods and facilities, the existence of a public culture. Raz also rejects the tenet, once thought central to liberalism, of the state's neutrality as between conceptions of the good. He argues in favour of a recognition that liberalism itself espouses what is in effect a conception of the good life, albeit one which leaves broad scope for individual choice and self-determination.[18] But even social democratic versions of liberalism have been thought deficient in terms of their commitment to a thoroughgoing conception of social justice. It is to some of these communitarian, feminist and socialist criticisms that I now turn, in order to focus on the first of my main questions: how far can liberal theories adequately cater for the welfare state?

One idea to which communitarian, feminist and socialist critics of liberalism tend to give emphasis is that human beings are necessarily and primarily social beings. In other words, not only our projects, tastes and commitments, but in some real sense our identities—our selves—are tied up with the sort of society in which we live, the communities to which we belong. This has generated a lively and now well-known debate about the appropriate conception of the person or the self from which political philosophy should proceed. Communitarians,[19] have taken liberalism to task for its assumption of a "disembodied" conception of the self, prior to its ends and abstracted from its social context—a self which is perhaps most graphically represented in Rawls' construction of the original posi-

---

[17] As the work of other political theorists like Ackerman (1980), Barry (1989), Kymlicka (1989) and Raz (1986) and (1995) shows.

[18] See Raz (1986) Chs. 5, 14, 15; see also Macedo (1990) Ch. 2, and Rosenblum (ed.) (1989).

[19] Notably Michael Sandel (1982) Ch. 1.

tion. This is argued to have led to an impoverished view of the potentialities of social life—to a focus on the priority of justice as between individuals and a relative lack of interest in collective values and in the scope for more affective virtues such as benevolence and altruism. Liberals have countered that communitarians' embodied, socially situated conception of the self encounters problems in terms of its fragmented and determined nature. For this conception appears to leave little scope for the notions of agency, will and subjectivity which are central not just to the liberal political vision but also to feminist and marxist views.[20]

Like most political debates, this communitarian/liberal argument has become unduly polarised, with each side constructing its opponents' position in terms of extremes. Clearly, both Rawls and Dworkin give significant recognition to the influence of the social in determining not just the conditions of persons' existence, but also those persons' commitments, conceptions of the good and so on. Conversely, Sandel, Taylor[21] and other communitarians do not see the agent as entirely victimised or engulfed by her social circumstances, and do see a role for reflection and decision. The recognition that humans are socially constituted does not entail the non-revisability of our ends and attachments, although it does explain why we often find such revision difficult and painful. The really interesting thing here, however, is not so much the choice between two radically different approaches to selfhood, but rather the starting point for reflection about the nature of a just social order. Where the communitarians and others seem to me to have an unanswerable point is in their identification of a certain *direction* of thought and argument in liberal theorising. For liberals like Rawls and Dworkin unarguably take the individual and his or her needs and interests as their starting point, and move from there towards inferred needs for collective provision. The ultimate value, reflected in Rawls' priority of liberty and Dworkin's emphasis on individual rights, is that of the life of self-determination, drawing on such public and collective goods and facilities as are necessary to provide for this valued possibility.[22] The

[20] The question of whether, and in what sense, feminist theory needs a concept of agency or of the subject is, of course, a contentious one. For a powerful argument against such a view, see Brown (1995); for further discussion see Chapters 4 and 6. On both this question and the distinction between methodological and substantive aspects of communitarianism, see Chapter 5 and Frazer and Lacey (1993).

[21] Taylor (1985) Ch. 7; (1989).

[22] This is not to say that Rawls and Dworkin are relativists, or uninterested in the relative value of different lives and conceptions of the good. As liberals they regard state

direction of argument, then, is from individual to collective; it is the life of the citizen, rather than the ideas of citizenship and a community of persons, which is their focus.

The social constructionist communitarian view would question this direction of argument. For if we can all agree, at least, that human beings are necessarily social—that we do live socially and could not live otherwise; that even the basic things valued by liberals can only be achieved in a social context—then social structure and collective provision appear to be either the most appropriate starting point for political theory, or, at least, an equally important starting point to that of ideas about individual personhood. From this point of view, the worry about starting with the individual and moving towards the social is that the social provision which, admittedly, theorists like Rawls and Dworkin justify, is valued only indirectly and contingently. If even a relatively weak socially constructionist thesis is correct, as I believe it is, then the usual liberal division between individual and society is conceptually problematic. The link between the individual and his or her community is more intimate, and the notion of public goods, collective values and social provision should be more central to political theory, than theorists like Rawls and Dworkin have acknowledged.

Clearly, recent arguments like Raz's argument about the importance of public culture[23] and Kymlicka's defence of the notion of cultural membership[24] move some way in this direction. Dworkin's more recent work, which gives a central place to the ideal of community structured by fraternal (sic) relations flowing from the right to equal concern and respect, seems to move in a similar direction.[25] However, it is unarguable that liberal political philosophy has been slow to develop a theory of public goods and collective values, of social virtues and roles such as citizenship, of similar detail and sophistication to its accounts of basic liberties, individual rights and so on. I emphasise this point because I think it helps to explain why, although modern liberalism can accommodate the welfare state, it has actually had relatively little to say about it, and has been content to leave detailed debate about the welfare state to feminist and socialist

neutrality and respect for liberal values as the appropriate political means for allowing valuable lives to be led. The real value lies neither in freedom nor in certain conceptions of the good: it is that good lives be led freely.

[23] Raz (1986) Parts III–IV.

[24] Kymlicka (1989) Chs. 8–10: it should be noted, however, that Kymlika's idea of cultural membership is an *individual* right.

[25] See Dworkin (1986), (1990).

theorists.[26] I would argue, then, that the insights of the social constructionist stance of communitarianism should lead us to a different direction or emphasis of argument in political philosophy—one which would give greater attention to the social in reflection on the just society, and one which would therefore develop a more concrete conception of the welfare state than has been the case with social democratic liberal theories.

Before moving to the feminist critique of the welfare state, I want to advert to one last issue on which liberal theories of justice have recently been subjected to criticism—much of it from feminist theorists. We have already seen the way in which communitarians have criticised liberals' conception of the "limits of justice", and have argued that other values such as solidarity, reciprocity and benevolence should be regarded as of *political* importance. The liberal idea of the priority of justice as a political virtue is tied up with the idea of the proper limits of the state. This is also true of the object of a converse (not necessarily conflicting) objection, which argues that liberals have failed to extend the notion of justice sufficiently far to realise even the liberal values and ideals by which they are motivated. Typically, this objection focuses on the liberal division of the world into public and private spheres: a strictly delimited public sphere is appropriate for the enforcement of justice, whilst the state leaves relations and distributions in the private sphere untouched.[27]

Both the liberal argument on which the objection focuses and the objection itself are obscured by the difficulty of actually identifying the public/private division. Ideas of what inhabits public and private realms are historically and culturally specific. Yet whatever the configuration of these realms at a particular time, a major difficulty arises from the question-begging way in which ideas of public and private tend to be used: public simply to denominate "that sphere in which state intervention is justified", and private the reverse, without any detailed argument about the actual justification. The justification has, of course, to do with the value of human freedom, which Mill's argument for the harm principle has the virtue of making clear.[28] But arguments about public and private spheres are all too often hived off from their underlying liberal rationales and used as if we were simply *describing* spheres of activity, obscuring the normative premises of the argument.

---

[26] See Campbell (1983); Hernes (1987); Miliband (1969); Miller (1990); Plant *et al.* (1980).

[27] See Okin (1989) Chs. 2, 6; O'Donovan (1985); Olsen (1983); for a more detailed discussion, see Chapter 3.

[28] Mill (1859).

Feminists, while recognising the importance of limits on state action, have criticised both this question-begging use of the public/private distinction and the substantive judgements which its use disguises.[29] For spheres of life which turn out to be private are disproportionately often those of particular importance to women. Their denomination as private has the consequence that the state both leaves in place the pre-existing power relations in these spheres (power relations which exploit women) and depoliticises women's central concerns and disadvantaged position. Furthermore, the appeal to "private spheres" is often disingenuous in social democratic discourse. If used "descriptively", there simply is no "private sphere" in which the modern state does not intervene: the oft-cited example of the family is in fact hedged about with legal regulation at every turn. Even the most extreme libertarian would not argue that the family sphere should be exempt from operation of laws such as those against serious assault; and even the most blinkered observer would have to acknowledge the influence of social welfare laws on family structure. If used presciptively, moreover, the notion of the unregulated family depends on a tenuous distinction between acts and omissions. The state claims it has no responsibility for what happens in the family—this is a private sphere. But where it omits to regulate, the state implicitly confirms the existing distribution of power and goods within the family. Failure to apply the demands of justice to the "private sphere"—for example the family—means that the guarantees of justice and equality held out to citizens in the public sphere are worth systematically less to those who are "pre-politically" disadvantaged. The limited scope of political justice asserted by liberals such as Rawls and Dworkin is, in other words, inconsistent with the realisation of the values which they claim to espouse. Unless the bounds of justice are widened, the idea that social democratic liberal theories are in any real sense egalitarian or socially progressive must be abandoned.[30]

In this section I have focused on two main debates around liberal egalitarian theories of justice: the communitarian and social constructionist critique of liberal individualism and the feminist critique of the public/private distinction. In the first case it seemed that the

---

[29] Young (1987); see further Chapter 3.

[30] Many of the problems of the distinction between public and private drawn by liberal political theory are reproduced in Habermas's social theory (Habermas (1975), (1987)). For feminist critique of his distinction between the systems- and life-worlds and his argument that we should decry the "colonisation of the lifeworld" by the systems world in the developed welfare state, see Fraser (1989) Ch. 6; Hernes (1987) pp. 153–63; see also Chapter 5.

emphasis and direction of liberal thought had inhibited the full development of a political-theoretical account of the welfare state. In the second, conversely, it seemed that the implications of a welfarist social democratic polity in terms of shifting and blurring the boundaries between public and private spheres have simply not been taken on board by liberal theorists. In each case, the move towards central accommodation of the welfare state and a thorough commitment to social justice appear to be pushing social democratic theories to their limits and perhaps beyond them.

WOMEN'S CITIZENSHIP AND THE WELFARE STATE: FROM PRIVATE TO PUBLIC PATRIARCHY?

I now want to shift perspective from political theory to political practice, to look at the ways in which welfare states have in fact developed. I shall then return to theories of justice to see how far the deficiencies in welfare states which can be identified from a feminist perspective relate to some more general theoretical problems. Since it is impossible to develop an argument which takes account of even a representative sample of welfare states within the scope of this chapter, I shall draw my examples from Britain. However, many of the points I shall make are of wider application.[31]

I said earlier that a commitment to the welfare state discloses a certain conception of citizenship—of the necessary conditions for membership of and participation in a polity and of what the polity sees as the most important interests of its members and their mutual obligations of provision and support. The needs met and goods and services provided by the welfare state disclose a conception of the necessary conditions of citizenship and the nature of the common life. When we look at the operation of welfare states, however, we all too often find that the egalitarian commitments which inform the idea of the welfare state are not realised in terms of equal eligibility for, let alone access to, its benefits.[32] Inequalities of access are strikingly patterned along class, race and gender lines: research shows clearly that the most generally provided benefits are taken up far more effectively by those who are relatively privileged in terms of education and resources.[33]

---

[31] See Hernes (1987); Watson (ed.) (1990).

[32] See Pateman (1989) 179 et seq; Fraser (1989) Chs. 7, 8; Dale and Foster (1986); Walby (1990).

[33] See Le Grand (1982).

Unfair inequalities of eligibility, however, are most likely to be patterned on racial or gender lines. Taking the example of gender, the welfare system in Britain was set up on the basis of the concept of the "family wage": hence the presumed contributor to the welfare system and recipient of welfare benefits was the "head of the family"— i.e. the man, presumed to be the breadwinner. Indeed it would not be going too far to say that the implicit construct of the citizen on the basis of which the welfare state was designed was that of a man, with single women gradually getting recognition. Some aspects of the welfare state were originally designed precisely to keep women, and mothers in particular, out of the paid labour market.[34]

Although most benefits are now formally equally available, in practice access to benefits is still structured along gendered lines. The rule, for example, that a member of a cohabiting couple has their claim tested in the light of the other member's earnings acts to disqualify far more women than men from access to benefits. There is a clear and disturbing echo here of Rawls' use of the concept of "heads of households" as the representative decision-makers in the original position: the apparently gender-neutral ideal of citizenship disclosed by the welfare state in fact turns out to be highly gendered.[35] The degree of accretion of rights to benefits such as state earnings-related pensions, unemployment benefits and so on depend on access to pre-existing benefits which are already highly unequally distributed along gender lines—most obviously because men on average still earn more and more often have unbroken career paths due to lower levels of domestic responsibility than women. Moreover, given the distribution of work in the "private" sphere, criteria of eligibility for (particularly full-time) work are often impossible for women with family commitments to meet, thus excluding them from the ambit of higher tier unemployment benefits and pensions which are generally related to past employment-related contributions. These differences are such that it has been argued that women are constructed as dependent clients of the welfare state. Whilst men are likely to be in the position of *entitled* claimants whose rights flow from economically recognised contributions, women's contributions of labour within the home are entirely disregarded.[36] The implications of the public/ private divide are obvious here.[37] Conversely, women are over-

[34] See Pateman (1989) p. 194.
[35] See Okin (1989) Ch. 5.
[36] See Fraser (1989) pp. 149–53; Hernes (1987) Chs. 1, 2.
[37] See Atkins and Hoggett (1984) Chs. 5, 6, 9, 10; Stang Dahl (1986) Chs. 7, 8.

represented among not only those employed by the welfare state but also those economically dependent on welfare benefits, because they are overrepresented among the poor.[38] This makes the fact that the benefit system is implicitly designed on a male model even more inappropriate. Women (and children, for whom women still bear primary responsibility) have therefore suffered disproportionately from the retrenchments in welfare provision undertaken by recent administrations in Britain.

What has liberal political theory had to say, of a perceptive and critical nature, about these deficiencies in the welfare state? Given what I have already said about liberalism's slowness to engage in reflection about public goods and provision, it is perhaps not surprising that the answer is, very little.[39] As Carole Pateman points out,[40] in a gendered society committed to liberal politics, women are caught in a dilemma. On the one hand, they can try to claim full citizenship on the male model—a possibility which is either ruled out for or unattractive to many women because of their social position and responsibilities. Alternatively, they can argue for the recognition of a female conception of citizenship based on women's special contributions—an avenue which is unpromising because those special contributions are seen as economically valueless and because the argument in any case threatens to undermine the foothold of women's claims to liberal equality. Even more significant, however, is the fact that liberalism's failure to address the gender deficiencies of the welfare state is simply one aspect of the almost total silence maintained by political theorists on issues of gender. The question which I now want to examine is how far this relates to general problems with the structure of modern political theory, and how far they can be overcome.

GENDER AND POLITICAL THEORY

First, let us return to the question of liberal emphasis on the individual. As we saw in our earlier discussion, the idea that liberalism assumes an atomistic and disembodied individual, abstracted from his

[38] Gender patterns in unemployment and labour markets have, of course, changed significantly over the last decade; however, gender continues to mark one of the most important divisions in these areas.

[39] There are, of course, a few honourable exceptions: see for example Gutmann (ed.) (1988).

[40] Pateman (1989) p. 197.

or her social context, has been exaggerated. Yet it is hardly to be doubted that liberalism's primary focus on the individual, on persons *one at a time*, abstracted from their social context, as moral units, is inimical to giving issues of gender the central place in political theory which their practical importance dictates they should have. The use of sex-inclusive language by political theorists may represent an advance in that they no longer implicitly represent the world as populated entirely by men, but the modern usage has its own dangers.[41] For it sends the message that gender equality in political life can be attained simply by means of gender neutrality, and obscures the fact that the practices and institutions being argued for are designed on the basis of strongly gendered assumptions about matters such as the structure of families and the division of labour.[42] Until political theorists begin to give social context greater attention, structural features like gender are likely to go on being ignored, in an unrealistically utopian world of genderless, classless, raceless persons (i.e. implicitly a world of white middle class men). Until the question of public goods, public culture and social structure, along with questions of substantive access to these goods, rather than formal opportunity to take them up, become a central concern of political philosophy, the questions which, for example, feminists and anti-racists want to prioritise will continue to be marginalised. And until social democratic political theory begins to address the limitations inherent in the public/private distinction as traditionally constructed, it will be structurally incapable of delivering justice to women, of counting women as full members of the polity, of developing a conception of citizenship which is not implicitly male.

I now want to make this argument more concrete by focusing on the public/private division. I do so both because the division is so central to the feminist critique of traditional political theory and because it has recently been developed by Susan Moller Okin in a persuasive form which illuminates its relevance to the feminist critique of the welfare state. I want to take up many of Okin's ideas, while also marking out some differences between her approach and mine. Okin argues powerfully that the way in which the limits of justice have been drawn by liberal theories of justice has marginalised and depoliticised women's disadvantages, setting them outwith the proper sphere of not only state action but also political concern and critique. Liberal theories have typically constructed the organisation

[41] See Okin (1989) pp. 10–13.
[42] For further discussion, see Chapter 7.

of family life, domestic work, sexuality and child-rearing as largely private matters, for the decision of individual citizens. They have therefore left untouched and implicitly colluded in the maintenance of the very areas of social life which disable women from participating equally with men in the public sphere. The division of labour within the family systematically inhibits women's participation in the paid labour force, particularly its more remunerative and prestigious areas; lesser access to resources, combined with the social construction of male and female sexuality and the structure of family and criminal law, means that women's power within the family is less than is men's; on divorce, women's work within the home is accorded small economic value, and her human capital investment in the family often accorded none at all. These and many other factors conduce to the relative poverty, lack of political power and low status of women and the children for whom they are disproportionately responsible. Outside the family, the mode or organisation of full-time, well paid work in the vast majority of areas is premissed on the unattached, full-time worker without domestic responsibilities; again, this is not seen as raising issues of justice. None of this is to deny that there are limits to both the efficacy and the legitimacy of state action. What the argument emphasises is a direct link between the distribution of power and resources in spheres not directly controlled by the state, and distributions within the public sphere. Injustices within one are bound to show up in the other. The guarantee of justice in the public sphere which Rawls, Dworkin and others hold out is illusory to women and others whose "private" experiences systematically hamper their abilities to take up the citizenship which liberals offer them on superficially gender-neutral terms. Okin shows how Rawls' own recognition of the importance of the family as the setting in which children develop their sense of justice must commit him to regarding the family itself as susceptible of critique on the basis of his two principles of justice: how, after all, can children acquire a sense of justice within a fundamentally unjust institution?[43]

Okin's arguments are persuasive, and many of her policy recommendations (such as compulsory compensation for human capital investment in childrearing on divorce, child care in the work place, parental leave) attractive. Some of her proposals raise serious questions about the potential efficacy of state action. But this can be no

[43] Okin (1989) pp. 97–101.

comfort to the political theorists whom she criticises: after all, political theorists are not widely known for their astute grasp of policy
practicalities, and usually defend themselves by retreating into arguments about what is desirable in principle. Moreoover, as Okin quite
rightly points out, even political theorists who have not espoused the
liberal division between public and private spheres—and those who
take a social constructionist line are certainly far more likely to see the
family as a genuinely political institution—have distinctly poor feminist credentials. Sandel, for example, who emphasises membership in
communities as the locus of both human development and political
value, has nothing whatsoever to say about gender, while MacIntyre
is almost wilfully blind to the sexism which is a pervasive feature of
the traditions which he would have us revive, and adds insult to
injury by using the female pronoun in discussing situations in which
those traditions would have excluded women. Walzer, although an
honourable exception in adverting several times to issues of gender
and giving at least some recognition to the question of distribution
within what liberals would regard as private spheres, gives the question of gender no systematic treatment. Not only have influential
liberal and communitarian political theorists therefore failed so far to
provide us with a sophisticated account of the welfare state, but certain *structural* features of their accounts actually prevent them from
doing so. Liberals' commitment to an under-theorised public/private
ideology inevitably blinds them to the ways in which the welfare
state's wholesale adoption of the traditional model of the family and
labour market as structural bases for the distribution of benefits raises
fundamental questions of justice to women. But communitarians are
unlikely to fare much better. For although they have the theoretical
equipment which would allow them to question the current pub-
lic/private divide and to see that private injustice will be directly
reproduced by a welfare state structured like that of Britain, their
myopia when it comes to gender issues means that they would be
unlikely to identify that obvious source of injustice in the first place.

In the face of these evident failings in contemporary political philosophy, Okin's strategy is to take up some of the basic substantive
prescriptions and methodological approaches which she finds most
satisfactory, and then to elicit their potential from a feminist point of
view. She points out that Walzer's principle of non-domination
between spheres has considerable potential in combatting the problem of private disadvantage engendering public injustice; she also
comments favourably on both Rawls' two principles of justice and his

methodology of the original position.[44] Whilst her argument about Rawls' commitment in logic to examining the family is unanswerable, I want to look more closely at Okin's general affirmation of Rawls' approach. Leaving aside the very challenging general critical literature on Rawls' two principles,[45] one of the problems for any feminist theorist in evaluating contemporary theories of justice is that, since gender has been virtually ignored, it is almost certainly the case that any reasonably liberal theory is going to have some untapped feminist potential, in the sense of positive implications for the treatment of women relative to our current social position. It is therefore quite difficult to get a grip on just what the limits of a feminist reading of these theories are. In my view, Okin exaggerates the potential of Rawls' theory, because she fails to see the fundamental problems with the structure of the original position.[46] The original position represents the political subject as essentially individual, disembodied, degendered. In decontextualising social decision in such an extreme way, Rawls inevitably marginalises issues such as gender (even if we can make sense of the idea of choice under conditions of such ignorance, as seems doubtful). Okin's response to this is to reply that the original position is not really about choice from a detached standpoint, so much as choice from the point of view of everyone: it captures the idea that fair choices only emerge when every decision-maker has made an attempt to enter into the perspective of people in other social positions.[47]

This is certainly an attractive reconstruction of Rawls' position, but it raises almost as many problems as the more traditional interpretation. Principally, it raises questions about the possibility of empathetic judgement, which are exacerbated by Rawls' stated conditions of ignorance. It assumes that a single individual can "get inside" the experiences of others, imagine what their lives might be, *without ever having actually to listen to anyone else*. This is a danger. The logic of Okin's position seems to lead to participatory democratic models in which people learn to speak and listen to each other, and take seriously each other's views:[48] translated into the terms of the original position, it conjures up a super-imaginative being. In particular, and

[44] Okin (1989) Chs. 3, 5, 6 and 8.
[45] See for example Barry (1973); Daniels (ed.) (1975).
[46] See for example Jaggar (1983) Ch. 3; Benhabib (1987); Frazer and Lacey (1993), (1995).
[47] Okin (1989) pp. 101–9; this reading is affirmed in Rawls' later work: Rawls (1993).
[48] Interestingly, Okin refers sympathetically to the feminist credentials of the kind of participatory politics advocated by Benjamin Barber (1984) (see Okin (1989) p. 200, n. 59). See also Phillips (1991); Mansbridge (1991).

of great concern to Okin, is the question whether the person in the original position could really empathise with the experience of being oppressed, in gender terms or otherwise. Either there really are a number of people in the original position, in which case men and women, black and white, rich and poor must be properly represented, or there is really just one representative person behind the veil of ignorance. On the latter model, we must presuppose the possibility of a degendered perspective—this person is neither male nor female.

Okin's own argument shows that the Rawlsian chooser is a man. She should be wary, I would argue, of the possibility of a genderless chooser for, given that all the societies we have known have been gendered, the idea of a viewpoint which is not formed in part by gendered experience is something which we have yet to encounter. Gender-neutrality is Okin's ideal.[49] Yet even if we endorse this ideal, to ask that the person in the original position think himself beyond the gendered conditions of the society he is allowed to know about into a society beyond gender is to put extraordinary demands upon him. Such demands stretch the limits of imagination, and possibly of logic, to breaking point. It is hard to resist the conclusion that the original position must dissolve into a conversation between real, socially situated people.[50]

CONCLUSION: A CRITICAL APPROACH TO SOCIAL JUSTICE

In the last two sections I have discussed the adequacy with which social democratic liberal and communitarian theories of justice have been able to account for the welfare state, and I have traced certain deficiencies in both practical and theoretical approaches to state welfare to certain deficiencies of emphasis in those theories. In particular, I have suggested that feminist criticisms of the construction of traditional political theory have identified many of the deficiencies which have led to an inadequate theorisation of the welfare state. I now want to conclude by drawing out some general implications for the best way to proceed in our theorising about social justice and the welfare state.

---

[49] On the issue of neutrality, see further Chapter 7.

[50] This is, of course, the position towards which Rawls has moved in his later work: Rawls (1980), (1985), reprinted in (1993).

In the first place, I have argued for a proper recognition of the social location of the individual: of the ways in which our communal ties and affective attachments, along with our cultural history, our geographical location and so on, fundamentally affect what we are like, our sense of our selves, *who we are*. Such a recognition dictates that political theory give a greater emphasis than has been the case with modern liberal theory to social context, social institutions, communities and cultures. This is not to say that our sense of ourselves as distinct and autonomous should not have an important place: clearly, it should. But the recognition that what is good for persons can only be fostered in social contexts must render those contexts at least as important a focus for political theory as the rights, interests and claims of the individual. The liberal ideal is that of persons living autonomous, choosing lives, pursuing their conceptions of the good. This carries with it, implicitly, a conception of political society and a public culture, and this must have more priority in political theory than most liberals have been willing to give it. If this kind of perspective were brought to bear in theorising about social justice, we should have a far more sophisticated theorisation of both social justice and the welfare state than we do.

Secondly, and implicit in any recognition of the primacy of the social, would be a greater emphasis on the importance of social context in influencing judgement. This has implications for the appropriateness of any kind of detached, ideal-observer starting point for political philosophy, and does, I think, point to a conception of political theory as a socially grounded activity which consists in the critical and constructive interpretation of certain traditions of thought. Even more importantly for the theorisation of the welfare state, it would bring political theory down from the heights of abstraction which characterise much of *A Theory of Justice* to the ground level of concrete social institutions: since such institutions have a decisive influence on how we think and live, an understanding of how they work and what their real impact is on people's lives must be central to political theory.[51] It is implicit in this view that political theory must concern itself with real, embodied, gendered, socially situated persons, and not persons in an idealised society which

---

[51] This is well illustrated in Walzer (1983). It is also reflected in the concern of at least some political philosophers with questions of the generation, as well as the redistribution, of wealth (Barry, 1989). This is a pressing question given that the rising cost of welfare provision is giving rise in many countries to retrenchments in social provision—retrenchments which push women back into the invisible welfare state of the "private" sphere.

we have never seen and which we have little idea how to bring about. It should also remind us that ideas which are seen as progressive in one social context may seem not to be so in another. For example, in more solidaristic and traditional societies such as Japan individualist libertarian theories may look progressive at the same moment that some aspects of communitarianism have looked progressive in the individualist cultures of Britain and the USA.

Thirdly, my discussion implies that a political theory which takes social justice and the welfare state seriously must focus on questions of distribution at a material level and not just at the level of formal equality of opportunity. As we have seen, one of the major drawbacks of actual welfare states is their failure to achieve the equality they aim for, and this has to do with inequalities not just in formal but in material access to their benefits. This has in large part to do with a failure in designing welfare institutions to think about access to their benefits from the point of view of the social locations of their likely clients, and with insufficient consideration of differences of social situation which will inevitably lead to perpetuation of inequalities of distribution by the welfare state. In terms of design of rules and their effects in practice, the welfare state must take account of our positions as women and men, working class and middle class, Asian, Afro-Carribean and so on. This means that issues of class, gender and race must be at the centre of political theory, rather than at the margins where they have been for so long. It also suggests that political theorists should be far more concerned with existing social worlds than they have traditionally been. Only once we abandon the idea that the starting point for political philosophical reflection is the non-socially situated individual, rather than the socially located woman or man from a particular class and race, implicated in certain kinds of networks, groups and communities, will we begin to generate theoretical ideas which could really help in designing effective and just welfare institutions.

Fourthly, the arguments of feminists like Okin and Jaggar dictate that political theorists subject the public/private distinction to a radical review. The overwhelming evidence that injustices in the private sphere carry over into material lack of access to justice in the public sphere dictates that we must reexamine the way in which the boundaries around the political sphere are currently drawn. This critique is often taken as asserting that there are no proper limits to state intervention. This is far from being the case. Most feminists certainly recognise the importance of a sphere of life left open to personal determination—indeed, this is one of the most important goods which women lack given the double burden inherent in current social arrangements.[52] But the current boundaries are unsatisfactory in that they leave uncorrected important sources of social injustice which government could tackle without more extensive intervention in personal lives than is already undertaken in areas such as the definition and regulation of marriage and divorce, the prohibition of surrogacy contracts and the invalidity of marriage contracts, and the regulation of adoption. The current construction of the public/private divide is both incoherent and disingenuous, for the family and sexuality are already extensively regulated. The current ideology of the public/private distinction cannot be maintained consistently with a commitment to gender justice from which most liberals and communitarians would be unwilling explicitly to dissociate themselves.

Fifth, and finally, I would argue that theorists of social justice need to reflect on whether the object of political allocation is appropriately to be limited to resources, or whether more intangible factors such as power and welfare should not also be objects of redistribution. The debate between theorists who favour equality of welfare and those who assert the ideal of equality of resources cannot be discussed here. It may well be that as a question of political means, only the equalisation of resources via welfare institutions is within the reach of the state. Indeed, we have so far been singularly unsuccessful even in our attempt to create greater equality of resources via our welfare systems. However, the ideal of social justice which informs commitment to the welfare state—particularly the ideas that people's needs generate obligations upon fellow citizens and that this recognition of mutual obligations of support defines the relevant political community— carries with it a commitment if not to equality of welfare at least to the idea that gross inequalities of welfare *are* states of affairs which should be of political concern.

Any political theory which does not recognise that power relations are relevant to the attainment of social justice is evading what is in fact a central question: indeed, just this kind of evasion is at the root of political theory's failure adequately to take on board questions of gender. To take one example, in many countries it either is or until recently has been the case that a man who has intercourse with his wife without her consent cannot be convicted of rape.[53] This quite

[52] Young (1987) 56.

[53] The position in England and Wales was modified by the House of Lords in *R v. R* [1992] 1 AC 599. The court rejected the idea that marriage implies a woman's irrevocable

evidently expresses and legitimises a view of unequal power relations within marriage. Any political theory which does not recognise this as a question of social justice, which tries to marginalise the question as one between parties in the private sphere, seems to me not to merit the name of a theory of justice.

consent to sexual intercourse on grounds of both the weakness of common law authorities for the marital rape exemption and its inappropriateness to modern conceptions of marriage. This change was confirmed by the legislature in the Criminal Justice and Public Order Act 1994. It remains to be seen how seriously the courts will treat marital rape in their sentencing practice. See Lacey and Wells (1998) Chapter iv.II. For further discussion, see Chapter 4.

3

Theory into Practice? Pornography and the Public/Private Dichotomy

"The feminist total critique of the liberal opposition of private and public still awaits its philosopher".[1] So concluded Carole Pateman in an important article written fifteen years ago. During the intervening years, there has been an explosion of feminist literature reflecting upon issues raised by public/private dichotomies in social and political thought. Much of this literature concerns itself with legal analysis or questions of legal policy and reform. Yet, notwithstanding this theoretical development, questions around public/private dichotomies have lost little of their power to bewilder, as each confidently asserted critique raises further questions of theory and strategy. Indeed, it sometimes seems that the more we talk and think critically about the public/private dichotomy, the more we get trapped within its conceptual framework.

In this chapter, I want to return to this well-worked terrain. I have two purposes in doing so. First, I want to distinguish several different concerns which have informed feminist preoccupation with the public/private dichotomy. Drawing on feminist political and social theory, I shall suggest the ways in which each of the different concerns which I shall identify feeds into questions of legal policy. Secondly, I shall turn my attention to one concrete area in which feminist activism—including that directed to law reform—has been informed by the public/private critique. The area I have chosen is pornography—an issue which perhaps above all others has been controversial *within* feminist thought, and in which issues of theory and strategy connect particularly closely. I hope to shed some light on why the pornography debate has been such a problematic one for contemporary feminism by looking at it again in the light of a more differentiated appreciation of the

[1] Carole Pateman, "Feminist Critiques of the Public/Private Dichotomy", in Pateman (1989) p. 118, at p. 136. The article was originally published in S. Benn and G. Gaus (eds.) *Public and Private in Social Life* (1983).

public/private critique. In particular, I shall try to identify the negative consequences which unjustified inferences from the public/private critique have had on feminist politics around pornography.

DISENTANGLING PUBLIC/PRIVATE DICHOTOMIES

The idea that "the personal is political" has been a central tenet of the contemporary women's movement. But the precise meaning of the slogan is less than clear. At its broadest, the idea implies a thorough-going reassessment of the traditional conception of what is properly within the realm of public debate and critique, most obviously by unearthing and making visible issues of gender which have been ignored in political theory and practice. One particular theoretical ploy has been to focus on a supposed liberal division of the world into public and private spheres: a strictly limited public sphere is appropriate for the enforcement of justice, whilst the state leaves relations and distributions in the private sphere untouched.[2] But though the idea of privacy as an essential constituent of individual autonomy has been central to the liberal tradition, public/private divisions are not confined to liberal or libertarian thought. The delineation of a "private" sphere which is beyond the scope of politics is a feature of Marxist thought, too: the sphere of reproduction within the family does not form the object of revolutionary critique or practice except in specifically feminist versions of Marxist theory.[3] Feminists have pointed out that, since women's lives have in many societies been lived to a greater extent than men's within the so-called private sphere, the implication of the public/private division has been that fundamental sources of women's oppression have been politically invisible and hence ignored. But both the arguments on which the feminist critique focuses and the critique itself have been obscured by the difficulty of identifying precisely what is meant by the public/private divide. In what follows, therefore, I shall try to distinguish between a number of different issues which are relevant to the debate.

[2] See Okin (1989); (1991); O'Donovan, *Sexual Divisions in Law* (1985); Olsen (1983); for further discussion, see Chapter 2.

[3] See Jaggar (1983) pp. 207–15.

Public and private spheres: normative and descriptive arguments

The claim most commonly associated with public/private ideology is that the world is divided into public and private *spheres*. Two questions immediately present themselves. First, what are these spheres— what do public and private denote in this context? Secondly, is this a descriptive or a normative claim? I want to look at each of these in turn.

As far as the identification of public and private spheres is concerned, two basic accounts have been influential. In the first, the division is between the state and civil society. Particularly in nineteenth century *laissez faire* versions of liberalism, a central idea was that the role of the state should be strictly limited, with the market governing relations other than family relations in civil society. The continuing influence of such ideas is reflected in the ideology of recent governments in Britain and USA. In the second account, the division is between the state and/or the market on the one hand and the family on the other. The family is constructed as the quintessentially private sphere in which human relations must be allowed to develop away from the scrutiny let alone intervention of state or market institutions. In each case, the ideas of "public" and "private" roughly correspond to "regulated" and "unregulated", and the claim is offered variously as descriptive and as normative. At one level, the idea of a division between state and civil society or between the market or state and the family is offered as a characterisation of the world. At another, it is connected with substantive political arguments about the appropriateness of regulation in the relevant areas.[4] Clearly, this means that we need to assess the various kinds of public/private sphere claims in terms of different criteria.

First, let us examine the descriptive version of the public/private dichotomy. To what extent is it sensible to see our social world as divided into spheres corresponding to state/civil society, market/family? Obviously, these categories have a degree of institutional validity. But at the level of political and sociological analysis, taking these categories as a starting point would be very crude. "The" state consists of many interlocking institutions and practices, as does

---

[4] Jaggar suggests that the state/civil society division is an analytical feature of liberal economics whilst the market/family division is an explicitly normative feature of liberal theory: Jaggar (1983) pp. 143–8. I do not dissent from this, but believe that the state/civil society dichotomy also has a normative dimension, whilst the market/family dichotomy is sometimes presented as a description.

"the" market; "families" can be defined in different ways and come in a variety of forms. Nor does this three-tier institutional character-isation seem an adequate starting point for social theory. For modern capitalist societies have also developed a "public sphere" or set of "publics" which constitute not the state or state institutions but non-state fora for public, political debate—social movements, trades unions, pressure groups and so on.[5] Here, too, politics, in the broad sense of "the critical activity of raising issues and deciding how insti-tutional and social relations should be organized",[6] goes on.

What of the specific attempt to understand social institutions as public or private in the sense of their being (at least predominantly) regulated or unregulated by state power? Thinking about this as an historically and culturally specific claim, it would certainly be fair to say that in, for example, mid-nineteenth century Britain the opera-tion of the market and contractual relations were relatively unregu-lated by the state, or that in mid-twentieth century Britain legal regulation was not applied to some significant aspects of family life and relations within the family. But we are talking here of *relativities* rather than clear divisions. The very institution of contract law in some sense regulates market transactions, albeit that developments since the late nineteenth century have enormously increased the degree to which the state controls the terms on which parties may contract with each other. Similarly, in spite of a great deal of rhetoric about privacy in the family sphere, a moment's thought reveals that many aspects of family life are hedged around with legal regulation—marriage, divorce, child custody, social welfare rules, to name but the most obviously relevant areas of law. Moreover, it would be wrong to see direct *legal* regulation as the touchstone for state involvement. In all sorts of indirect ways—economic, administrative and politi-cal—state institutions have a crucial and often deliberate impact on the conduct of family life.[7] Indeed, it might be argued that in the late

---

[5] Habermas (1981), Vols. 1, 2, (1984), (1987). For a feminist commentary on this and related aspects of Habermas's social theory, see Nancy Fraser, "What's Critical about Critical Theory? The Case of Habermas and Gender", in Fraser (1989) p. 113. On the idea of "civic publics", see Young (1990a) Ch. 7; (1990b) Chs. 3, 4 and 6.

[6] Young (1990b) p. 240; see also Fraser (1989) pp. 166–71. The importance of this kind of public sphere to social theory is shown by the way in which writers like Arendt and Habermas have been preoccupied, in various ways, with a reduction in the vigour and rich-ness of debate in non-state public fora, and with the importance of "communicatively achieved action contexts". The idea of the "decline of the political" as a symptom of a wor-rying dilution of democracy identified by civic republican theory is in stark contrast to the emphasis on the state which characterises dichotomised public/private analysis.

[7] Donzelot (1979); Naffine (1990) pp. 69–71; Smart (1984).

twentieth century in Britain we have seen an increasing willingness to regulate the family, whilst *laissez faire* attitudes to the market (not always realised in political practice as opposed to rhetoric) have experienced a revival. As for the non-state "publics" referred to above, the question of regulation or non-regulation seems inapt, yet their importance to the conduct of social life further blurs any supposed division between public and private spheres. We may be able to make relative judgements, and draw crude distinctions between family, market and state at an institutional level. But the search for the public/private division in terms of the presence or absence of state-directed or state-sponsored regulation is as hopeless as the analysis of society merely in terms of state, market and family is inadequate.

This conclusion becomes even clearer when we take into account the difficulty in attaching any general significance to a distinction between regulation and non-regulation, or between intervention and abstention. In any given case it can be unclear analytically whether to characterise the state's position as one of regulation or non-regulation.[8] For example, the exemption of married men from charges of rape of their wives which persists in some jurisdictions is generally seen in terms of non-regulation. Yet it discloses a certain view of the marriage relationship which is positively inscribed in law. In such cases, abstention amounts to a form of regulation. And even where a regulation/non-regulation distinction can be drawn analytically, its significance is called into question by the fact that decisions *not* to regulate made by state or other institutions with the power to do so are every bit as much *political* decisions as are decisions to regulate. Clearly, both within and beyond liberal theory, the shape of arguments for regulation and non-regulation cannot be taken to be identical. But the strong liberal presumption in favour of non-regulation which proceeds from the commitment of some of the most influential versions of modern liberalism to a *negative* conception of freedom—freedom as the absence of constraint—has obscured the way in which state decisions not to regulate are themselves political and call for justification.[9]

Another problematic feature of the characterisation of family or civil society as private in the sense of unregulated has to do with what

[8] See Olsen (1985).

[9] The distinction between negative and positive freedom is discussed further below: see also Chapters 2 and 4. The preference for negative as opposed to positive ideas of freedom does not characterise all forms of liberal thought: see, for example, Mill (1859); Haksar (1979); Raz (1986). But the idea of freedom as non-intervention has continued to dominate liberal political theory; see Isaiah Berlin's influential *Four Essays on Liberty* (1989).

such a characterisation presupposes about the regulator. This is generally conceived in simple terms as "the state". But, as I have already observed, the state is not monolithic; it is rather a set of diverse institutions. This gives rise to further complexities in identifying regulation or non-regulation. What are we to say of issues such as wife-battering—always "regulated" in the sense of being within the purview of criminal law, but frequently "unregulated" because of the decisions of law enforcement agencies? The picture is fragmented even if we leave aside the operation of powerful regulation which cannot be identified with "the state". Once we incorporate non-state power, and acknowledge the difficulty of distinguishing between state and non-state bodies in a world where "public" and "private" power are inextricably linked with each other, the picture threatens to disintegrate.[10] Can we deny, for example, that the economic influence of multinational corporations accords them a measure of political power, or, conversely, that government's economic power can be used as a tool of policy? Are influential institutions which are state subsidised or regulated to be regarded as part of "the state" or not? The very idea of power as something which is deliberately exercised by identifiable agents, as opposed to, or also, subsisting in discourses and practices spreading throughout the social body—including those other "publics" ignored by the traditional public/private distinction—misses important aspects of how subjects' positions are constituted and maintained in the social world.[11]

Finally, the descriptive association of women with "the private sphere", particularly in the sense of the family, is itself problematic. For whilst it is both true and highly significant that women still bear a disproportionate responsibility for domestic labour, the converse suggestion that women have lived their lives exclusively or even mainly in the private sphere of the family is quite unsustainable. Working class women in particular have worked outside the home to a far greater degree than the public/private critique has tended to acknowledge; and in many other respects women's lives have not been lived in any real sense in a "private" domain. At a descriptive level, the idea of a private, unregulated family quite simply collapses when subjected to scrutiny.

---

[10] See McAuslan and McEldowney (eds.) (1986).

[11] This broader theory of power derives from the work of Michel Foucault; see in particular Foucault (1980), (1981) pp. 90 *et seq.* For discussion of the implications of this theory for debates around the public/private dichotomy, see Rose (1987) and Chapter 5.

Now let us move from the descriptive to the normative. The idea that the state's use of coercive force to curtail citizens' behaviour calls for special justification lies at the heart of liberal political philosophy. In Mill's famous formulation, the only justification for state intervention to curtail individual freedom lies in the prevention of harm to others.[12] Individual freedom is the paramount liberal value. State power threatens that freedom in a peculiarly dangerous way, and must be strictly limited. Mill's argument was framed, of course, at a time when the state was less extensive and was regarded as having fewer legitimate functions than is the case in post-welfare state societies. Leaving aside for the moment his unitary conception of state power, the implications of his argument depend on how freedom is conceived. To the extent that we recognise that genuine freedom depends not only on being left alone—not interfered with, not regulated or scrutinised—but also on being provided with certain positive goods and facilities, we will be alert to the freedom-enhancing as well as the freedom-threatening potential of state or state-sponsored action. This, certainly, was a position to which Mill was sympathetic, and it has come to be known as the idea of *positive freedom*. However, in modern debates about the proper limits of state action, the tendency has been to focus on *negative freedom*—freedom as being left in peace.[13] On this view, a conceptually neat and rhetorically powerful way of realising the argument from human freedom is in terms of the delineation of a "private sphere"—famously described in the Wolfenden Report as that which is "in brief and crude terms, not the law's business".[14] The central thrust of feminist critique has borne upon this normative interpretation of liberal theory. For, it has been argued, the practical consequence of non-regulation is the consolidation of the *status quo*: the *de facto* support of pre-existing power relations and distributions of goods within the "private" sphere. In effect, if not explicitly, much feminist critique espouses a positive conception of freedom. It exposes the way in which the ideology of the public/private dichotomy allows government to clean its hands of any *responsibility* for the state of the "private" world and *depoliticises* the disadvantages which inevitably spill over the alleged divide by affecting the position of the "privately" disadvantaged in the "public" world.

---

[12] Mill (1859).
[13] Berlin (1989); Hart (1961).
[14] Wolfendon (1957).

The feminist critique, then, is a direct attack on the idea of public and private spheres, which it sees as a politically and ethically inadequate realisation of liberal arguments about individual freedom and the proper role of the state. The attack consists in both a normative argument about positive freedom and an analytical argument about the interdependence of regulated and unregulated spheres. Liberal theory which depends on the public/private distinction is self-defeating in that the guarantees of justice and equality held out to citizens in the "public" sphere are worth systematically less to those who are pre-politically disadvantaged. The limits of the scope of politics and justice asserted by liberals such as Rawls, in other words, are inconsistent with the realisation of the general values which they claim to espouse.[15] Also notable from a critical point of view is a tendency to couch the normative argument in superficially descriptive terms, in a way which is at once intellectually indefensible and rhetorically powerful. As we saw above, the project of delineating public and private spheres at a descriptive level is fraught with difficulty. Yet the substantively normative argument often proceeds by simply announcing a particular issue to fall "within the private sphere" and "hence" to be inappropriate for regulation. The statement of the Wolfendon Committee quoted above is an excellent example. What happens in this kind of rhetoric is that the labels "public" and "private" are used in question-begging ways which *suppress* the normative arguments which they actually presuppose. This means that the debate sounds common-sensical rather than politically controversial. Hence one of the main tasks, as well as the main successes, of feminist critique has been to expose the *politics*—the "power-laden" character[16]—of "privatisation" of this kind. It ought to go without saying that this repoliticisation of attributions of "privacy" is quite different from an argument for the propriety let alone the efficacy of state regulation: to say that what has been thought of as private is within the scope of political *critique* is not to say that it must necessarily be *regulated*. Unfortunately, as we shall see, this crucial distinction has not always been observed.

---

[15] For a particularly clear statement of this position, see Okin (1989) Chs. 1, 2, 5, 8. Much of Okin's immanent critique in these chapters is directed to John Rawls' *A Theory of Justice* (1971). For further discussion, see Chapter 2.

[16] I take this expression from Nancy Fraser: Fraser (1989) p. 110, n. 24. Her argument in this note accords closely with the general position which I want to defend in this chapter.

Public and private values

At an explicit level, most of the debate around the public/private dichotomy (or more properly, dichotomies) has centred on the idea of public and private spheres. But just below the surface has been another, equally important set of ideas. These have to do with the place of the public/private opposition within a set of dichotomies which structure our thinking in the Western world. Other dualisms include objectivity and subjectivity, reason and passion, self and other, culture and nature and, crucially for feminist thinking, male and female. Many feminist theorists have argued that the male/female opposition maps onto these other dichotomies, identifying, for example, femaleness with emotion, passivity, subjectivity, nature; male with reason, objectivity, activity, culture.[17] They have also observed that in Western culture one half of each pair is valued above the other, and that the halves with which women and femaleness are associated are the less valued ones. This kind of analysis in turn maps onto the public/private dichotomy. For, it is argued, what we need to focus on is not so much empirical claims about women's lives being lived disproportionately in the private sphere—claims which are problematic for the reasons already canvassed—but rather *cultural associations* between femaleness, the private and under-recognised values and attributes. On this view, the importance of the public/private dichotomy lies in the fact that the cultural construction of the public sphere as the sphere in which universal reason holds sway implicitly marginalises or is inhospitable to women. This is because reason, and hence the public, are culturally associated with the masculine, whereas the private, conversely, is associated with the feminine—with particularity, with emotion, with the body, with *otherness*. The task of feminist critique, then, is to expose the gendered nature of the concepts in terms of which our notions of "the public sphere" are constructed, and to offer alternative conceptions which would render the "public" genuinely accessible not just to women as well as men, but also to all those whose "particularity" currently marks them as "different" and hence as excluded from the unity of the public.[18]

Another aspect of this feminist argument has to do with the very nature of public/private and the other dualisms as *dichotomies*. Here

---

[17] See for example Lloyd (1984). For further discussion of dualisms as an object of feminist critique, see Chapters 4, 5 and 7.

[18] See Young (1990b) Ch. 4.

feminist thought participates in a broad project of exposing and challenging ways in which our thinking is structured around pairs of ideas which are opposed in the sense that the attribution of one excludes the other: that which is public cannot be private; that which is male cannot be female and so on. By showing how each side of each dualism depends on the other for its own meaning—subectivity can only be understood by differentiating itself from objectivity, maleness takes its meaning by differentiation from femaleness and so on—this "deconstruction" shows how the less valued half acts as a "dangerous supplement" to the other. Each member of the pair refers to the other at the same time as it suppresses it. Thus the self-sufficiency of the more powerful side of the dichotomy is fragile: it could be said to be undermined in the very moment in which it is expressed. This kind of deconstruction proceeds on the assumption that we need to erode the power of the hierarchically ordered dichotomies, including that between public and private, as part of a liberating political programme.[19] For the fact that one side of the dualisms has cultural status helps to invest people associated with those attributes or values with greater power. Hierarchically dichotomised thinking operates by way of suppressing the implied reference to the "other"; by marginalising that "other", it forms an important part of the politics of the powerful as realised through language.

As always, it is easier to identify the problem here than to find a way of resolving it. Some deconstructionists affirm the inevitability of working *within* the dichotomies: since they are part of our cultural and linguistic heritage, they cannot be left behind by an act of political will. There must therefore be a phase—for some deconstructionists it is a phase which will never end—in which we work to unearth the "dangerous supplement", to effect a revaluation of that which has been suppressed. Since gender neutrality is unrealisable, the only possible immediate goal is to attack gender hierarchy—to expose the contingency (and hence the *politics*) of the current cultural hierarchy. This is disappointing, for to the extent that we stay within the dichotomised categories, our only political option seems to be to change the position of particular groups within those structures—merely substituting one oppressed, marginalised group for another. The hope of a genuinely radical politics would be to escape oppression altogether, and this, in the view of many critical theorists, entails

---

[19] On the relationship between feminist legal theory and deconstruction, see Chapters 6 to 8: see also Cornell (1991), especially pp. 92–106.

PORNOGRAPHY AND THE PUBLIC/PRIVATE DICHOTOMY   81

transcending the dichotomies rather than reversing them.[20] In so far as there will be room for reconstructed notions such as public and private, they will not relate to each other as hierarchised dichotomies. But how is such a project to be effected; how is the logic of binary oppositions, in which deconstruction itself seems to participate, to be escaped? Two possibilities (they are not mutually exclusive) have been suggested. The first is exemplified by Cornell's feminist reading of Derrida (see for example Derrida (1992)). Whilst Cornell acknowledges the need to "take off" from within the dichotomies, the openness of language, particularly as realised through devices such as metaphor and metonymy, opens a utopian moment within deconstruction. Different meanings and possibilities can be glimpsed or imagined, and they may gradually allow us to transcend the oppressive social relations expressed in the current dichotomies.[21] In the work of other theorists such as Young, in which deconstruction plays a less central role, the possibility of transcending the dichotomies proceeds from a decided rejection of the idea that the world must be understood in terms of their binary straightjacket. Rather, it is argued, we can move to a realisation of difference as multiple and relational, hence undermining the dichotomised construction/understanding of the world and rejecting the limited political options that its either/or analysis seemed to force upon us.[22] Each of these strategies needs to be borne in mind in considering feminist critique of public/private dichotomies.

The value of privacy

One final aspect of the debate about public and private needs to be distinguished. This is the argument about what, if any, value should be ascribed to privacy. Clearly, the idea that privacy in the sense of a space around the individual or a particular association from which she or it is entitled to exclude others connects closely with liberal notions of individual freedom. As such, it has contributed to liberal arguments about the desirability of an unregulated private sphere, particularly in the sense of the family. But a commitment to the idea that

---

[20] See for example the vision sketched in the final pages of Olsen (1983).

[21] See Cornell (1991) Ch. 4; for discussion of this aspect of Cornell's work, see Chapter 7.

[22] Young (1990b) pp. 169 et seq. On the danger of deconstruction's re-erecting binary oppositions where our critical thought has begun to escape them see Radin and Michelman (1991) at p. 1053.

privacy can be of value and should sometimes be respected does not entail a commitment to a private *sphere* in any of the senses generally understood by that term. Evidently, the value of privacy is contextual—it depends on the particular area of life we are thinking of, and the circumstances which prevail. This means that an approach to protecting privacy which operates by delineating a relatively concrete *sphere* seems inappropriate. But, from a feminist point of view, it is far from clear that a critique of the public/private dichotomy should bring with it a total rejection of the notion that privacy can be valuable and ought sometimes to be protected by state and other powerful institutions.[23] Indeed, given the double burden inherent in current social arrangements, privacy is one of the many things which women tend to lack. This needs to be emphasised because some feminist critiques have been taken (not always without justification) to imply that privacy is a value which has nothing to recommend it to women.[24]

PROBLEMS FOR THE PUBLIC/PRIVATE CRITIQUE

Now that we have a clearer view of the different aspects of the public/private dichotomy and the critique which it has generated, we can begin to focus on some of the specific difficulties which the critique has encountered. The main problems associated with the division between public and private spheres can be summarised as follows. In its "descriptive" guise, it inappropriately "reifies" spheres which cannot be clearly identified by means of careful sociological analysis. The construction of public and private spheres as analytical categories exaggerates the extent of actual institutional divisions, suppresses the ways in which women's as well as men's lives are lived across "public and private spheres", and gives insufficient attention to concrete social practices and historical changes. Secondly, the analytical categories are used in a question-begging way, being applied to

[23] Privacy has, of course, been an important strategic counter in certain feminist legal arguments, notably that for the prohibition of state proscription of abortion decided by the US Supreme Court in *Roe v. Wade* 410 US 113 (1973). This is not to say that privacy was necessarily the most advantageous conceptual framework for the protection of abortion: see MacKinnon (1989) Ch. 10.

[24] For a useful discussion of privacy in terms of of personhood and in the context of a clear rejection of any public/private *separation*, see Radin (1990) and Michelman (1990). For discussion of the relationship between autonomy as privacy and the issue of rape, see Chapter 4.

particular areas and practices as if descriptively, but with normative conclusions being drawn from the "descriptive" denotation of publicity or privacy. The premises on which these conclusions are based are hence obscured and protected from critical scrutiny. Thirdly, the assumption that the world can be divided into separate spheres obscures the interdependence of those spheres and the spill-over from oppression in one sphere to subordination in another. This point is important both as an observation about social realities and as raising some very broad questions about the pitfalls of dichotomised thinking. Finally, the analysis is crude in its focus on "the state" and "state intervention" as the touchstones of "the public" and of "regulation", when in fact both the state and means of regulation are multiple rather than unitary. Many different modes of regulation exist—overt and covert, legal and administrative, more or less coercive—operated by a variety of state institutions. Indeed, the very idea of state as opposed to non-state agencies (yet another form of public/private dichotomy) is inapt in a world where "public" and "private" power are inextricably linked. The critique of the public/private dichotomy questions a fundamental assumption of post-enlightenment political theory: that politics has to do exclusively or at least primarily with the state. It also suggests that we should reject the idea that power can be understood exclusively in terms of sovereignty: rather than seeing power as something which is wielded by particular persons or agencies in a conscious or overt way, we must also attend to the operations of power in a diversity of state and non-state institutions, practices and discourses.[25]

Unfortunately, however, the critique of the division between public and private spheres which has generated these insights has not itself always escaped the problems it has identified. The difficulty lies in the fact that once one engages in a critique of the division, it is almost impossible to avoid framing one's arguments in its terms—in other words, one gets sucked into the very categorisation one is attempting to undermine. One good example is provided by the last two chapters of Katherine O'Donovan's *Sexual Divisions in Law* (1985). This book, which broke new ground in feminist legal scholarship in Britain, devoted much of its argument to a critique of the public/private dichotomy. O'Donovan's models of reform, canvassed in the last two chapters, essentially consist in turning the values which characterise one side of the dichotomy against practices on the other. In

---

[25] This view of power derives from the work of Michel Foucault: see note 11 above.

doing so, O'Donovan elides two aspects of the public/private divide which we have distinguished: public versus private *spheres* and the sexualisation of the public/private dichotomy at the level of *values*. Evidently, the idea of "making a man more like a woman", and the public more like the private, precisely does not transcend the dichotomy it critiques, for it is speaks in the unreconstructed terms of the dichotomy itself. And, despite her vision of transcending the dichotomy via a world of reds and greens and blues, Frances Olsen's sophisticated analysis too makes limited progress in this transformative direction. In "The Family and the Market" (1983), most of her argument, like O'Donovan's, consists of an analysis of the way law reform has mapped the values associated with the private onto the public, and vice versa. Because the critique of the ideological power which the public/private dichotomy has as part of a sexualised and hierarchical cultural discourse is mapped back on to a division between public and private spheres which has effectively been exploded as a myth, the argument reaches a kind of deadlock in which the promise of genuine transformation cannot be made good. In Olsen's metaphor we begin to escape the binary and the dichotomised, but the utopian vision opened up by deconstruction is glimpsed rather than developed.

Another way of looking at this problem is to think of the public/private critique as operating at several different levels. At one level, the dichotomy is criticised as being impossibly indeterminate or even analytically incoherent; as being an inaccurate description of the world; and as implying an unattractive prescription for social organisation. At a rather different level, the critique focuses not on the dichotomy itself but on the power which that dichotomy—incoherent, inaccurate, unattractive though it may be—has actually had in constructing or consolidating certain features of women's oppression. In spite of all its glaring defects, in other words, its discursive power in our culture is acknowledged. This involves feminist critique in a delicate balancing act, and one which can all too easily appear to lose its equilibrium. It can seem, in other words, as if our theoretical critique of the public/private distinction undermines our critique of its power: if the division is so hopelessly indeterminate—if public and private spheres cannot even be identified, and if women have in any case always inhabited public and well as private worlds—to what concrete political practices is the normative liberal argument and, more importantly, the feminist critique of it, meant to relate? It is extremely difficult, in other words, to engage in critique of the public/private dichotomy or its effects without speaking as if it had an analytic and empirical validity which the critique denies. The way out of this impasse lies in seeing that the dichotomy has operated, and continues to operate, ideologically—and that ideological power does not necessarily depend upon empirical validation or logical coherence. This suggests that the critique may have focused to too great an extent on the idea of public and private *spheres*. For the ideological role of the dichotomy can be—and has been—played *without* necessarily being realised in any empirically identifiable separation of institutions, activities or areas of life.

A final problem encountered by the critique has to do with the conclusions which are to be drawn from it. Critique of the public/private dichotomy has been of particular interest to feminist lawyers. This is hardly surprising, given that one important general mode of regulation, the presence or absence of which links with ideas of public and private, is legal regulation. Feminists are bound to be concerned with the ways in which laws have been implicated in constructing and maintaining ideologies of public and private, and the gendered divisions and subordinations which they have sustained. Yet, all too often, we have made the assumption that a critique of the depoliticisation of the private should go hand in hand with change in the form of greater legal regulation. Consider the assumption tucked away in Alison Jaggar's otherwise careful analysis: "By defining sexual and family relations as private . . . liberal theorists provide grounds for arguing that these assaults are no business of the law *and so* for allowing them to continue" (my emphasis).[26] It is perhaps unfair to attribute to Jaggar a general view on the basis of a particular example in which law is arguably a rather obviously apt response. Nonetheless, the passage makes a strong assumption both about the appropriateness of legal intervention as a remedy for the ills of privatised wrongs and about the efficacy of such legal intervention. Both of these assumptions call for much more argument—argument which needs to be fleshed out in particular contexts.

Whilst feminist lawyers have debated widely about the strategic implications of legal regulation, the normative arguments have been less fully developed. This is perhaps because of a pervasive and understandable scepticism in feminist thought about the utility of normative theories which pretend to a politically dubious universalism and fail to articulate the position from which they speak. Nonetheless, it

[26] Jaggar (1983) p. 145.

is of the first importance that feminists should address the underlying substantive political and ethical issues which have been skated over by both public/private dichotomised discourse and its critique. This must be part of a larger feminist enterprise of reconstructing concepts such as autonomy and privacy in terms of which political debate goes forward in non-dichotomised terms.[27] The kind of enterprise I have in mind is well illustrated by the following passage from feminist philosopher Iris Marion Young:

> Instead of defining the private as what the public excludes, I suggest, the private should be defined, as in one strain of liberal theory, as that aspect of his or her life and activity that any person has a right to exclude others from. The private in this sense is not what public institutions exclude, but what the individual chooses to withdraw from public view. With the growth of both state and nonstate bureaucracies, the protection of privacy has become a burning public issue. In welfare capitalist society, the defence of personal privacy has become not merely a matter of keeping the state out of certain affairs, but of calling for positive state regulation to ensure that both its own agencies and nonstate organisations, such as corporations, respect the claims of individuals to privacy.
>
> This manner of formulating the concepts of public and private, which is inspired by feminist confrontations with traditional political theory, does not deny their distinction. It does deny, however, a social division between public and private spheres, each with different kinds of institutions, activities and human attributes.[28]

This passage captures the importance of reconstructing an adequate distinction between public and private—a distinction which is neither dichotomous nor mapped onto separate spheres—and shows how such a reconstruction connects with ethical considerations. It also implies that adequate notions of public and private do not automatically map on to conclusions about regulation and non-regulation. I shall now move on to consider these theoretical points in the context of the specific issue of pornography.

PORNOGRAPHY AND THE PUBLIC/PRIVATE DICHOTOMY

Feminist concern with pornography is certainly not new, but it has taken a particular shape and gained a new intensity over the last twenty years. In a period of reflection upon the implications of the

27 See Nedelsky (1989) pp. 7–36; see further Chapters 4 and 8.
28 Young (1990b) pp. 119–20.

sexual "liberation" of the 1960s, many women began to be concerned with the proliferation of pornography and its ready availability. They began to ask questions not just about the relationship between pornography and sexual violence, or about the exploitation of women involved in the production of pornography, but also about the broader cultural implications of the spread of pornography for the status and citizenship of women. In the work of Andrea Dworkin, for example, pornography is seen as central to the maintenance of women's oppression: heterosexuality constructs women as the sexual objects of men, and this objectification finds its most graphic as well as one of its most powerful expressions in pornographic material.[29] On this view, sexuality is the fundamental site of women's oppression, and pornography, like rape, wife-beating, sexual harassment and other forms of sexually specific violence, represents the social practices which both express and cause women's subordination and powerlessness. The analysis of pornography issuing from this critique emphasises its implicit or explicit violence, its dehumanisation of its objects—mostly women or children, disproportionately often black women—by representing them in positions of servility, as enjoying pain or humiliation, by reducing them to particular body parts.

A somewhat different account has emphasised the ways in which the proliferation of pornography has affected other areas of life. Pornography, on this view, is a regime of representation through which we see the world. Once widely available as a genre, the regime of representation which pornography engenders is not restricted to the viewing of pornographic materials themselves. It affects the way in which consumers of pornography look at other genres—advertising, novels and so on.[30] On this view, the question of whether or not pornography contributes to actual sexual violence—whether or not men try to live out pornographic fantasies as a result of pornographic consumption—is not the exclusive or even the central concern. The point is that the profusion of the pornographic regime of representation inevitably affects the social constitution of femininity—affects the ways in which women can be represented and can represent ourselves across all social practices—and hence directly and adversely, albeit intangibly, affects the status of women.

[29] A. Dworkin (1981). Similar analyses are to be found in MacKinnon (1987) and Jeffreys (1990).

[30] See Kappeler (1986); Coward (1984). For an analysis of the differences between conceptions of pornography as violence and pornography as representation, see Smart (1989) Ch. 6.

My concern here is not to engage in any further analysis of pornography, for this has been more than thoroughly done elsewhere. I want instead to focus specifically on the contribution which the critique of the public/private dichotomy has made to feminist analyses of pornography. In the first place, pornography in liberal society has largely been constructed as a matter of private consumption, and hence as outside the ambit of political critique or action. Absent proof of the contribution of pornography to overt acts of violence, violence or coercion in its production, or indecency thought to impinge on public order, pornography has been taken to be either an instance of expression or a form of sexual practice and hence within the sphere of individuals' privacy. Feminist critique has brought pornography into the sphere of the public and has insisted upon its political relevance. This is both because of the interdependence argument—the argument that private oppression inevitably leads to public disadvantage—and because the traditional denomination of pornography as private can itself be shown to be disingenuous. The liberal analysis which constructs pornography as a matter of private sexual preference in one breath constructs it as a matter of public right to free expression in the next. In what might be called a "no-lose situation" for the producers and consumers of pornography, the production of pornography is seen as a matter of public right, and hence protected, whilst its consumption is constructed as a matter of private interest, and hence also protected. Both public and private sides of the dichotomy are manipulated in ways which exclude anti-pornography arguments. Another twist to the conundrum comes from the ways in which the public right to pornographic expression has often been limited to the private sphere: legal regulation of pornography tends to focus on public manifestations which cause offence. As many commentators have suggested, this policy compromise may be functional to the meaning of pornography by in effect making pornography easily available whilst maintaining the illusion of illicitness which forms part of the power of pornography to arouse.[31]

In several senses, then, issues of public and private suffuse the feminist analysis of the traditional construction of pornography: the private consumption of pornography inevitably impacts on the public status of women—on women's citizenship. However, in the work of

[31] See for example Coward (1984). Catharine MacKinnon, too, has made this point (MacKinnon (1983)), although in her later work her acceptance of it is less decisive (see MacKinnon (1989) pp. 200–1).

several feminist lawyers, the critique of the privatisation of pornography has been developed in the form of inferences from critique to practice, and to practice in a very specific legal reformist guise. I want to consider this specific attempt at reform, because I think it illustrates some of the theoretical problems I have identified, as well as some of the pitfalls of making simple inferences from theory to strategy.

In response to a local grassroots movement in Minneapolis, American feminists Andrea Dworkin and Catharine MacKinnon were invited to draft an anti-pornography ordinance.[32] The political process included lengthy hearings in which many women gave painful and appalling evidence about the effect which pornography had had in their lives. The hearings helped to produce a political atmosphere in which pornography was widely acknowledged to be a serious social harm with a specific impact upon women. The ordinance which Dworkin and MacKinnon drafted enunciated a very broad definition of pornography as the "graphic, sexually explicit subordination of women through pictures and/or words" which also exhibits one or more of a number of further features. These further features included the presentation of women as dehumanized sexual objects; as experiencing sexual pleasure in rape, incest or other sexual assault; and, perhaps most controversially, in postures of positions of sexual submission, servility or display. Pornography in these senses was conceptualised as sex discrimination—that is, as behaviour which exploits and differentially harms women. The ordinance went on to give civil causes of action for injunctions and/or damages to anyone coerced, intimidated or fraudulently induced into performing pornography; to anyone on whom pornography is forced in a place of employment, education, home or any public place, as against the person forcing it on them; to anyone assaulted, attacked, or injured in a way that is directly caused by specific pornography; to anyone defamed by the unauthorised use of pornography in their proper name, image or recognisable likeness; and to any woman acting against the subordination of women or other person who alleges injury by pornography, against anyone who produces, sells, exhibits or distributes pornography, including through private clubs.

In many respects, the ordinance represented an inspired piece of feminist legal politics. In the first place, the conceptualisation of pornography as sex discrimination placed at the heart of the legislation

---

[32] See Dworkin and MacKinnon (1988). The text of the ordinance is also to be found in Graycar and Morgan (1990) and is dicussed in MacKinnon (1987) Part III. See also Smart (1989) Ch. 6.

a feminist view of pornography. Moreover, by pitching one constitutional standard (free expression) against another (equal protection) it in effect forced the American courts into a position where, if they were to hold the ordinance unconstitutional, they had to do so in terms which were easily interpreted as valuing an at best dubiously worthwhile form of expression over and above the removal of sex discrimination, and as valuing men's expression over the worth or even possibility of women's. Indeed, the United States Court of Appeals, which did find the ordinance to be unconstitutional, underlined these embarrassing implications of its decision by making it clear that it accepted the premises on which the ordinance was based.[33] Secondly, the reform process itself was a model of feminist political practice. The hearings gave a public voice to women whose suffering had been hidden and silenced; indeed, they constituted precisely the kind of civic forum which illustrates the inadequacy of the traditional public/private distinction and its focus on the state. The legislative process responded directly to the experiences expressed by women in the hearings. Thirdly, the choice of civil rather than criminal enforcement was important. It helped to some extent to defuse the accusation that the ordinance was an attempt at censorship. More significantly, the process of giving individual women rights of action was symbolically apt. It sought to empower women to use a legal process whose terms are generally constructed in ways which are inattentive or even hostile to the interests and needs which many women may wish to defend legally. Finally, by defining pornography *as* sex discrimination, causal links between pornography and harms to women were taken as being already established. Hence the legal process was relieved from having to deal with intractable questions about the relationship between pornography and sexual violence: these would only arise legally in the specific cases where this was what the cause of action alleged.

As is well known, however, the ordinance also raised some very difficult questions for feminist politics, and generated a bitter controversy within the women's movement. At its heart, this controversy had to do with the basic shape of the feminist analysis on which the ordinance rested: in short, the claim that pornography is a *central* means of perpetuating women's oppression. Many feminists see pornography and sexual violence as epiphenomenal rather than as central: as the product of economic and other material means of sub-

---

[33] See *American Booksellers Association, Inc et al v. William Hudnut III, Mayor, City of Indianapolis, et al* 771 F 2d 323 (7th Cir 1985). The decision was summarily upheld by the Supreme Court: 475 US (1986).

ordination.[34] For the purposes of this discussion, I shall make an intermediate assumption: that pornography in the forms which predominate in our culture, whilst not being a root cause of women's oppression, is a practice which does contribute to sex discrimination, not just in the sense of sexual violence but also in the sense of contributing to the low esteem in which women are held by men and, all too often, hold ourselves. Pornography is by no means the only or even the most important means of degrading objectification to which women (and indeed men) are subjected in our society, but as one such form, it is of political relevance and concern. To this extent, incorporation of the *issue* of pornography in public debate, and the recognition of the interdependence between privately consumed pornography and the public status of women, is entirely progressive.

However, reflection on the instrumental and symbolic implications of anti-pornography legislation of the kind embodied in the ordinance gives serious pause for thought about how the public/private critique is to be realised in political practice. A legislative strategy such as the anti-pornography ordinance exhibits two features which I have already suggested are among the failings of the feminist development of the critique. First, it participates in an over-concentration on the public/private *spheres* aspect of the critique at the expense of its ideological or discursive aspects. It recognises the discursive power of pornography, but adopts a strategy which, though it has short-term attractions because of its concreteness, is likely to be discursively counter-productive in the medium term. The price of this way of constructing pornography as a public wrong is that it has to be fitted into the conceptual straightjacket of an already legally recognised harm: in the case of the ordinance, sex discrimination. But it is unlikely that all the important aspects of the feminist critique of pornography can be captured in terms of the individualised and relatively tangible harms to which both criminal and civil law have tended to address themselves and which the idea of sex discrimination evokes.[35] Secondly, and closely related to the first point, a legislative strategy risks falling back into the assumptions made by the public/private dichotomy itself about the importance of the state as the main source of political/regulatory power. If the

[34] For varied contributions to the debate, see Cameron and Frazer (1987); Coward (1984); A. Dworkin (1981); Jeffreys (1990); MacKinnon (1987); Rich (1977); Segal (1987) pp. 105–16.

[35] On the individualism of anti-discrimination law, see Chapter 1, the argument of which would suggest the need to think in terms of collective rather than individual rights and remedies.

power which has kept in place the negative aspects of public/private thinking inheres, on the other hand, in a wide variety of institutions and discursive practices, the resort to state/legal reform as a means of undermining this aspect of public/private divisions looks less promising than the proponents of the legislative strategy have assumed.

Of course, the relative costs and benefits of pursuing a particular legislative or other legal strategy as one aspect of feminist politics vary in different jurisdictions. The virtually absolute constitutional protection of free speech in the USA presented Dworkin and MacKinnon with a very constraining legal and political framework. Conversely, the greater salience of litigation strategies as part of political life in the USA (a situation which, particularly since the introduction of the Charter of Rights, also obtains in Canada[36]) means that the gains to be expected of such a strategy may well have been greater than in Britain. Some of the most important problems presented by a legal reform strategy against pornography, however, would arise in most jurisdictions. It is worth considering what concrete instrumental effects might be expected to follow such a legal reform in Britain. How many women would be able to gather the resources, financial and otherwise, to bring cases against pornography? The experience in Britain and elsewhere of individual-initiated sex discrimination litigation is not encouraging: the experience of taking cases is hardly an unambiguously positive one. Even in the few cases where the best legal representation is available, and even where litigants have a very firm political commitment to their cause and a great deal of emotional and material support, research suggests that they may find it a disempowering experience rather than the reverse.[37] Strategic litigation funded by pressure groups may be a more realistic possibility, but

[36] In Canada, the Women's Legal Education and Action Fund (LEAF) has pursued an active litigation strategy geared to developing the potential of sections 15 and 28 (the equality provisions) of the Charter of Rights and Freedoms. The litigation has covered a large number of areas, including sexual harassment, protection from sexual assault, reproductive choice and, most recently, pornography, in a case in which an analysis of pornography as a sex equality issue was accepted by the Supreme Court (*R v. Butler* [1992] 1 SCR 452). Nonprofit interest groups and individuals have been helped to bring test cases on the Charter's guarantees of equality rights and language rights by a federally funded Court Challenges Program, administered by the Canadian Council on Social Development. The issue of the costs and benefits of Charter ligitation continues, however, to be a controversial one among feminists and other groups pushing for political change in areas covered by the Charter: see Fudge (1989); Fudge and Glasbeek (1992).

[37] For an assessment of the strengths and weaknesses of the individual enforcement model in sex discrimination law, see O'Donovan and Szyszczak (1988) and Chapter 1. The limitations of the individual enforcement model are certainly not confined to Britain: on the position in Australia, see Thornton (1990), and in the USA, see Freeman (1978).

the knock on effects of local cases such as could have been brought under the ordinance can easily be overestimated, whilst the resources which would have to be devoted to litigation strategies, as some womens groups in Canada can attest as a result of their experience under the Charter of Rights, are enormous.[38] Conversely, we have to consider the extent to which the law may be used by litigants other than those convinced by the feminist analysis which inspired it. Given the breadth of the ordinance's definition, it is hardly to be doubted that such a law could be exploited by conservative litigants to attack a wide range of sexually explicit art and literature including that evoking or expressing lesbian sexuality. These, of course, are forms which radical feminists would not see as coming within the ambit of the definition because of the background equality which may be argued to be possible in principle in homosexual but not heterosexual relations. It seems unlikely that judges would confine themselves to such an interpretation. A feminist conception of pornography, already moulded to fit a legal framework, could be further distorted in the interpretive process so as to push it towards a conservative conception inimical to the direction of feminist analysis.

Nor can we assume that a reasonable proportion of cases challenging pornographic material would be successful. Problems of proof— particularly of requirements such as being "coerced" into pornography, "forcing" pornography on a person, an attack or injury being "directly caused by specific pornography"—give strong reason to think that cases would be fraught with practical difficulties, and that the success rate, like that in other sex discrimination cases, would turn out to be low.[39] In any event, would the remedies envisaged by the ordinance be instrumentally effective? What level of awards of damages could be realistically expected in the cases where the harm involved is intangible? How often would courts be willing to award injunctions, and how effectively would or could these be policed? If injunctions were to be awarded and enforced, the argument that the law is not a form of censorship would be hard to sustain. More importantly, what would be the impact on working conditions in the pornography production industry? The ordinance focused on consumers of pornography and on victims at the production stage only in so far as they had been coerced into performing. Such a law would have no bite against the social conditions which put women into the position where they are able to be so coerced, particularly

---

[38] See Fudge (1989); Fudge and Glasbeek (1992).
[39] See Lacey (1987).

where their performance for pornography is a rational way of making a living because of the poverty of their other options.[40] It seems unlikely that a broad interpretation of coercion such as would cohere with a feminist analysis of this issue would gain a secure foothold in legal practice.

A supporter of the legislative strategy against pornography could justly object that I have been assuming that legal reform intervenes only at a concrete, material level. This is to underplay the discursive aspects of law. It is also to exaggerate the difference between the discursive and the material. If power inheres to an important extent in discourses, as I have argued, then influential discourses such as law *are* material in constituting social relations, and legal interventions can deploy discursive power in seeking to change the world, as well as operating at the level of the concrete. We need, then, to look also at what are sometimes called the "symbolic" aspects of this kind of law reform. Here again, several considerations suggest that a law such as the ordinance might be counter-productive. In the first place, if the instrumental arguments just rehearsed are correct, a symbolic message follows from them: the political meaning of having an unenforceable or unenforced law on the statute books is, at best, ambiguous and, at worst, suggests that legal policy is being used as a sop to political sentiment and as a way of avoiding the need for more effective political action. An interesting analogue here is the (criminal) law in England and Wales on incitement to racial hatred—an offence which is sometimes suggested as a model for anti-pornography legislation.[41] The number of successful prosecutions since the introduction of the first form of this offence has been miniscule, and the law is widely regarded as a costless (for government) sop to concern about racism which merely serves to legitimate government's relative inaction in other more potentially fruitful areas.[42] In addition, each unsuccessful prosecution implies the *legitimacy* of the racist conduct thereby condoned. A second symbolic worry about this sort of anti-pornography law lies in its openness to use by litigants motivated by other than feminist concerns, and indeed in the need (realised in the political process in Indianapolis) to build political alliances with those on the (evangelical) right in order to enact and sustain the legislation.[43] In

---

[40] See Cornell (1995) Ch. 3; Roberts (1986).

[41] See Graycar and Morgan (1990) p. 398.

[42] For comment, see Lacey and Wells (1998) Chapter 4.III.c; see also Fitzpatrick (1987) and Chapter 1.

[43] See Segal (1990) p. 225.

certain quarters the pornography debate in the USA has increased the image of feminism as moralistic and potentially repressive. Doubtless this is to some extent inevitable: the charge of moralism is one way of trying to marginalise a view with which one disagrees. But the feminist position has been made more vulnerable than it needed to be because of the quick inference from the theoretical reconstruction of pornography as public to the idea that *some* instrumental regulatory strategy must be appropriate, and hence by a failure to engage in a sufficient debate about not just the efficacy but also the ethics of legal control. At a discursive level, the implications of the legislative strategy seem, at best, uncertain and, at worst, damaging.

FEMINIST CRITIQUE AND FEMINIST STRATEGY: A FALSE DICHOTOMY?

I have suggested that the legal reform strategy encapsulated in the Dworkin/MacKinnon anti-pornography ordinance makes some unjustified inferences from the theory of the public/private critique to the political practice of regulation. The idea that rescuing an issue like pornography from the insulation from political critique implicit in its "privacy" entails a regulative strategy gets stuck within the very categories of public and private criticised earlier in this chapter.[44] For it buys into the idea of the private as the unregulated/not to be regulated and the public as the regulated/to be regulated, and to the idea that the relevant regulator is the state. It misses out on, or gives unsufficient emphasis to, the substantive normative arguments underlying attributions of public and private which I argued earlier were a useful part of the public/private critique. It also assumes that feminist critique is in some sense deficient unless accompanied by feminist strategic action. This entails a strong dichotomy between critique and action which is questionable, not least in the light of feminist emphasis on forms of consciousness raising as a political practice. It underestimates the importance of undermining the discursive power of attributions of public and private by reconstructing conceptions of privacy and the public adequate to the explication and defence of feminist politics. This is a project which has to be realised through a diversity of political practices—debates, boycotts, satire, counter-propaganda, pickets and so on. Of course, the publicity which tends

[44] For a more general discussion of the relationship between feminist critique and reformist strategy, see Chapter 8.

to be given to legal fora means that a court-centred strategy may have
positive secondary effects for these extra-legal politics. But the risks
attendant on legal strategies are acute where we try to use new legal
regulation instrumentally, to realise values which command little
acceptance among those who will administer the laws in question.[45]

The idea that feminist critique *necessarily* implies a reformist regulatory strategy is, however, one which has often recommended itself to
feminist lawyers. Since in my view the elision is an unfortunate one,
I want to try to unsettle it by sketching the kind of feminist politics
which an adequate reconceptualisation of public and private would
engender. To do so, I want to return to Young's idea of the public as
openness to political debate and dialogue and the (legitimate) private
as that area of life from which people have the right to exclude
others. This conception of public and private is entirely consonant
with the idea expressed earlier in this chapter that human autonomy—
the value *allegedly* respected by the traditional public/private divide—
may require not, or not only, non-intervention, but also positive
regulation, the provision of goods and facilities, education and so
on.[46] Feminist critique has exposed the ways in which sexuality, an
area of life traditionally constructed as private, impacts upon women's
lives in an adverse way which should not be beyond the sphere of politics. It has argued for, *and has actually engendered*, a *public*, a political
debate about sexuality, and about pornography in particular. Feminist
arguments are perfectly consistent with the idea that sexual practices
are among those from which people have the right to exclude others
and the state, but point out that the range of seriously autonomy-
reducing sexual practices which call for political critique and,
sometimes, action go beyond those, such as rape, traditionally
acknowledged to be harmful. Feminist critique, to put it broadly, has
put *women's* autonomy as well as men's on the political agenda.[47] By

[45] In my view, the case of pornography can be distinguished from, for example, current
court-centred debates around provocation, diminished responsibility and "battered women's
syndrome". Here, the burden of the feminist campaign has been the oppressive way in
which the existing legal position fails to recognise arguments which have already attained a
degree of acceptance outside the legal sphere. The issue to which the campaign addresses
itself is already and unavoidably constituted in legal terms.

[46] Young herself wants to draw a distinction between autonomy and empowerment:
Young (1990b) p. 251. Her distinction is blurred by my formulation, but the difference
between us on this point does not, I believe, affect the way in which I have drawn on her
views about public and private.

[47] This is not to say that autonomy is the only value which should be of political concern. It is rather to address the influential liberal argument, and show it to be wanting, even
in its own terms.

making the link between sexual subordination and citizenship status, and by pointing out the impact of oppressive sexual practices on the value of women's speech, Dworkin, MacKinnon and others have already begun to effect a process of social re-education, consciousness raising and change. Their political critique has itself undermined the traditional public/private divide in that it *constitutes* a form of political action—a discursive intervention in the production of dominant meanings, albeit one which still has an uneven hold. Unless we were to believe that a legal reform strategy was likely to be very effective in furthering this discursive and educational process, a less formalised process of campaigning and consciousness-raising in regional and national political fora seems a more sensible feminist strategy in this field.

In short, the inference from the reconstruction of pornography as a political issue to the strategy of legislating against it seems to me to be unjustified. First, it takes an unduly narrow view of the power and role of feminist critique conceived as a form of political practice. Secondly, it falls into the trap of thinking that as feminist lawyers we have to be lawyers first and feminists second—in other words, that we have to find legal solutions to all the problems identified by feminist critique. As a general assumption this is dangerous, for questions about law reform are essentially strategic and have to be assessed carefully in the context of particular reform possibilities. At least in Britain, such an assessment in the case of pornography leads, I have argued, to the conclusion that legal reform of the kind attempted in Minneapolis is likely to be a counter-productive feminist strategy. Finally, the history of the pornography debate illustrates the importance of distinguishing between different aspects of the public/ private dichotomy and its deconstruction in feminist theory. The critique of public/private divisions in social, political and legal thought cannot of itself recommend particular political strategies. What it can do, properly differentiated, is to give us a broader conception of the political and a sense of the questions we have to confront. In their work on not only pornography but also a range of other issues— abortion, sexual harassment, rape and so on—radical feminist lawyers have made an invaluable contribution to feminist politics, irrespective of their activities around law reform. To regard legislative reform as the *invariable* core of feminist legal politics is to exaggerate the power of such reform and to undervalue the power of legal critique.

4

Unspeakable Subjects, Impossible Rights: Sexuality, Integrity and Criminal Law

As Michel Foucault famously observed,[1] the nineteenth century's construction of sexuality as an unspeakable subject paradoxically generated an extraordinary amount of talk about sex. This chapter engages with another paradox in the same field: for my main thesis will be that the criminal law which purports to regulate sexual behaviour has, in an important sense, very little to do with sex at all.

Perhaps this rather startling aspect of my argument explains the difficulty which I had in writing this chapter. It probably had more to do, however, with the fact that it was originally written as an inaugural lecture. I want to begin by describing the history of the lecture—for this history is, I think, an integral part of the present chapter's argument.

Writing and delivering an inaugural lecture is, in my experience, a uniquely challenging process, which forces one to think in a particular way about the place one sees one's work as having in and beyond the academy. For a woman, there is an added complication which probably (though subconsciously) informed the reference to "unspeakable subjects" in my title. The delivery of a lecture is an authoritative activity culturally marked as masculine. This issue about, as it were, the sex of lecturing came home to me very forcefully when I asked a friend to read a draft of the lecture: a few pages into the text, she observed: "so far, the tone is more woman than professor . . .". Having completed my higher education without once being taught by a woman, it perhaps wasn't surprising that I was having trouble finding a feminine professorial voice. But my friend's comment touched also on a deeper issue. This lies in the controversial philosophical and psychoanalytic literature which equates the

---

[1] Foucault (1981).

feminine with a state of lack, abjection and silence.[2] If a woman professor is in some sense "speaking as a man", and if, as a feminist and a woman, one wants to find an authentic voice and style, the inaugural lecture presents at once the forum in which one's responsibility to do so is greatest, and that in which success is most elusive. I spoke, then, as a subject of the unspeakable sex, exercising the apparently impossible right of speaking on the unspeakable subject of sex.

I wanted to present a lecture which would express my intellectual commitments: both my substantive interests—criminal law and criminal justice—and the diverse theoretical resources which have informed my work. In this context, I decided to organise my lecture around the theme of sexuality and criminal law. The decision, I have to confess, came as something of a surprise to me. Up till that point, I had studiously avoided working on the sexual offences. The reasons were a combination of the political and the aesthetic. Criminal law, for some doubtless interesting reason which exceeds the ambit of this chapter, has tended in Britain to be a male preserve. There is one, all too predictable exception to this norm: sexual offences in general, and the law of rape in particular, are often taught and researched by women.[3] For eleven years of my career, I worked as Fellow in Law at New College Oxford. As someone who spent a large part of that time struggling to change its Senior Common Room from something resembling a gentlemen's club into a female-friendly workplace, joining what I saw as a feminine (even if feminist) intellectual ghetto wasn't entirely to my taste. Whilst I certainly felt a responsibility to spend a considerable amount of my time in another feminine ghetto—counselling students, campaigning on various issues of sexual politics—by the time I got to the library I was damned if I was going to occupy the pigeonhole which both feminist and other scholars seemed to have created. Female criminal lawyers' specialism in sexual offences seemed to me to reflect a pervasive cultural tendency to accord women responsibility for certain aspects of human existence—those having to do with bodily and emotional life—with which it is then pretended that men need not concern themselves.

[2] Much of this work derives its theoretical framework, albeit with modifications, from the psychoanalytic theory of Jacques Lacan: see for example Moi (ed.) (1986); Luce Irigaray (1985a), (1985b); Drucilla Cornell (1991). For a critical appraisal of the influence of such work in legal theory, see Chapter 7 below; and in political theory, see Fraser (1997) Ch. 6. For further discussion of the implications of psychoanalysis for feminist theory, see Chapter 5.

[3] See for example Temkin (1987).

I also had a number of intellectual doubts about the direction which feminist work in the area of sexuality and criminal law was taking in the early 1980s. In the first place, some radical feminist literature had the effect of replaying and hence confirming the very stereotypes of active and aggressive masculinity and passive and victimised femininity which it is one of the main projects of feminism to unsettle.[4] In both radical feminist and some psychoanalytic literature, a rather hopeless picture emerged.[5] It was a picture of a world of pathological and uncontrolled male sexual athletes, armed with a weapon—the penis, or was it the phallus?—which we were now told gave them not only physical power but also the power to control language and meaning. Of course, there was a great deal of scope for engaging in the strategy of satirising the patent contradictions which inform contemporary discourses of feminine and masculine sexuality: the rational male whose sexuality is so potent is, after all, that same poor creature who is driven to rape by the urgings of his uncontrollable sexual drives, and whose cognitive capacities are so fragile that he is at times incapable of recognising the distinction between that apparently rather straightforward dichotomy, yes and no.[6] Similarly, the poor, passive female—the very same subject who, according to the English and Welsh law of incest,[7] does not, like a man, "have" sexual intercourse but rather (and graciously?) "permits" a man to have sexual intercourse with her—is also the calculating and deceptive seductress who uses her sexuality to entrap men very much as a capitalist uses wealth to control actors in the market. Yet these contradictions occupied a relatively small place in feminist legal analysis of that time.

Curiously, and conversely, much of the feminist literature which painted such a depressing—dare I say structuralist—picture of male and female sexuality, at once generated a relatively optimistic reformist literature in the legal sphere.[8] It was as if the powerful cultural forces which shaped male and female, gay and straight sexualities would simply fall away as soon as the power of law was invoked.

---

[4] The direction of such work is perhaps best exemplified by Catharine MacKinnon's *Feminism Unmodified* (1987).

[5] For discussion and critique of these tendencies, see Gibson (1993); Jackson (1992); Butler (1997) Ch. 2; Brown (1995) Ch. 4.

[6] For an excellent discussion of the use of satire as a strategy of rape prevention, see Marcus (1992).

[7] Sexual Offences Act 1956, ss. 10, 11.

[8] See MacKinnon (1979), (1987), (1989).

At best, this seemed implausible.[9] At worst, it threatened some unpromising reforms, and the construction of some dubious political alliances. A relevant factor in the criminal justice arena was an alliance with a certain wing of the victims' movement which argued for greater general severity in sentencing. Whilst feminist activism undoubtedly made an extraordinary contribution to the better treatment of sexual assault victims, our grasp of how such reformist projects might contribute to a more radical reconstruction of sexual relations remained tenuous.

Nonetheless, it is the relationship between sexual offences and the sexed body which forms the main object of my analysis in this chapter. My choice of topic was premised on a number of changes in the cultural and intellectual environment which had altered my view of the potential contribution to be made. Unfortunately, sexual abuse of various kinds, and the denigrating attitudes towards women, gay men and others which feed and legitimise those abuses, still constitute a major social phenomenon. Nonetheless, there has been a genuine change in the cultural climate in countries like Australia, Britain, Canada and the USA towards the acknowledgement and critique of a number of such abuses which were invisible and even nameless a generation ago. Child abuse, marital rape, "date" rape, homosexual rape, domestic violence and sexual harassment, notwithstanding the many problems which remain, are all instances of the kind of change to which I am alluding. In the legal sphere, the American tort of sexual deceit is reconstructing masculine sexual power as not so much an offer which can't be refused as one which can be very expensive if it isn't fulfilled.[10] In each of these areas, questions formerly thought of as matters of private responsibility have begun to be reconstructed as matters of public concern. It is therefore appropriate to think about why, notwithstanding significant legal reforms, criminal law still falls so far short of providing an adequate construction of these phenomena.

To date, feminist scholarship in the area of sexual offences has been primarily concerned with the inequities (or perhaps iniquities) of the prosecution and trial process, and with what these inequities reveal about the legal construction of female and male sexualities.[11] In this

---

[9] One of the first British scholars to express caution about the reformist optimism of feminist legal theorists was Carol Smart: see in particular Smart (1989); for further discussion of the relationship between critical, utopian and reformist projects, see Chapters 3 and 8 of this book.

[10] See Larson (1993).

[11] See for example Smart (1995); Lees (1996); Temkin (1987).

chapter, rather than focusing on specific features of the criminal process, I shall address the question of how criminal law itself constructs the wrong of rape. I shall argue that the inadequacy of the sexual offences identified by feminist critics flows at least in part from the law's impoverished conception of the value of sexuality. In making my argument, I shall draw on recent work in feminist philosophy which engages with the place of the body—or, more properly, of corporeality—in social theory. While voicing some reservations about this work, I shall suggest that the impoverished evaluative framework of the sexual offences indeed relates to their very partial idea of the body, and to the virtual absence of affectivity from criminal law's doctrinal scheme. This analytic argument leads, in the final section of the chapter, to a set of normative questions. To the extent that criminal law replays an unsustainable mind/body dualism and a downgrading of the importance of the bodily and the affective, could this be corrected? Could corporeality be inserted within, spoken by, legal discourse? And what would be the implications of such an incorporation?

RE-READING CRIMINAL LAW'S CONSTRUCTION OF SEXUALITY:
SEXING THE BODY OF THE LAW?

To begin to address these questions, I now have to spend a little time introducing, as it were, the relevant body of criminal legal scholarship. In the arena of sexual offences, the most productive scholarship to date has read criminal law as a powerful social discourse from which much can be learnt about the social order of which it is a part.[12] It interprets criminal law not only as an index of powerful social attitudes about the form of behaviour in question but also as a discourse which produces certain kinds of sexual subject. How, then, does criminal law construct sexuality in its various senses? In particular, what assumptions about normal and abnormal sexuality does criminal law embody?

In the criminal law of England and Wales, a relatively clear picture emerges:[13] criminal law produces, both explicitly and implicitly, a norm of adult heterosexual sexuality, and of penetrative heterosexual

---

[12] See for example Moran (1996); Zedner (1995); O'Donovan (1991); Wells (1994); Naffine (1994),(1997).

[13] My analysis is drawn from a wide range of offences contained in the Sexual Offences Acts of 1956, 1967 and 1985 and the Sexual Offences (Amendment) Act 1976.

sexual intercourse as the paradigm of normal sexual behaviour.)
Whilst certain forms of male homosexual behaviour have gradually
gained some implicit legitimacy, this change has arrived late and is
extremely partial. This is reflected by features such as differential age
limits and offences specifically addressing male same-sex sexual conduct. As for lesbian sexuality, it enjoys the dubious privilege of literal
legal unspeakability. We can read off a conception of abnormal
sexualities—and perhaps still of sexual taboos—which are structured
around the axes of bodily sex, age, relationship, and place: normal sex
happens in the private sphere; it is not part of an overt commercial
transaction; it happens between persons with differently sexed bodies, of certain ages, within certain kinds of relationships. Crucially,
both the "normal" and the "deviant" sexualities of those with male
and female bodies are very different. The heterosexual male who
stalks the sections of the Sexual Offences Acts is a creature who pen-
etrates, who procures, who threatens and coerces; with consummate
economic rationality, he lives off the earnings of prostitution. Whilst
women are occasionally allowed to step into the domain of action
and control—exercising control over prostitutes and, curiously, living on the earnings of male prostitution—their predominant role is
one of passivity and victimisation.

   The resources for this kind of reading are as rich as they are diverse.
They lie in the structure and substance of offences, with their messages about normal sexualities and the relative power and autonomy
of different sexual subjects. They lie in the details of linguistic formulation: references to "unnatural intercourse"[14] or the construction
of different subject positions in relation to sexual conduct as in
incest—men have sex: women permit men to have sex with them.
They lie also in what we might call the semiotics of statutory and
reformist frameworks—the elision of prostitution and homosexuality
in the important Wolfenden Committee Report[15] is perhaps the most
spectacular British example.

   Building on the insights of this scholarship, I now want to pose a
further, incredibly obvious question, yet one which, as far as I am
aware, has occupied almost no attention in criminal law theory.
Reading across and between the lines of the sexual offences, what
can we tell about their implicit conception of what is valuable about
sexual experience, sexual expression, lived sexuality? Conversely,
what is their implicit view of abuses of sexuality?

[14] Sexual Offences Act 1956, s.44.
[15] Wolfenden(1957).

LIVED SEXUALITY AND SEXUAL OFFENCES

The question of what it is which is valuable about sexuality as a field of human experience is one to which it would be reasonable to expect to find some clues in the structure and substance of criminal law. It is, after all, a prime tenet of criminal law in supposedly liberal societies that it exists to protect certain especially valued interests. Even granted that criminal law is primarily concerned not so much with rights as with wrongs, it would be difficult to conceive ·of wrongs without some initial conception of what is socially valued. In a professedly liberal system in the late twentieth century, the most obviously relevant interest—and one which forms the normative framework for many academic commentaries on the sexual offences[16]—is *sexual autonomy:* the freedom to determine one's own sexual experiences, to choose how and with whom one expresses oneself sexually.

   This is not to say, however, that the sexual offences in fact express this liberal ideal. The discourse of sexual autonomy is, of course, a recent one. It is therefore not surprising that a reading of the diverse array of such offences, scattered across several English statutes of the post-war era, suggests on the contrary that criminal law evinces only an uneven commitment to sexual autonomy. Certainly, the modest liberalisation of criminal law, particularly in the field of male homosexuality, has been informed by the idea of autonomy and an associated (though markedly spatialised) notion of privacy.[17] In so far as it is possible to infer a commitment to any other positive values, these have to do with maintaining a rather nebulous idea of social order and upholding a set of moral conventions historically associated with Christian sexual mores.[18] The vast majority of sexual offences amount, in short, to public order offences. What is conspicuously missing is any sense of why sexuality matters to human beings in the

---

[16] See for example Lacey and Wells (1998) Ch. 4; Ashworth (1995) pp.337–58.

[17] Since the enactment of the Sexual Offences Act 1967, consensual adult male same-sex sexual conduct has been lawful, but only when it takes place "in private" (s.1).

[18] Good examples here include the offence of indecent assault (Sexual Offences Act 1956 ss. 14, 15), which turns on the jury's assessment of what "right-thinking people" would regard as indecent (*R v. Court* [1987] 1 All ER 120);the various offences relating to prostitution contained in the Sexual Offences Act 1956; the offence of kerb-crawling created by the Sexual Offences Act 1985, s.1; the offence of incest (n. 7 above); and the recent rejection of consent as a defence to assaults occasioning actual bodily harm in the course of (male homosexual) sado-masochistic sexual conduct *(R v. Brown* [1993] 2 All ER 73). For comment, see Naffine (1997); Weait (1996).

first place—something which contemporary understandings of sexuality have put at the centre of cultural debate, and of which one might therefore expect to find traces in the more recent statutory formulations and judicial interpretations.

Leaving aside the apparently public order offences and special cases such as offences relating to children, where the normative framework of autonomy remains to some extent inapt, I want now to focus on the one offence whose structure may most plausibly be argued to be consistent with a commitment to sexual autonomy: that of rape.[19] The idea of autonomy is one which, it should be noted, assumes rather than explicates what is valuable about sexuality itself. Liberals, of course, value autonomy for its own sake: its discrete value lies in the centrality of self-determination to the meaningful pursuit of human life. On a liberal view, the capacity for autonomy is central to what it means to be a person, just as the social and political recognition of autonomy is at the heart of respect for persons. Yet to the extent that criminal law respects or restricts autonomy, it inevitably makes judgements about the nature and context of a subject's autonomous choices: even in the most thoroughly liberal theories, the acceptance of a proper sphere for criminal law entails that moral self-governance is not total, and autonomy, therefore, is filled out by other values and interests. Probably the most obvious supplementary interest recognised in liberal theory is the value of avoiding the infliction of harm—a principle whose common-sensical resonance disguises, however, some fundamental problems of determinacy.[20] These problems about determining the concept of "harm" are relatively easily disguised in cases such as homicide, assault or theft. In the area of sexual offences, however, the nature of the relevant harm and,

[19] In England and Wales, the principal elements of the offence of rape are defined in the Sexual Offences Act 1956, s. 1, as amended, as follows:

"1. (1) It is an offence for a man to rape a woman or another man.

(2) A man commits rape if—

(a) he has sexual intercourse with a person (whether vaginal or anal) who at the time of the intercourse does not consent to it; and

(b) at the time he knows that the person does not consent to the intercourse or is reckless as to whether that person consents to it.

(3) A man also commits rape if he induces a married woman to have sexual intercourse with him by impersonating her husband."

[20] The "harm principle" derives from John Stuart Mill's essay *On Liberty* (1859); for critical discussion of the difficulty of establishing both its determinacy and its independence from the principle of utility, see Frazer and Lacey (1993) Ch. 2; Honderich (1982). The liberal literature on concepts of freedom and autonomy is, of course, vast; see in particular Berlin (1989); and Ryan (ed.) (1979).

hence, of the precise value to be attached to defendants' and victims' autonomy remain, as I shall show, deeply contested.

Leaving aside for the moment the question of precisely how the idea of autonomy should be understood, let us turn to the ways in which it has been interpreted in the law of rape. It is well known that the history of the offence of rape expresses a commitment not so much to sexual autonomy as to property rights: its essence was damage to the proprietary value of virginity or chastity to an "owning" male rather than any recognition of a women's interest in her own sexual freedom. In other words, the value of property to male autonomy rather than the value of female sexual autonomy was the object of the offence. Even modern commentators on the law of rape sometimes argue that it protects a proprietary interest in sexuality: a woman or man has a right in her or his body much like that in other property, and it is the right freely to dispose of this odd form of property which rape violates.[21] According to the definition of rape in England and Wales,[22] the core of the legal wrong lies in the lack of the victim's consent: it is this which turns sexual intercourse into the conduct element of rape. Arguably, this definition coheres with the view that the offence of rape protects an interest which the (disembodied) subject has in controlling access to a rather curious object to which she stands in a position of ownership—her body.[23] This understanding of rape, and its relationship to ideas of autonomy and property, is something to which I shall return shortly.

There is little trace in criminal law, then, of those things which contemporary social discourses of sexuality mark as its values and risks. Ideas of self-expression, connection, intimacy, relationship—those things which surely underpin contemporary understandings of what is valuable about sexuality—are absent. Conversely, violation of trust, infliction of shame and humiliation, objectification and exploitation find no expression in the legal framework, albeit that they surface with increasing insistence in argument at the sentencing stage. Why should it be that the contemporary criminal law dealing with sexuality has such an oblique relationship with social attitudes about what is valuable about sexual experience and what is wrong with or abusive about certain forms of sexual behaviour? Certainly,

[21] For a very clear expression of the commodity theory of sexual autonomy, and hence of the view of rape as an offence against the proprietary interest in control over one's body, see Dripps (1992): I am grateful to John Samson for referring me to this article.

[22] See above n. 19.

[23] On the relationship between the body and ownership, see Church (1997); and Diprose (1996).

the answer lies in part in the history of sexual offences and the
recency of these ideas about the value of human sexuality. However,
this is not a complete explanation: cultural changes in ideas about
sexuality predate some of the relevant legislation, and legislative definitions are in any event open to judicial interpretation, which might
have been expected to infuse legal discourse with at least some modern ideas about sexuality. To suggest a more complete answer to the
question, I shall now make a short excursion into the terrain of
feminist philosophy.

FEMINIST CRITIQUES OF DUALISM:
A NEW BODY OF KNOWLEDGE?

In a wide range of recent philosophical work, it has been argued that
the Cartesian tradition in Western thought has proceeded on the basis
not only of a dualism between mind and body, but also of a privileging of mind over body.[24] From a feminist point of view, there are two
important arguments here. The first points to the relative absence or
invisibility of the body in philosophy and social theory. It traces the
implications of the primacy of the mental and the rational for women
in a culture which also associates masculinity with the mind and with
reason. The second, conversely (but consistently) points to the lin-
gering relevance of the repressed body: since persons, as legal or other
subjects, indeed inhabit bodies (just as we have emotions), implicit
assumptions about the embodied and affective aspects of life surely
inform social practices. Hence the project is one of reading between
the lines to discover *what kinds of bodies* are, to borrow the
Foucaultian term, "normalised" and inscribed in social discourses
such as law. For only subjects with normal bodies can claim full legal
privileges, including, on occasion, the privilege of corporeal invisibility. In other words, having a "normal" body allows a subject to fit
the culturally privileged model of the rational choosing individual.

[24] See for example Gatens (1996); Grosz (1994). These books have a distinctively feminist orientation, but they also draw upon a number of non-feminist philosophical traditions,
in particular the ideas of Deleuze, Foucault, Freud, Merleau-Ponty, Nietzsche and Spinoza.
These and other books exemplify an increasing pre-occupation with the body in feminist
theory and a turn from the category of "gender" to that of "sex" in feminist analysis. For
recent examples, see the essays in Meyers (ed.) (1997); in Cheah et al (eds.)(1996); and in
Naffine and Owens (eds.) (1997); see also Young (1990a) Part Three. For an early analysis
of the relevance of the body for feminist legal theory, see Eisenstein (1988).

An influential strand of feminist theory goes on to argue that, notwithstanding changes in the social understanding of sex and gender during the course of this century, the normal body remains the male body, and that the female body continues to be constructed in significant ways as abnormal, disruptive, problematic.[25] This visibility or intrusiveness of the female body marks the cultural association of the feminine with the corporeal, with disorderly materiality rather than with controlled form. Woman becomes the sex which, as Elizabeth Grosz implies, bears the burden of physicality,[26] sustaining men's position as the rational individual in just the way that women's private labour sustains man's public status.[27] The implication of this elision of the feminine with the corporeal is graphically evoked by the concept of hysteria, which ties etymologically a condition of both pathology and irrationality to the physical possession of a womb.

Feminist philosophers like Elizabeth Grosz, Luce Irigaray[28] and Judith Butler[29] have thus argued that we need to reconstruct our view of the world so as properly to accommodate the inevitably corporeal aspect of human being. This reconstruction is no easy task, for it has to replace the body in ways which escape both mind/body dualism and a materialist or idealist reduction from one pole to the other—mind to body or vice versa. Clearly, such a project cannot leave the concepts of mind and body, as it were, intact: nor can it easily rely on the language of mind and body—a language which is deeply embedded in Western categories of thought. Accordingly, these philosophers have sought distinctive linguistic terms and written styles in which to express their ideas, speaking the unspeakable by transgressing conventional borderlines as in the idea of "body-writing". Grosz, for example, speaks not of mind and body, but of the interconstitution of the inside and the outside, of depth and surface, in human subjectivity. She seeks to reposition the body as a vantage point connecting or relating various different aspects of human life.

Accompanying this effort to rethink and write the body, feminist philosophers have also been concerned to accord the body a certain

---

[25] This feminist argument has a close analogue in theories about the operation of racial oppression through the objectification and exoticisation of the non-white body. In the legal sphere, see for example Harris (1990); Williams "On Being the Object of Property", in Williams (1991) p. 216.

[26] Grosz (1994) p.22.

[27] I shall return below to the question of how far this remains a convincing account of legal discourse. On feminist critique of dualisms, see Chapters 3, 5 and 7 of this book.

[28] See Irigaray (1985a), (1985b), (1991).

[29] See Butler (1990), (1993), (1997).

priority. There is, of course, an apparent paradox in this feminist discovery of the germ of intellectual liberation in the very body which
has so often been the basis for the denigration of women. The idea
that the shape of women's lives is determined by the shape of our
bodies is precisely what feminism has attacked, and what the concept
of gender as social construct has sought to undermine. Yet in so far
as gender difference continues to be mapped rather consistently onto
differently sexed bodies, it has begun to appear that the issue of the
body is one which feminism cannot, after all, spirit away. There are
thus some persuasive strategic reasons for embracing the paradoxical
feminist espousal of the sexed body.[30] For if corporeality is the dominant framework of analysis, women's bodies—indeed many different kinds of bodies—are put into the conceptual picture, and sexual
(as well as other bodily lived) differences are placed at the centre of
the philosophical agenda.

The feat which has to be accomplished, of course, is the reinsertion of the body without a return to an essentialist, fixed view of
sexual (or other) differences. This entails that sex as much as gender
must be understood as a social construct—a concern which is nicely
expressed in the title of Grosz's recent book, *Volatile Bodies*. A yet
more radically constructionist understanding of the sexed body is
Judith Butler's idea of gender as performance or masquerade—a
process most vividly played out in the practices of transvestism
explored in her book *Gender Trouble*. The corporeal frame within
which gender is performed is strongly emphasised in Butler's more
recent book whose title—*Bodies that Matter*—neatly encapsulates
both her analysis and its political implications.[31] Analytically, bodies
are actively materialised through iterative practices of citation within
established cultural discourses such as law. This means not only that
such practices give meaning to bodies but also that they shape the
powers and capacities of different bodies. Politically, this process of
cultural materialisation produces some bodies which matter, and
some which do not. Another striking example is Luce Irigaray's lyrical meditation on the role of feminine embodiment in the generation
of distinctive sensibilities and knowledges: the idea of knowledge as
embodied here disrupts the terms of a conventional mind/body

---

[30] For a more detailed discussion of this paradox, see Lacey (1997) p. 65 *et seq.*

[31] Butler (1990), (1993); Butler's most recent work, *Excitable Speech* (1997), makes yet
more explicit the links between the linguistically oriented notion of gender as performance
and the body; it draws on Bourdieu's notion of the "habitus" to construct an argument about
the embodied nature of performativity.

dualism.[32] Irigaray, like Foucault, also draws on corporeal metaphors to express analytic ideas: for example, she uses the image of lips as a way of expressing a form of feminine and relational human subjectivity different from that of the unitary and rational individual of modern thought.[33]

Before moving on, I want to voice one important reservation about this stream of scholarship. My reservation derives from the constant risk of reaffirming an untenable mind/body dualism, as well as a certain genre of essentialism, in the attempt to reassert the importance of corporeality. To assert the need *both* to deconstruct the mind/body dichotomy *and* to (re)prioritise the body sounds, after all, like wanting to have one's cake and eat it (perhaps a reasonable enough desire for anyone concerned with the corporeal . . .) But the real importance of the debate lies not only in the emphasis on the sexed body as social construct but also in its relationship to the deconstruction of yet another powerful dichotomy: that between reason and emotion. Thus the key argument must be not about reprioritising the body as a "thing", but rather about affirming the inevitably corporeal frame through which affective *and* intellectual life is lived.[34] As we shall see in relation to sexual offences, it is the positioning within social theory of the affective and intellectual as much as the physical aspects of human embodiment which is at issue.

AUTONOMY, CORPOREALITY AND THE CRIMINAL LEGAL SUBJECT

I now want to demonstrate the relevance of these philosophical debates for criminal law by posing a few salient questions. To what extent does mind/body dualism and the privileging of the mental and rational over the material and experiential realise itself in criminal law doctrine and practice? In what ways, if any, is the body represented or implied in criminal law categories? The arena of sexual offences is a particularly powerful one in which to explore these questions. This is not only because sexuality is an area of human experience in which the body is vividly implicated, but also because sexual offences are unusual in that they lift the veil of legal neutrality. They explicitly

---

[32] This is perhaps most vividly and lyrically represented in Irigaray (1991).

[33] See Irigaray (1985b).

[34] On the tension between (equally problematic) conceptions of body as "thing" and body as "person", see Diprose (1996); Brison (1997); Church (1997).

construct subject positions specific to differently sexed bodies: only men, for example, can perpetrate rape in English law.[35] I have already suggested that the inadequacy of rape law derives from its impoverished conception of sexuality. I now want to argue that this has to do with two discrete but related factors: first, the general conceptualisation of legal subjects as rational and disembodied individuals; and secondly, rape law's underlying notion of sexual autonomy. Each of these issues relates closely to the feminist critique of mind/body dualism just canvassed.

Let us examine first the idea of the criminal legal subject. The paradigm legal subject is defined in terms of a certain set of cognitive capacities combined with the power to master the will, and hence to control one's behaviour. What is at issue here is therefore the mind: the embodied aspects of human life are in general not acknowledged as either important or problematic. We see this reflected very clearly in the key doctrinal question in criminal law: what justifies the imposition of criminalising power on the individual? This is answered in terms of a conception of responsibility which is both rationalist and mental; criminal responsibility depends on the capacities of understanding, reason and control.[36] The binary division of the conceptual framework of criminal liability into conduct and fault elements, traditionally expressed in the telling labels, *actus reus* and *mens rea*, posits a strong mind/body dualism. Moreover, the doctrinal focus on *mens rea* places the argumentative fulcrum of many appellate cases on questions about the cognitive or volitional capacities of the legal subject: in the normal subject, the mind is not only well informed, it is also master of the body. To the extent that feminist philosophers are correct in assuming that physicality is associated with the feminine, then, one might argue that the criminal legal subject is implicitly marked as masculine.[37]

[35] Furthermore, until the Sexual Offences Act 1956 was amended by the Criminal Justice and Public Order Act 1994, only women could be raped.

[36] For further discussion, see Chapter 7 below; see also Norrie (1993a).

[37] A somewhat different and perhaps yet more radical critique of the unitary and rationalist conception of the legal subject, and of the Cartesian image of the body as animated by the soul, is that deriving from psychoanalysis. Legal theorists influenced in particular by the work of Jacques Lacan have argued not only that the human subject is split on its entry into language, but also that the structure of language, which inevitably marks the body, is masculine: see Cornell (1991). My reservations about the Lacanian view of language are discussed in Chapter 7. Though a full discussion of psychoanalytic accounts is beyond the scope of this chapter, I hope that it is evident that a complex view of the body as marked by (among other things) language is necessary if feminist critique is to avoid both dualism and essentialism.

In criminal law, the critique of mind/body dualism therefore has its most obvious applications in relation to the binary division between *actus reus* and *mens rea*—between conduct and what makes one responsible for it. In the definition of offences such as rape, however, a "mental" element is part of not only the *mens rea* but also the *actus reus*: whilst the defendant's lack of belief in the victim's consent is part of the *mens rea* requirement, the victim's lack of consent itself is part of the *actus reus*. Hence the contemporary debate about mind/body dualism and the privileging of mind over body become relevant to the very constitution of criminal wrongs. This brings us to the second factor which explains the inadequacy of rape law: infringement of (a certain conception of) sexual autonomy as the core idea underpinning the wrong. As I have shown, feminist philosophers' entry into the mind/body dualism debate has focused upon the sexual marking of the mind as masculine and the body as feminine, and the hierarchical positioning of mind over body. The bodily and the affective, they argue, are repressed within Western metaphysics, and this repression is replayed in social institutions and categorisation systems. To the extent that this critique is applicable to the constitution of criminal wrongs, therefore, we would expect to find either a predominantly mentalist construction of the wrong in question, or at least an impoverished conception of its embodied or affective aspects. If the incorporation of the corporeal aspects of human existence is attenuated even in sexual offences—where ideas of wrongdoing are most insistently inscribed upon different bodies, and where the experience of victimisation is vividly embodied—this would be persuasive confirmation of the feminist hypothesis about the repression of the corporeal in Western social practice.

And, as we have seen, the idea of harm communicated by the legal definition of rape is indeed a peculiarly mentalist, incorporeal one. Its essence lies in the violation of sexual autonomy understood as the right to determine sexual access to one's body. Thus it might be inferred that rape amounts to something between expropriation of a commodity and violation of a will. The ultimate trespass on the liberal legal subject's sexual personhood is that his sexuality is appropriated without his consent. Whilst that lack of consent is indeed mapped onto a bodily experience, the dualistic framework of criminal law blocks the articulation of the inextricable integration of mental and corporeal experience: nothing in criminal law doctrine invites any expression of the corporeal dimension of this violation of choice. For the purposes of criminal law doctrine, sexual autonomy simply *is* proprietary autonomy: the choice to exclude another from access to bodily "property".

If we look, conversely, at the conception of wrongdoing implicit in the definition of rape, we might also infer that the perpetrator is punished precisely for his failure to control his body, and hence for slipping from his pedestal as the rational subject. In Western culture, the most obviously valued image of the masculine body is, after all, that of the athlete, whose body is shaped by his mental determination and ambition. Yet the picture is complex. While the perpetrator of rape is certainly sometimes censured for failing to repress his body—particularly so where his body does not conform to the white heterosexual paradigm—norms about appropriate male bodily reactions can also operate to excuse his conduct. For example, the defendant who suggests that the victim "led him on" has not infrequently found a sympathetic audience in court—something which has led to feminist jibes about "the myth of the uncontrollable phallus" . . . Significantly, however, if such a story is to generate an excuse within the doctrinal structure of criminal law, it has to be translated to the mental plane: assuming it to be accepted that the victim did not consent, the defendant must argue that the victim's behaviour was such as to induce him to form a mistaken *belief* in his or her consent.[38]

To date, feminist scholars have focused their critique of the role of consent in rape law on intractable problems about the conditions under which consent is "real" or meaningful. In particular, they have focused on the way in which existing law, in apparently abstracting the victim's "choice" from its material location, in fact contextualises that choice within a prevailing system of sexual stereotypes which denigrate female sexuality and personhood. This approach sidelines the relevance of contextual factors such as unequal power relations between the parties. It also has the effect of concentrating attention at the trial on the victim's rather than the defendant's conduct and credibility.[39] Whilst I am in broad agreement with this critique, my own argument is a different and, in some ways, more fundamental one. For it is that an abstract notion of non-consent as the core of

[38] For reasons of space, I shall concentrate in what follows not on the idea of wrongdoing implicit in the definition of rape but rather on that of harm. However, I think that a more comprehensive analysis of the idea of wrongdoing would also generate interesting insights, notably into the representation of the male body in criminal law and the criminal process.

[39] See MacKinnon (1989) Ch. 9; West (1993); Temkin (1987); Brown, Burman and Jamieson (1993). For a thorough exploration and feminist critique of the ideas of consent and contract in political theory, see Pateman (1988).

rape provides a distorted or (at the very least) partial representation of the real wrong of rape, in that it displaces the embodied and affective aspects of the offence. Indeed, one might go further and suggest, as has Wendy Brown, that the very constitution of rape in terms of the victim's lack of consent presupposes a subordinate position for the victim. The victim's consent responds to power by conferring legitimacy, rather than shaping power in its own terms: consent is currently understood not in terms of mutuality but rather in relation to a set of arrangements initiated, by implication, by the defendant, in an asymmetric structure which reflects the stereotypes of active masculinity and passive femininity rehearsed above.[40]

As in the best murder mysteries, however, the body is generally somewhere to be found, and it would be quite false to suggest that the doctrinal focus on consent means that the body finds no place in the court room or the criminal process. When we move from legal doctrine to the legal process, the balance of representation in the dualist picture undergoes a striking change. As empirical studies of rape trials show all too clearly, it is very much the body which is in question: the mental legal issues of consent and belief are sought to be proven in terms of a set of inferences about bodily submission, and indeed pleasure, which threatens to turn many rape trials into what Carol Smart has memorably called a "pornographic vignette".[41] In legal doctrine the prevailing image is that of body as property—as something owned by and hence separate from the legal subject. As we have seen, this has the effect of displacing the body—the move which has called forth feminist demands for a "reprioritisation" of the corporeal. In enforcement practice, by contrast, we see a different implication of mind/body dualism: an equation of (the female) subject with her body: the person *as* body.[42] This move relates to another aspect of the feminist critique of mind/body dualism: the association of woman (as of racialised "others") with the (devalued) body. As Jennifer Church has noted, this alternative picture, though resonant with some radical feminist literature, is no more satisfactory than the vision of body as "thing"; as rape trials show, its consequence

[40] Brown (1995) p.163; cf. Butler's analysis of the individualism of models of consent: Butler (1997) p.95.

[41] Smart (1989) Ch. 2, (1995) Chs. 4, 5.

[42] The very recent inclusion of male homosexual rape within English criminal law means that it is too soon to know how these factors will affect the construction of male victims of rape in the trial process. My analysis would suggest, however, that they will encounter very similar processes of objectification/identification to those described here in relation to women.

is that of changing the meaning of a woman's speech in ways which undermine her credibility as an autonomous subject.[43] The discursive practices which materialise bodies in rape trials are not ones which any liberal would want to commend, and this should remind us that merely "reprioritising or reinserting the body" is hardly a panacea from a feminist or any other politically progressive point of view.

We appear to be caught, then, between two equally unsatisfactory poles generated by mind/body dualism. Let us now consider a little more closely the images of the body produced by criminal law itself. The explicit images evoke once again the murder mystery genre, consisting as they do in dismembered body parts divorced from any sense of their status as integral constituents of human personhood— ones which are related in an intimate albeit complex way with human subjectivity. The implicit picture is yet more significant. Ngaire Naffine has pointed out that the implied body of the criminal legal subject is essentially the bounded body which finds expression in some aspects of Kantian philosophy: the emphasis on cognitive and volitional capacities of control in the construction of criminal respon-sibility cashes out in terms of an image of the self-contained and con-tinent body—a body which is not breached, penetrated or invaded.[44] This image of bodily normality is one which informs the construc-tion of the bodies of gay men and all women, of small children, the disabled, the elderly, as exceptional and as marginal to legal subjec-tivity.[45] It is an image of the body as territory, in the sense of both bounded space and property; divorced from both reason and emo-tion, bodies are boundaries which separate autonomous individuals rather than aspects of lived subjectivity through which people relate to one another. This atomistic vision marginalises relational values which one might hope to see criminal law seeking to protect.[46]

What of the other aspect of the wrong of rape which I have argued to be obscured by the doctrinal framework: its affective dimensions? Certainly, the emotional damage which flows from the embodied experience of unwanted, violent or otherwise abusive sex has increasingly found its way into criminal justice practice. It operates as

[43] See Church (1997); Diprose (1996). The sexualisation of women's speech has been thoroughly analysed in Catharine MacKinnon's work on pornography and on sexual harass-ment: see for example MacKinnon (1989) Ch. 11; see also Butler (1997) pp. 82–6.

[44] Naffine (1997); see also Nedelsky(1990) p.162 *et seq*.

[45] The same applies, though for more complex reasons, to people from particular racial groups: see Williams (1991).

[46] This argument is developed in more detail below. On ideas of relational autonomy, see Nedelsky (1989),(1995); for a critical discussion of Nedelsky's ideas, see Friedman (1997).

an informal means of grading the seriousness of the offence, albeit as often in terms of mitigation of the offender's culpability as of recognition of the victim's experience. In other areas of law, the emotional meaning to be given to physical or indeed mental or economic experience has gradually come to be recognised, for example in the law of torts' recognition of nervous shock, and in the place of self-esteem as grounding the wrong of defamation.[47] Yet the language of embodied existence—of pain, shame, loss of self-esteem, the sense of violation and objectification—find no place within formal legal categories: nothing in those categories invites the victim to construct her testimonial narrative in the terms which empirical research suggests would best relate her experience. At the level of doctrinal construction of criminal wrongdoing, affective experience is, if not absent, more or less invisible behind the veil of rational and abstract legal subjectivity. Rape victims giving evidence in court are effectively silenced, caught between the equally inept discourses of the body as property, framed by legal doctrine but incapable of accommodating their experience, and the feminine identity as body, which pre-judges their experience by equating it with stereotyped and denigrating views of female sexuality—views which are themselves filtered through a variety of further prejudicial assumptions based on factors such as race and sexual orientation. This silencing effectively denies rape victims both the status of personhood and the chance to approach the court as an audience capable of acknowledging their trauma—a process which is arguably crucial to surviving the trauma and among the most important things which a public rape trial should achieve.[48]

Would it be advantageous, in feminist terms, to attempt to reframe criminal law so as to reflect a richer conception of the wrongs it seeks to proscribe? Specifically, should we try to reconstruct criminal law

[47] The law of criminal libel, of course, did recognise damage to reputation long before the twentieth century. However, this recognition of a property-like right in reputation was premised on a social order organised around relatively rigid distinctions of status, and was hence rather different from the recent developments which I have mentioned.

[48] On the importance of finding a community to acknowledge trauma, see Brison (1997). In making this argument, I should not be taken to suggest that victims' narratives have the unassailable status of truth; indeed, I concur with Wendy Brown's argument that feminist theories which rely heavily on the "discovery" of "authentic women's experience" engage in a form of essentialism (Brown (1995) Ch. 2). Rather, as I hope will become clear in the final section, my aim is to reconstruct the trial process as a political space in which precisely the contestation of meanings which Brown envisages might take place. I do, however, believe that it is crucial to this broader project to trace the ways in which current legal and procedural arrangements close off the articulation of certain arguments and points of view.

in terms which express the affective and corporeal aspects of both
criminal wrongs and criminal victimisation, and which provide a
framework within which victims' narratives would be less constrained and distanced from their embodied experience than is the
case at present? Some tentative responses to these two questions
occupy the final section of this chapter, to which I now turn.

REINSERTING THE CORPOREAL: FROM AUTONOMY TO INTEGRITY?

I have suggested that the primary good which a liberal theory of
criminal law would expect the sexual offences to respect is that of
sexual autonomy. As usually understood, this idea of what is at issue
in the area of sexual harm is one which expresses precisely the eleva-
tion of mind over body to which feminist criticism has drawn our
attention. In focusing on an individualised notion of consent, rather
than the conditions under which choices can be meaningful, the
prevailing idea of sexual autonomy *assumes* the mind to be dominant
and controlling, irrespective of material circumstances. Furthermore,
the liberal discourse of autonomy appears to leave no space for the
articulation of the affective and corporeal dimensions of *certain* viola-
tions of autonomy—in other words, it closes off the possibility of
developing a sophisticated conception of sexual harms. While the
idea of autonomy as independence seems directly relevant to the
wrong of rape, it dominates at the expense of the development of a
positive conception of what kinds of sexual relationships matter to
personhood.

Might it be possible to reconstruct the idea of autonomy or to find
an alternative analytic and normative framework within which to
rethink the sexual offences—one which might allow repressed corporeality to be thought and spoken, which would contextualise the
victim's and the defendant's encounter more adequately, and which
would accord the embodied aspects of human existence their proper
place? I should like to suggest we can draw on the work of two feminist legal theorists, Drucilla Cornell and Jennifer Nedelsky, to make
significant progress in just this direction.

In her most recent work, Drucilla Cornell has argued for the
importance of what she calls the imaginary domain.[49] The imaginary

---

[49] Cornell (1995).

domain generates the psychic and political space within which sexual equality might be realised. Taking one step back from the quasi-contractual starting point of much recent political theory, Cornell focuses on those conditions under which a human being can pursue her life project of becoming a person. These conditions, Cornell asserts, include a fantasy dimension: the psychic space in which each of us can imagine ourselves as whole persons. The core of a substantial liberalism, in Cornell's view, is the political and legal guarantee that this space will be equally open to all.

Cornell's imaginary domain consists in three elements: bodily integrity, access to symbolic forms sufficient to achieve linguistic skills permitting the differentiation of oneself from others, and the protection of the imaginary domain itself. Central to each of these elements is the fact that a crucial part of existence for all humans is our status as sexed and embodied beings, and our sexual desire: without access to the means of expressing one's desire, and of having one's sexuality accorded such respect as is consistent with a similar respect for others, one can never have the psychic space to pursue the project of personhood.[50] For one is barred from the identification with one's sexual imago which is central to the possibility of imagining oneself as a whole being, worthy of respect and capable of self-esteem.

Might the notion of sexual integrity which we can derive from Cornell's argument constitute a better analytic peg on which to hang our framing of sexual offences than the mentalist conception of autonomy? Certainly, the idea of integrity, as developed by Cornell, puts the bodily and affective aspects of sexual life more directly in issue, quite simply because the body is implicated in the relationships which are central to human integrity.[51] Within the language of integrity, the real damage of rape might be expressed more fully, recognising the way in which rape violates its victims' capacity to integrate psychic and bodily experiences. Understood in this way, respect for victims' integrity seems an eminently worthy ideal for rape law and its enforcement. But it is also worth thinking carefully about the potential for reconstructing the ideal of autonomy so as to escape its dualistic implications. Many critics of atomistic versions of

[50] In affirming that legal arrangements may *positively* facilitate the expression of desire, Cornell appears to be breaking with Lacanian views about the structural relationship between desire and law as obstacle: see Salecl (1994).

[51] Cornell is one among many feminists who have explored the idea of integrity. See for example Urban Walker (1997).

liberalism, from Marx to the present day, have shown that the idea of autonomy can be reconstructed in positive terms. Autonomy, in this sense, focuses on the capability of persons to realise their life plans as much as on formal choice and the negative freedom not to be interefered with.[52] But even among those who embrace the positive conception of freedom, the emphasis has tended to be on the provision of goods and resources external to the person. Because of its close association with the dominant image of the abstract, choosing subject, the history of the concept of autonomy conduces to the body's concealment.

More recently, however, Jennifer Nedelsky's important work on the concepts of autonomy and rights has demonstrated that these ideas can be reconstructed so as to encompass the body.[53] The core of Nedelsky's argument is that human autonomy is fundamentally premised upon the relational aspects of life—our bodily and psychic dependence upon others. This inevitable relational interdependence renders the very idea of atomistic autonomy nonsensical. Without sustaining and respectful relationships, we cannot realise our personhood; and relationships inevitably implicate the corporeal. Hence the connection between autonomy and the repression of the body, and the supposed opposition between the feminist prioritising of the body and the liberal value of autonomy, begins to unravel. Embodied autonomy becomes, by contrast, a precondition for the pursuit of personal integrity. In Marilyin Friedman's terms, recent liberal conceptions do recognise the importance of relationships as *external* conditions necessary to the realisation of autonomy, but they fail to acknowledge that certain kinds of relationship may be conditions *internal* to autonomy itself.[54] This is not to deny the importance of autonomy as, on occasion, the power to exclude others or to maintain separateness and privacy, nor is it to deny the importance of distinguishing between connections which are valuable in the sense of fostering personhood and those which may be oppressive.[55] It is,

[52] For contrasting views on this point, see Berlin (1989); Frazer and Lacey (1993) pp. 53–60; 124–7. For further discussion of positive and negative freedom, see Chapters 2 and 3.

[53] Nedelsky (1989), (1995).

[54] Friedman (1997) pp. 56–8. Friedman takes the view that recent liberal versions of autonomy do allow for the importance of social relationships to autonomous life, but she remains agnostic on the question of whether such relationships are in some sense definitional of an autonomous life.

[55] On these problems, see Brison (1997) pp. 28–9; Friedman (1997) pp. 44–5. Friedman suggests that Nedelsky's framework needs to be supplemented by a conception of the distinction between substantive and procedural independence, and by the recognition that only

rather, to affirm the need to locate our assessments of autonomy in the context of the relational conditions which obtain between human subjects.

The interdependence of autonomy and integrity may easily be demonstrated. In Cornell's sense, integrity embraces both physical integrity and the affective sense in which access to bodily or sexual integrity also depends on a host of social and psychic conditions. These range from external conditions such as adequate sustenance and medical care through to the conditions of respect for differently embodied subjects, different sexualities—respectful relationships as conditions internal to human integrity. A recognition of the value of integrity invites the incorporation of implications of sexual abuse such as shame, loss of self-esteem, objectification, dehumanisation. These are, of course, features central to the emerging social under-standings of the wrong of sexual assault, and ones which have led feminist legal scholars such as Robin West to equate rape with "mur-der of the spirit".[56] When combined with the emphasis on person-hood as project—as a process of becoming which has an imaginary dimension and no definite end—the idea of integrity promises to escape the dangers both of essentialising a particular conception of the body and of propagating a vision of feminine empowerment which is premised, paradoxically, on a victim status which accords access to "truth".[57] It conduces rather to reflection on the conditions under which a multiplicity of bodies and sexualities can be lived by full cit-izens, and to the opening up of a political debate about the nature of those conditions.

The right to bodily integrity which Cornell advocates is, in one important sense, impossible: it is not something which can be realised or determined institutionally; rather, it operates as a vision which generates both individual ideals and critical standards for the assess-ment of existing legal and political arrangements. There is an asym-metry in the imaginary domain: it cannot be captured or realised by institutions, but it can be killed or closed off by them. The vision of sexual integrity is at once a necessary condition for the ongoing pro-ject of personhood and an impossible ideal which forms a motivating horizon in political rhetoric.

---

some relationships foster autonomy. I am in broad agreement with Friedman on the latter point, but do not think that this jeopardises the basic validity of Nedelsky's insight.

[56] West (1993) at p.1448; cf. Brison (1997) at p. 18, citing rape as "social murder".
[57] See above at note 48.

It is interesting to consider, nonetheless, what a rape law framed around the ideal of sexual integrity and relational autonomy as opposed to proprietary autonomy would look like. I would argue that an analysis in terms of sexual integrity and relational autonomy has implications for each of the features of rape law discussed in this paper; for the definition of rape; for evidential and other aspects of the trial process; and for a rethinking of the symbolic role of the criminalisation of rape. As far as the definition of rape is concerned, the most obvious change would be a move away from the emphasis on lack of consent understood in abstract and asymmetrical terms as the central determinant of sexual abuse.[58] Rather, it conduces to a more complex sexual assault law which articulates a distinctive conception of sexual as opposed to proprietary autonomy, specifying particular conditions under which coercive, violent or degrading sexual encounters should be prohibited. In rethinking the idea of autonomy as integrity, we are led to a rethinking of consent itself in both broader terms and ones which assume a mutuality of relationship and responsibility between victim and defendant. The argument, for example, would unambiguously support the proposal currently being advanced by the British pressure group, Women Against Rape, which calls for a legislative definition of consent in the following terms: "A person shall not be deemed or presumed to have consented to sexual intercourse if that person agreed to it under coercion, including the use of threat or physical violence . . . economic deprivation, abuse of authority, deception, or threat to the welfare or security of a child".[59] Even this broad statement of the conditions which may undermine the "reality" of consent, however, does not address the question of mutuality. This, I would argue, could best be dealt with by moving towards some form of "positive consent" standard: for example, by the institution of a negligence-based fault standard supplemented by a "no-negligence" defence. While no such reform is a panacea, it would express far more nearly than does the current law in England and Wales a vision of the parties as presumptively equal partners in sexual encounters, adjusted to account for the asymmetry of possible harms arising out of misunderstandings about mutual willingness.

---

[58] On possible ways of reconstructing the idea of consent, see Bronnit(1994); for critical discussion of consent, see O'Donovan (1997). The revised laws of sexual assault now prevailing in Canada and in Australian states such as New South Wales and Victoria come considerably closer to meeting these ideals thant does the law of England and Wales.

[59] See Hall and Longstaff (1997).

Even more directly, the analysis of rape in terms of relational autonomy and integrity would necessitate the reform of rules of evidence so as to allow victims more fully to express their own narrative in the court room setting, as well as ensuring that they are able to do so without having the rape trial turned into an at large examination of their sexual history.[60] This is not to imply that women's narratives produce unassailable truths. It is rather to argue that unless the rape trial is constructed in terms which allow all parties to advance their points of view, the valuable prospect of the trial as a space not only for the examination of past events but also for political contestation of their interpretation cannot be realised.

Finally, however, it should be noted that the value of sexual integrity would not direct a very great reliance on criminalisation as a mode of protecting the imaginary domain. On the contrary, criminal law is likely to be an effective defender of the imaginary domain at a symbolic rather than an instrumental level. Though lawyers are inclined to lose sight of this obvious fact, the most important conditions for sexual equality and integrity lie in cultural attitudes rather than coercive legal rules. Nonetheless, as I have argued throughout this chapter, legal rules may be inimical to these ideals, and the need to avoid this situation is among the most pressing reasons for rape reform in Britain as elsewhere. Symbolically, it is therefore crucially important that rape law be reformed so as to express an unambiguous commitment to the positive integrity as well as the full humanity of both rape victims and men accused of rape. In my view, this militates towards the maintenance of a distinctive offence rather than a subsumption of the law of rape within the general law of assault.

A rethinking of the philosophical framework of criminal law in terms of a shift from autonomy to integrity might prompt some fruitful ideas, then, for reshaping the law of sexual offences. Though I have not in this chapter pursued the argument, I think that the same might well be true in relation to non-sexual offences of violence. I do, however, want to make one important caveat. I referred earlier to the bounded conception of the body which feminist scholars have argued to haunt criminal law. Might a reassertion of the value of bodily and sexual integrity serve precisely to reaffirm this insulated vision of the body, with excluding consequences for other bodies? This is of particular concern in the light of the power of another sexualised dichotomy: that between form and matter. Feminist theory has

---

[60] On the iniquitous use of sexual history evidence in English and Welsh rape trials, see Temkin (1987).

traced the association of the feminine with matter rather than deter-
minate form, and has associated the fear of woman with images of
incontinence, flow, viscosity which are connected culturally with
various female bodily traits. Whilst the flows associated with the male
body have been interpreted in terms of potency or, in Mary Douglas's
famous term, purity, menstrual blood in particular has, in many
traditions, represented danger, disorder, contamination.[61] In the context of this cultural history, the association of integrity with *physical
wholeness* is therefore a dangerous one.

To evade these dangers, two aspects of Cornell's account need to
be emphasised, and the link between her argument and that of
Nedelsky very firmly grasped. First, the idea of integrity as project
rather than as end-state serves to displace the misleading idea that
some particular shape must be sought as the "integral" basis of
personhood. As Margaret Urban Walker has argued, integrity should
be seen as an ongoing process of integration, and the political issue
here is how to secure the conditions under which women as well as
men have a real chance to develop a coherent set of relationships
between the corporeal, affective and mental aspects of their lives.[62]
Such integration is accomplished through the construction of narratives of value, identity and relationship, and it is the framing of an
appropriate institutional audience for the construction of as well as
debate about such narratives which is precisely what is missing in the
domain of legal responses to rape and sexual abuse. Only if we find
new ways to allow women to tell their stories, and, crucially, be
heard, will we transcend their "states of injury"[63] and allow the rape
trial to become an—always risky—space for recovery rather than for
continued victimisation. Secondly, the link between bodily integrity
and psychic and social space reminds us that the possibility of the continuing search for integrity depends precisely on the multiplicity of
socially endorsed images of bodily integrity.

Each of these points is in turn underpinned by the ideal of
relational and embodied autonomy, which serves to deconstruct
the image of the autonomous subject as bounded or atomistic.
Understood in this way, the ideals of autonomy and integrity might
have the power to disrupt the implicit construction of the masculine,
white, able-bodied, heterosexual body as norm. A move to a conceptual framework incorporating the value of integrity alongside that

---

[61] Douglas (1966).
[62] Urban Walker (1997).
[63] See Brown (1995).

of autonomy, like the feminist reassertion of corporeality, might serve productively to put sexual and other embodied differences at issue. In doing so, it might open the path towards both a more inclusive sexual politics and a richer understanding of sexual harms.

IN CONCLUSION

I want to return, finally, to my point of departure, and hence to my decision to speak on the unspeakable subject of sex. And, having spoken at length, I want to consider once again the proposition that women who speak with institutional authority occupy a socially masculine position. Clearly, it is a proposition which contains a grain of truth. But I should prefer to think—and I hope that this is implicit in my argument—that institutional power can be transformative: that it can liberate women to speak in their own voices, from their own bodies, on topics of their own construction, combining, as I have tried to do, subjects and methodologies formerly marked as masculine and feminine in novel and productive ways. The progress of both women and feminist scholarship in the academy—something which I wanted specifically to recognise and celebrate in my inaugural lecture—has gradually broken down the ghetto walls which I once feared, and has redefined the nature of men's and women's space in the legal academy. The scope further to disrupt the difference made by sexual difference in and beyond the academy is among the many exciting prospects for the future of feminist legal scholarship.

5

Community in Legal Theory: Idea, Ideal or Ideology?

"There is no politics without fantasy" (Renata Salecl, *The Spoils of Freedom* (Routledge, 1994) p. 37).

"[C]ommunities tend to constitute themselves by excluding difference, but . . . the task of a philosophical politics is to conceptualize new forms of association which let the differend appear in their midst" (Seyla Benhabib, "Democracy and Difference: Reflections on Rationality, Democracy and Postmodernism" (1994) p. 30).

"There was something Gabriel's father always said to him on the bridge . . . 'The law is like railway lines, Gabriel, straight and true. The law protects the truth. What the law decides *is* truth.'
    'I suppose', Gabriel said, 'it's the kind of thing fathers say to sons, especially when they've made up their minds their sons will study law. I suppose it doesn't mean anything'." (Janette Turner Hospital, *The Last Magician* (Virago, 1992) p. 199).

These words of a father—himself a judge—express the much remarked upon power of law to accord its own definitions the status of epistemological objectivity. Spoken to his son, they also evoke the powerful draw of membership of law's community—both through the legal profession, and, in the weaker, but still significant sense, of living one's life within the boundaries imposed by legal truths—toeing, as we might say, the line. The draw consists in law's promise of order, of security and of identity for those who are both eligible for and willing to accept membership of its community—those who know where to draw the line. Its hidden face is its power to silence and exclude those who insist on reading between its lines or who live on the wrong side of its tracks, whilst effecting the discursive alchemy of nonetheless *including* them in the universal reach of legal subjectivity.

Janette Turner Hospital's novel provides a powerful literary anecdote symbolising many of the issues which confront contemporary critical legal theory. It is a story of the inclusions and exclusions implicit in the constitution of law's truth; of the erotic and fantasy dimensions of law's power; and of the ultimate violence of law's determinations.[1] As the author moves back and forth in time to tell the story of *The Last Magician*, we learn the further tensions which underlie the conversation between Robinson Gray and his son. At the centre of Turner Hospital's narrative is an incident in which the future judge was involved as a child: an "accident" on these very railway tracks, in which the brother of Cat Reilly was killed by a train. Robinson's experience of cross-examination in court has given him a strong sense of his investment in the legal constitution of truth:

> " 'And what were you doing at the railway cutting, young man?' the judge asked Robinson Gray. Robbie was wearing his Grammar uniform and looked very smart.
> 'I tried to look after Cat, sir', Robbie said. 'I felt responsible for her. She doesn't know the meaning of fear.'
> 'But you went along with the game, I understand?'
> 'I pretended to, sir, but it frightened me.'
> The judge nodded sympathetically. 'As it would any sensible person', he said. 'Anyone with a grain of sense.'
> 'We couldn't stop her, sir', Robbie said. 'I think she loves danger, sir.'
> 'And you, young woman', the judge asked Cat sternly. 'What do you have to say for yourself?'
> Cat stared at him silently.
> The judge frowned a little. 'Did you, or did you not, start this game?' he asked.
> Cat said nothing.
> 'Young lady', the judge said sternly, 'your attitude to authority is very revealing, I'm afraid. Very revealing indeed. This tragic death was clearly an accident, but I fear a long trail of family negligence leads to this sad place. A runaway mother, I understand. A father who leaves his children to run wild. A reckless little girl, product of a broken home . . .'."[2]

Overdrawn as this courtroom episode may seem, it serves to illustrate a number of pervasive features of legal community. Those

---

[1] The figure of law's mode of operation as a form of violence finds vivid expression in Jacques Derrida's "Force of Law": Derrida (1992). It has also been used by Boaventura de Sousa Santos, who distinguishes between violent, bureaucratic and rhetorical repertoires of legal governance: Santos (1982).

[2] Turner Hospital (1992) pp. 218–19.

whose ethnicity, class, gender or political position sets them askew the tracks, or who refuse—like Gabriel—to "inherit" the lines—are, in Turner Hospital's narrative, struck dumb, afflicted by madness, or consigned to the ultimate silence of death.[3] The position of those who go "off the rails" is one of abjection. What unacknowledgeable trauma underpins the denial which realises itself in the violence of this reaction? Particularly threatening to Robinson Gray is the insight of the son whom he hoped to become a lawyer. Relating his father's obsession with revisiting the railway bridge and staring at the tracks, Gabriel observes:

> " 'It was a very strange state he got into. Looking back from here, I'd be tempted to say it was sexual excitement.' . . . *Was* the law the arbiter of truth? His father's agitation on the bridge was part of the riddle and also part of the clue. That strange state of excitement had suggested to Gabriel, long before he could articulate it to himself, something lurking underneath his father's dogma: heresy, perhaps; a countertruth; a lie."[4]

Robinson Gray's access to membership of law's community protects him from the guilt which derives not only from his part in a child's death but also from the excessive enjoyment of his connection with that child's wild sister. As Willy Reilly dies, Robinson Gray submits to the castration implicit in the entry into law, language and the train on the tracks. He accepts (and symbolises) the Law of the Father. Yet the status and security which come with inclusion are illusory: the fragile fixity of Robinson's identity is constantly disrupted by the return of what has been repressed. Cat Reilly is silenced but survives to be pursued by Robinson throughout his life, as the figure who simultaneously confirms and undermines his own identity, and who evokes the bodily sensuality which his place as the rational legal subject forces him to repress. The fantasies and displacements which constitute the surmise of legal ideology,[5] as well as the power of law's ideologically asserted autonomy in "giving truth", are the central concerns of both *The Last Magician* and critical legal theory, broadly understood.

[3] The courtroom dialogue also serves to illustrate the potentially negative implications of a broad contextualisation of the legal subject—*i.e.* the judgement of the person as socially located as opposed to judgement in the limited terms of a particular action. Although broad contextualisation is often argued to be a feature of informal processes of justice (see below), Turner Hospital's instance alerts us to the potential influence of factors technically outwith legally relevant categories even in formal legal processes. See further Chapter 7.

[4] Turner Hospital (1992) pp. 199, 266.

[5] On the notion of surmise, see Salecl (1994) pp. 34–6; see further below.

In this chapter, I want to reflect on the significance of one particular discursive figure in contemporary Anglo-American legal theory:
that of community. My interest in this topic derives both from a
straightforward recognition of the frequency of appeals to ideas of
community in jurisprudence, and from a perception that these
appeals mark out issues which are of central importance not only to
legal but also to contemporary political and social theory. In particular, certain apparent paradoxes in the contemporary appeal of
"community" suggest that there is something interesting "lurking
underneath its dogma" which a critical interpretation may help to
reveal. I shall have three main concerns. First, I shall explore the
relevance for law and legal theory of the main currents of argument
within the liberal-communitarian debate in political theory. I shall
suggest that, by subjecting this debate to psychoanalytic interpretation and to a feminist critique, we can gain some insights both about
what the emergence of discourses of community signifies culturally
and about the promises and dangers which that emergence represents
for social theorists committed to a radical politics. Secondly, I shall
assess the significance of the currency of discourses of community in
legal theory in terms of a constellation of ethical, psychoanalytic and
sociological questions. What connects diverse appeals to "community", and how should we understand the rhetorical function of these
appeals, given that their rational basis is often obscure? Finally, I shall
explore the implications of this analysis for the relationship between
various different theoretical projects around law—notably critical
legal studies, socio-legal studies or law and society work, post-
modernism and critical theory. In doing so, I shall draw some tentative but general conclusions about the significance of the debate for
the revival of a concern with the ethical in some recent legal theories, and about the implications of this revival for the future direction
of radical legal analysis. In particular, I am concerned to explore
whether the commitment to a project of normative reconstruction of
the political, eloquently expressed by Seyla Benhabib in the passage
quoted above, can be translated into a similar project of legal reconstruction or re-imagination which reaches beyond the confines of
theoretical abstraction to engage with the particularities of legal institutional practices.[6] I shall realise this specific concern through an
analysis of recent debates about alternative legal forms, notably those
associated with "informal" or "popular" justice—practices which

---

[6] For a more extended discussion of the idea of "normative reconstruction", see Chapter 8.

have themselves frequently been couched in the discursive framework of "community".

Characterising communitarianism

One of the main spheres in which the idea of community has assumed a salient position in contemporary intellectual discourse is the liberal-communitarian debate in political theory. A review of that debate therefore provides a convenient starting point for my analysis. The delineation of a communitarian position is, however, notoriously difficult. This is both because of the variety of positions espoused by writers associated with communitarianism,[7] and because of the fact that contemporary communitarianism has developed as a critique of certain features of influential liberal political theories[8] rather than as a political doctrine in its own right. However, for the purpose of my argument it will be sufficient to note that communitarians typically align themselves with one or more of three distinctive positions. First, at an ontological level, communitarians espouse a social constructionist stance in relation to both human identity and the creation of value. This stance brings with it an analytic focus on not only individual subject and state but also intermediate "community" practices as important sites for the construction of subjectivity and political value. Secondly, at a political level, communitarians are concerned to develop substantial conceptions of collective values such as solidarity, reciprocity and community itself and of the institutionalised public goods which would help to sustain a rich collective life. Thirdly, at the level of method, communitarians adopt an interpretivist approach to social theory.

Conceived in this way, the communitarian critique of liberal individualism can immediately be seen to connect with a number of related yet relatively discrete debates in a range of social sciences and cultural studies. Of most obvious relevance to law would be the civic

[7] See for example Sandel (1982); MacIntyre (1981); Selznick (1987); Taylor (1985), (1989); Walzer (1983). For further discussion of communitarianism and legal theory, see Chapters 1, 2 and 6 of this book.

[8] Notably that of John Rawls: Rawls (1971).

republican and "new public law" debates.[9] But critical legal studies[10] and in particular feminist legal theory[11] also share certain concerns with communitarian thought. More broadly, links can be traced between the communitarian critique of liberal universalism and the revival of pragmatist thought in the USA.[12] Looking to Europe, intellectual links include hermeneutics, the critical theory of the Frankfurt school, and post-modernism—theoretical resources which had already made their way across the Atlantic in more or less modified form by the time the liberal-communitarian debate was beginning to flourish in the USA.[13]

Of particular significance is the political context within which the liberal-communitarian debate came to have a strong resonance. On the face of it, the extent to which the main themes of Sandel's *Liberalism and the Limits of Justice* were taken up and debated in British and North American universities is rather puzzling. After all, neither the argument about liberalism's ontological atomism nor that about its impoverished political individualism were entirely unfamiliar: both had featured prominently in critical social thought at least since Marx. Nor had the liberal assertion of a priority of the right over the good ever effaced alternative ethical positions in which reflection on the good or the virtuous were regarded as central features of political life. Where the communitarian position came to have a particular salience, however, was in the context of a more general critique of modernity and its moral impoverishment. This is most graphically captured in Habermas's vision of the colonisation of ever greater fragments of the lifeworld by the logic of the systems world, with money and power becoming the increasingly dominant frameworks of exchange and the fora for the symbolic reproduction of values being attenuated or effaced.[14]

The substantial economic and social changes which have marked the recent history of post-industrial countries have doubtless exaggerated a distinctive consciousness which has come to be associated with "the experience of postmodernity"—of disenchantment, alienation, uncertainty, fragmentation, loss of stable identities.[15] In Britain and North America, this post-modern moment coincided with a

[9] See Michelman (1988); Sunstein (1988); Kahn (1989).

[10] Unger (1983), (1987).

[11] Rhode (1990); Sherry (1986).

[12] Rorty (1989); West (1989).

[13] Goodrich (1993a); Frazer and Lacey (1993) pp. 101–7.

[14] Habermas (1986); cf. Bauman (1993); Lash and Urry (1994).

[15] For an excellent discussion, see Wagner (1993).

period in which central political power was held by right wing governments which had eschewed to a large extent traditional Tory or Republican values in favour of an intensely libertarian (and largely fiscally driven) commitment to rolling back the frontiers of the state and re-emphasising the responsibilities of the individual citizen. It is, of course, one of the ironies of these governmental regimes that they in fact gathered a great deal of power to the centre, albeit in the name of decentralisation: "community-based" criminal justice policies, for example, tend to be both sponsored and, in more or less overt ways, controlled by the state.[16] Nonetheless, their market-oriented policies which introduced the language of managerial efficiency and the practices of auditing into ever wider areas of social life can hardly be doubted to have accelerated the process identified by Habermas.[17]

For the purposes of my argument, however, the most interesting feature of both Reagan and Thatcher administrations was the effective use to which they put the rhetoric of community in constructing and legitimising various policies whose most obvious ideological ancestry lies in monetarist economics. Notable examples would be "community policing", "community-based penalties", "community 'care'" for the mentally ill. In each case, the delineation of the relevant "community" was obscure: indeed, the strength or even existence of what might have been relevant and meaningful communities had often been undermined by market-oriented and socially divisive policies of the governments themselves. Arguably, what gave the language of community such rhetorical force in these areas, notwithstanding the ease with which it could be exposed as disingenuous or as downright hypocritical window-dressing, was that it spoke to our fears at the same moment as it whispered to our fantasies. We—or perhaps parts of us—like to think that we live in real, identity-fostering, caring communities, yet part of the post-modern experience is precisely the fear—indeed the knowledge—that we do not. In this context, the rhetoric of community assumes a particular power in the hands of government and other purveyors of influential social discourses. An essentially pre-modern idea finds, as it were, its post-modern moment.

This sketch of its political context makes some contribution to explaining what Anderson calls "the profound emotional legitimacy" of the appeal to community.[18] But, as Anderson's phrase itself

---

[16] See Abel (ed.) (1982); Cohen (1985); Scull (1983); Lacey and Zedner (1995).
[17] Lacey (1994a); Power (1994).
[18] Anderson (1983) p.14.

implies, there may be more to the power of "imagined communities"
than that which can be explicated at the level of ideological meaning.
The ideological power of signifiers such as "community" may itself
derive from their "fantasy structure":[19] their role in organising subjects' desires by standing in for traumas which cannot be symbolised
directly in language. According to Salecl's and Zizek's development
of Lacanian psychoanalytic theory, it is the role of political signifiers
as the "surmise" of political discourse—their capacity to act as a "later
discourse" which provides us with a space within which we can
organise our desire and make sense of the world—which underpins
their ideological power. As Salecl puts it:

> "The 'trick' of a successful political discourse is not to directly offer us
> images with which to identify—to flatter us with an idealized image,
> an ideal ego, to portray us the way we would like to appear to our-
> selves—but to construct a *symbolic space*, a point of view, *from which* we
> could appear likeable to ourselves."[20]

Central to this psychoanalytic view is the idea of human subjectivity as split: on its entry into language, the subject submits to a law
which entails the perpetual finding of a lack in both the Other and
itself. This lack is premised on the fact that certain features of pre-
linguistic experience—the excessive enjoyment of the original relationship to the mother, for example—cannot be acknowledged: as
the subject's needs are articulated as demands, something of that original *jouissance* is lost and is experienced as a lack in the Other and, by
implication, in the subject him- or herself. But this unacknowledgeable and unrepresentable Real—itself paradoxically created by the
very process which makes it unrepresentable—returns to haunt the
subject and to destabilise her sense of identity. This underpins our
need for signifiers to "stand in for" the unrepresentable—to act as the
Lacanian '*petit objet à*'—so as to allow the subject to interpret herself
and the world as coherent and manageable.[21]

---

[19] Salecl (1994), Chs. 1, 2; Zizek (1989), Chs. 1–3; Butler (1993) Ch. 7.

[20] Salecl (1994) p.33.

[21] The suggestive power of this account is not, it should be noted, tied to a specifically
Lacanian approach. The central analytic tool here is the unconscious: that which is repressed
yet which returns to disrupt the surface level of rational discourse and action, and which
motivates human practices in ways which cannot always be acknowledged. Any account
which mobilises the idea of an unconscious and which recognises the implications of the
unconscious for the dichotomy between reason and affectivity could be used to engage in
the kind of analysis which I am here drawing out from Lacanian thought. It should also be
emphasised that such psychoanalytic accounts are complementary to the foregoing (and basically sociological) analysis of the fragmentation of the post-modern world and its implications for human experience and consciousness. To draw on a psychoanalytic frame as a

There are several reasons to think that the figure of "community" may be operating in something like this way. In the first place, such an account may help to explain the appeal of "community" notwithstanding the vagueness or even illusoriness of its apparent institutional reference points. In his powerful analysis of the rise of nationalism, Anderson makes the important point that "imagined communities" such as "nations" are not "imaginary" or merely "postulated"[22] in the sense suggested by a constrast with "real" communities. The latter, after all, are a social form which existed, if ever, only in face to face village societies long since extinguished in Western countries. Nonetheless, it is a striking feature of contemporary political discourses of community that they appear to presuppose at least partial forms of association based on kinship, residence, common interests or other features which *could*, in principle, exist, but whose existence in fact appears to be more or less irrelevant to the power of the political rhetoric. For example, the attraction of Thatcher's evocation of "care in the community" for the mentally ill was seemingly relatively unaffected by the fact that many of the institutional bases on which what might reasonably have been called "community" care could have rested had been eroded by her own Government's policies— particularly those in relation to the funding of local government, the distribution of welfare benefits and the structure of the labour market. The psychoanalytic account helps to explain this apparent disjuncture between the shape and meaning of the political discourse on the one hand and the policies it engendered and the social formations to which they were applied on the other. For it argues that the power of political signifiers lies precisely in their "contentlessness".[23] Ideas such as "democracy", "human rights" or "community" remain to be filled out by the fantasies of the subjects to whom they are addressed: the signifiers construct rather than describe the entities to which they refer. This feature also helps to explain the instability of such

theoretical resource for understanding the lacks and anxieties which motivate certain political discourses is not to imply that those lacks and anxieties are unrelated to the material conditions of the world at any given moment; it is rather to acknowledge that the experience of those changing historical conditions are inevitably mediated by underlying psychic dynamics. Further theoretical work remains to be done on the precise relationship between these and indeed other explanatory frameworks: important questions include the extent to which what Lacanian thought denotes as the "Real" is invariant or rather related to changing social conditions and the degree to which the "Real" is genuinely unspeakable rather than generally unspoken. For a feminist analysis of the deficiencies of Lacanian theory's treatment of these questions, see Chapter 7.

[22] Bauman (1993) p. 44.
[23] See Salecl (1994) p. 131.

discourses. They promise to assuage the anxiety or hopelessness attendant on the lack inherent in human subjectivity. But because the traumas which they stand in for are unrepresentable, political signifiers can never, by definition, deliver what they promise. The contentlessness of political signifers also entails, of course, that their democratic or anti-democratic tendencies are not fixed: they can express different fantasy structures, different economies of desire, for different subjects and at different times.

This raises the question of what contribution a psychoanalytic account can make to an understanding of the salience of the specific figure of "community" in certain realms of contemporary Anglo-American legal and political discourse. Clearly, a full answer could only be provided by means of a finely grained interpretation of particular instances—a project to which the later parts of this chapter seek to contribute. Nonetheless, a tentative general hypothesis may he helpful in guiding the local project. The general hypothesis is that "community" speaks to aspects of the Real which concern the role of the Other in underpinning (yet constantly threatening) the subject's identity. The subject's identity is premised on its entry into language and hence its separation from a primal enjoyment and connection which is subjected to legal prohibition. Yet the unspeakable fact is that it is the Other upon whose existence the subject's own existence is premised. In psychoanalytic thought, this Other is typically the feminine image of the mother. However, as Judith Butler has argued,[24] the insights of the psychoanalytic framework can be mobilised without our accepting an invariant account of this originary story. In the attempt to apply psychoanalytic insights in social theory, a broader conception of relevant figures of Otherness—those based, for example, on race or religion—have come to play an increasingly important role. What is central is that the logical relation of identity to otherness has to be denied, but constantly threatens to surface again.

Discourses of community, then, may be thought of as speaking to the longing for a primal unity and connection; yet, much like the liberal universalist signifiers which they in part purport to replace (individual human rights, to name but one), their underside is always a process of differentiation and exclusion. The community which promises to connect and include is itself defined in oppositional relation to an Other who is excluded from membership and whose

[24] Butler (1993) Ch. 7.

existence is denied. Furthermore, the community which promises to fix a stable identity is defined in relation to other communities whose existence whispers the possibility—indeed the inevitability—of a more fluid, mobile experience of subjectivity. In the quest for identity, the Other thus becomes an object of hatred and fear; but this hatred of the Other is in fact a displaced hatred of the self—an inability to acknowledge or own one's own enjoyment which the Other represents. This means that a central part of the *political* project of interpreting the role of signifiers such as community is the unearthing of the distinctive fantasies of Otherness—the particular exclusions and denials—for which they stand in particular discourses. In this context, as Salecl puts it, the democratic project is not so much to prohibit the articulation or to change the content of fantasy, but rather to create a political space in which, for example, the racist implications of particular fantasies have no effect.[25] This entails a very close connection between the project of psychoanalytic interpretation and that of reflection upon the institutional structure of social orders. In attempting a critical interpretation of the place of appeals to "community" in legal and political discourse, then, it is important to bear in mind the level of the hidden "surmise" as well as that of ideology.

Feminism, communitarianism and conservatism

In our work on political theory, Elizabeth Frazer and I were concerned to explore what we saw as an interesting but, as I shall argue, disturbing resonance between the communitarian critique of liberalism and certain features of feminist thought. It is worth noting the main points of political and methodological contact. First, as I noted in the introduction to this book, a social constructionist stance has always been central to feminism, for it brings with it the possibility of critical analysis and transformation of the processes whereby, for example, masculine and feminine identities have been formed and entrenched. Social constructionism is therefore a clear affinity between feminist and communitarian thought, opening up as it does (at least when combined with an adequate account of human subjectivity) the possibility of imagining and working for a world in which these and other features of social reality are otherwise. The recognition of the social constitution of human identity is also

[25] Salecl (1994) p. 37.

resonant with feminist concerns with connection and intersubject-ivity—persistent albeit controversial features of feminist thought.[26]

Secondly, the communitarian commitment to constructing a rich conception of collective values and the institutional public goods which would facilitate their realisation has clear resonance for femi-nist politics. For it connects with a number of persistent issues on the feminist agenda—for example, child care, public safety, environmen-tal concerns—all areas in which liberal market-based solutions are arguably unstable or otherwise inadequate.

Thirdly, the communitarian recognition of the "situated" subject brings with it the possibility of accommodating as politically relevant the embodied aspects of human subjectivity. This is clearly an impor-tant matter from a feminist point of view, given the ways in which female bodies have been inscribed with meanings inimical to women's full instantiation as citizens, whilst male bodies have been constructed as "normal", hence, paradoxically, enabling men to func-tion culturally as disembodied. In Lacanian thought, woman is not entirely determined or bounded by the phallic function which struc-tures the symbolic order: hence there may be a psychoanalytic dimension to this aspect of the resonance between feminism and "community"—one which could be expressed by borrowing Salecl's figure: woman as a symptom of community.[27] The socially situated subject of communitarian thought is identified closely with its ends and attachments in a way which clearly sits unhappily with any dichotomised conception of reason and emotion—another advantage from a feminist point of view. Again, there is a link here with psy-choanalytic theory, which has seen human subjectivity as destabilised by the division between the conscious and unconscious, or as split on the entry into language. These ideas have made an important contri-bution to feminist and other critiques of the unified, rationally choos-ing subject of classical liberal thought.[28]

[26] See for example Gilligan (1982); Noddings (1984); Ruddick (1990).

[27] The body and its enjoyment remain, according to Lacan, within the unrepresentable Real, to which woman has more direct access than man. Many feminists (myself included) have been exercised by the disturbing resonance between this argument and the discursive construction of women as "close to nature" or as identified with the body—constructs which have, historically, been important in underpinning women's subordination: see Chapters 4 above and 7. However, read as a cultural interpretation of how sexual difference is *imagined*, others continue to believe that the argument's apparently essentialist implications may be avoided, and that it can be mobilised as an aspect of feminist thought which seeks to reconstruct the scope and shape of the values endorsed by established moral and political orders: Braidotti (1991) Ch. 8; Butler (1993) Chs. 1–3.

[28] See Barron (1993).

Fourthly, the focus on "community" as a source of political value and a forum for political activity resonates with the powerful feminist critique of the dichotomisation between public and private which characterises modern liberal thought.[29] The recognition both of the political relevance of sources of disadvantage hitherto discursively located within the private, and of the relevance of practices and institutions intermediate between state and individual in sociopolitical analysis and projects of political activism, are sympathetic to feminism. For the women's movements of the latter part of the twentieth century are social movements whose political practices have been located in just such intermediate spheres and which have often been characterised (particularly in Britain) by scepticism about reformist or revolutionary activity which places its faith in the state, political parties or the public legal system. Finally, the interpretivist methodology espoused by communitarian writers is resonant with the strong currents in feminist thought devoted to deconstructing claims to objective truth and exposing their gendered partiality.[30]

For all these reasons, it is not surprising to discover shared concerns and commitments characterising feminist and communitarian literature in political theory. Notwithstanding the resonance, however, it is also important to see that the very connections mark up points of difficulty for not only feminism but any other genuinely radical politics. Most obviously, commentators have pointed out the actual or potential conservatism of communitarian thought. This is of particular concern given that the history of women's movements has been punctuated by disturbing overlaps between feminist and conservative constructions of certain political positions. A striking recent example here is that of anti-pornography campaigns, in which, perhaps to their mutual surprise, radical feminists and right wing moralists have found themselves sharing both political platforms and strategies, albeit not basic political analyses.[31]

Why should communitarianism be thought to be potentially conservative? A number of explanations suggest themselves. First, there is the possibility that the constructionism and interpretivism of communitarianism collapses into a radical relativism in which all political positions have equal status and no footing for political critique can be found. Whilst this explanation arguably poses a false dilemma in

---

[29] See Olsen (1983); Pateman (1988), and Chapters 2 and 3: on feminism and communitarian models of democracy, see Mansbridge (1991).

[30] Harding and Hintikka (1987); Jaggar and Bordo (1989).

[31] For more detailed discussion, see Chapter 3.

implying that any move away from objectivism entails a slide into total subjectivism,[32] it is not clear that all communitarians have set out their position with sufficient subtlety to avoid the force of some such critique.[33] Secondly, there is the argument that communitarians" failure adequately to characterise the various senses in which the notion of community is being used contributes to the development of an essentially uncritical and even obfuscating political discourse. Notably, it could be argued that there is a productive slippage in communitarian discourse between what might be called "institutional" or "sociological" notions of community and "ideological" notions of community. This conduces to a situation in which the recommendations of "community-based" this, that or the other are taken as incontrovertible, without allowing space for much needed political critique of the actual communities from which particular practices and conceptions of value emanate, let alone of the content of those practices and values. References to an apparently sociological *idea* of community, in other words, implicitly evoke a cluster of unexamined *ideals*. From a feminist or any other radical point of view, this is clearly disastrous, not least because the various available communitarian models—the family, the club, and so on—all mark forms of association which have historically subordinated or excluded women and which need to be subjected to a critical analysis which communitarian theory seems incapable of generating the conceptual tools to undertake. It is therefore crucial to expose the slippage between institutional and ideological appeals to community, and to trace the structure of the surmise which underpins the ideological appeal, whilst recognising that the slippage itself is central to the discursive power of community in the contemporary Anglo-American world.

The potential conservatism of communitarian thought can also be linked to its failure to generate an adequate account of the conditions under which subjects gain access to membership of powerful meaning-generating communities, and under which that membership includes the power not only to speak but also to be heard. A similar lack of critical analysis characterises communitarian literature in terms of the question of power relations *between* communities. Indeed, it is a curiosity as much of communitarian as of liberal political theory that the concept of power finds practically no place in the conceptual framework which the theories elaborate. Amid the welter of cosy

[32] A dichotomy which has been convincingly undermined by Bernstein (1983).
[33] See Frazer and Lacey (1993) Ch. 5; Frazer and Lacey (1994).

preoccupation has been with both the collective or socialistic aspects of the communitarian ideal and the effectiveness (or ineffectiveness) of "communities" of various kinds as alternative sites for practices of dispute resolution or other means of problem-solving, both at the level of determining standards and of developing processes.[41] Resisting classification in terms of the public/private divide, these practices seek to play a regulatory role independent of or complementary to that of the state legal system, and one in which different forms of popular participation are realised.

Finally, the idea of community has a significant place in the work of critical theorists—notably that of Roberto Unger. It has also featured, both as a focus of critique and as a reconstructive tool, in the post-modern feminist theory of Drucilla Cornell and in the post-modern jurisprudence of Costas Douzinas and Ronnie Warrington and of Peter Goodrich.[42]

Is it possible to make sense of the varying appeals to ideas of community among these diverse discourses in legal theory? At first sight it seems implausible to argue that these writers, with their very different intellectual and political preoccupations, can usefully be seen, as it were, as members of a community of those appealing to "community". Yet the sociological and psychoanalytic arguments sketched in the last section suggest a diagnosis of these disparate appeals to community as representing a shared preoccupation with those same anxieties about fragmentation and fluidity, that same unarticulated concern with identity and connection, which was argued to motivate political discourses of community. Jurisprudential discourses of community, in other words, stand in for a sense of lack which they express the desire to fill: to infuse, perhaps, the rational-instrumental space of the legal with something affective and committed. Yet they simultaneously represent a need to intellectualise, and hence to distance, the fundamentally emotional impulses which appeals to community express. Within this tentative and general framework, we may hope to find some more specific links which will help to unearth the metaphoric structure and rhetorical role of ideas of community in legal theory.

It is useful to begin by making some basic analytical distinctions between different ways in which the notion of community is being

---

[41] Braithwaite (1993).

[42] See Unger (1983), (1987); Cornell (1987), (1991), (1992a); Douzinas and Warrington (1991), (1994); Goodrich (1986). For a general assessment of communitarian aspects of critical legal theory, see Bauman (1988).

invoked. Starting with the notion of the *"interpretive community"*—
those who have the power to generate the meanings which law
expresses and imposes—we already begin to encounter deep fissures
and obscurities in contemporary jurisprudence. If we accept that
"[t]he context of legal decision-making is that of the legal community
and the values that legal order exists to protect",[43] we nonetheless
need to identify what—or whom—this "legal community" consists
in. It is this very question which is notoriously clouded in Dworkin's
work. On the one hand, *Law's Empire* evokes an intensely democratic image of all as equal members of the interpretive community—
legal subjects in the double sense of those who both create and submit
to the law. Yet in its substantive analysis, Dworkin's argument implies
that some members of the interpretive community are, as it were,
more equal than others. The intepretive community whose voice can
be heard is, after all, a professional community, access to membership
of which is carefully policed in terms of a historically embedded set
of norms, rites of passage, social and technical qualifications. Like all
communities, its identity is marked by exclusionary criteria.

This professional community invites the creation of communities
which in one sense or another define themselves in relation to it. For
example, the academic or pedagogic community has, to different
degrees in different times and places, an influence on the construction and rationalisation of the practices engaged in by the professional
community, not least in the sphere of legal education and textbook
writing. Conversely, critical and oppositional communities—critical
legal scholars, radical practitioners, pressure groups—develop in relation to the dominant professional community, challenging both its
epistemological pretensions and the content of its practices. The
interventions of non-legal interpretive communities such as those
which produce commentaries disseminated by news media are also of
relevance here, as are the interpretive practices of a large array of
more or less official regulatory agencies such as the police, health and
safety inspectors and so on. Even that paradigm site of legal definition, the court, is not entirely insulated from the influence of
external discourses: as for what gets into court in the first place, the
influence of communities auxiliary to the paradigm legal community
is the decisive one, with legal discourse acting as a structuring device
whose power is heavily context-dependent. Whilst the legal-
professional interpretive community will often have the final say on

---

[43] Goodrich (1986) p. 149.

what direction the rails should take, and whilst their apparent straightness is a product of rather specific legal ideologies, the cargo which they carry is determined to an important extent by interpretive communities outside the legal paradigm.

Conversely, the power of official legal constructions of community may well infuse regulatory practices which are in fact attempting to operate autonomously. For example, the critical literature on informal justice has demonstrated convincingly that institutions of popular or community justice often (perhaps inevitably) develop in "the shadow" of state justice.[44] The methods by which cases are referred to and resolved within institutions of informal justice tend to mirror, more or less obviously, those of the formal system. Their constant danger is therefore that they tend, paradoxically, to institute an increase in the overall level of state power rather than the reverse.

So far I have been talking about legal community in the sense of the set of practices and groups in terms of which legal meanings are articulated and enforced. But there is a converse and closely-related sense of community which is equally important in contemporary legal theory. This is the recognition of the sense in which *legal practices themselves create or legitimate "communities"* whose identity or sphere of existence itself reaches beyond the legal—a curious capacity of law to overreach itself in constitutive terms. Clearly one could think of professional interpretive communities from this point of view, but perhaps the most interesting focus here is the role played by law in constructing or underpinning the identity of national communities—political society—or indeed of local, international, supranational or federal communities. Not only is law arguably of fundamental importance in the identification of, for example, the national community, but the (actual or imagined) distinctiveness of particular legal traditions—the common law, to take a prime example—can also be mobilised in resisting the modification or reconstruction of that identity. This is arguably the situation which characterises contemporary British debates about national sovereignty and the limits of European integration, even in the commercial sphere. Crucially, this constitutive role of law is premised on the negation of the Others excluded from law's imagined communities. In creating the discursive space from which we can appear likeable to ourselves—as members of the "nation" or the "law-abiding community"—these legal discourses always embody the hatred and the

---

[44] Fitzpatrick (1992b), (1995b); Harrington (1985).

desire which cannot be acknowledged: its traces appear, if at all, only in the slips which pepper judicial and other legal utterances.[45] The other side of legal community—both formal and informal—is the dangerous or suspect community which must be managed and policed by law.

Locating the communitarian impulse in contemporary legal theory

Underlying these explicit references to the idea of community in legal theory are some persistent sources of contemporary preoccupation with the idea. These tie up closely with communitarian discourses in political theory. First, the idea of community in legal theory speaks to the *critique of the individualism of liberal legalism*, and does so in at least two senses. At an ontological level, talk of community connects with questions about the atomistic and abstracted nature of the liberal legal subject, and the ways in which the culturally contingent but politically significant contours of its construction serve to marginalise certain sorts of legal actors or claims. They also serve to limit recognition of intersubjectivity or reciprocally-constituted subjectivity, because the prevailing system of legal argumentation and reasoning depends upon the construct of a stable and closed subject about whose identity and history only a very circumscribed set of questions can be asked.[46] One way of understanding the feminist demand for a greater contextualisation of legal reasoning is in terms of the need to bring into the courtroom precisely these questions about how legal subjects are constituted by contingent yet extremely powerful discursive manoeuvres. Similarly, visions of a genuinely alternative "collective" justice are often premised upon a non-individual conceptualisation of both the legal subject and the object of legal claims. The critique of individualism gestures towards a recognition of the legal subject as fragmented rather than unitary: as defined in terms of a number of "community" attachments articulated in terms of factors such as race, ethnicity, class, gender, age, sexuality, occupation. Thus the position of a particular individual as subject of and to the legal order is neither fixed nor stable. Politically, the idea of community evokes a transcendence of the liberal legal emphasis on individual rights as the basic units of both constitutional entitlement and legal reasoning, and promises to reconceive legal

[45] See Goodrich (1994).
[46] For further discussion, see Chapters 4 and 7.

justice and equality in terms which reach beyond the formalism of liberal individualism to a recognition and even realisation of alternative goals and values—the assertion of collective over individual interests, of reintegration over exclusion, the pursuit of empathy, solidarity, reciprocity and care—within legal practices.

Secondly, at a structural level, the notion of community speaks to the *growing recognition of the diversification and fragmentation of the legal form*. The modern explosion of legal regulation into ever wider areas of social life has often been remarked upon, not least in terms of its fracturing of received notions of public and private spheres. Equally significant, however, is the extent to which the relevant professional communities and means of realising legal regulation have consequently diversified. Regulatory agencies, arbitration and mediation schemes and administrative tribunals, staffed by a wide array of professional actors, elected officials and volunteers, abound; whilst circulars, informal rules, and codes of practice supplement or replace case law or statute as tools of legal or quasi-legal articulation or enforcement.[47] In political theory, the institutional idea of community promises to accommodate a recognition of the decentring of the state and the genuine political relevance of what were hitherto either non-existent or "private" practices: in legal theory it provides an analogous framework for understanding the diffusion of state legal authority hitherto imposed in an unambiguously vertical way from the various summits of legal and political hierarchy. Significantly, this institutional conceptual flexibility also touches an evaluative nerve: the diversification of legal forms threatens the nightmare of ever more extensive, discretionary, unaccountable quasi-legal power. Yet it also holds out the hope of experimenting with novel legal forms which might be more normatively attractive—not so much vertical as horizontal or consensual. Once again, the slippage between the institutional and the ideological is an important one.

Finally, partly because of the normative dimension of each of the factors mentioned so far, the contemporary salience of community stands for a growing recognition that the *moral, substantively political or evaluative aspects of critical legal analysis need to be embraced more explicitly by legal theorists*.[48] This has at least two sources. In the first place, it is part of the impulse to expose and articulate "the politics of law"—in other words to deconstruct law's claims to neutrality and objectivity, and to unearth the substantive ethical and political judgements which

---

[47] See Hunt (1993).
[48] Selznick (1987), (1989); Cotterrell (1992).

underlie ostensibly procedural or formal determinations within modern legal forms. Secondly, in some of its manifestations it represents the pursuit of a utopian project which explores the place of the ethical *within* the deconstructive enterprise. There is an increasing emphasis in critical legal theory on the relationship between law and justice, and a marked stress upon the utopian aspects of the critical project—a development which is nicely symbolised by the title of a recent collection of essays: *Deconstruction and the Possibility of Justice.*[49]

The idea of community, then, stands as a useful metaphor for a number of coalescing analytical and political concerns, a cluster of ideas, ideals and ideologies, in contemporary legal theory. In this respect, its place in legal theory is much like its place in political theory. Not surprisingly, the problems it raises in the legal sphere are also similar.[50] With its productive combination of institutional and evaluative resonance and its role as a signifier which stands in for the unspoken and the repressed, the idea of community in legal theory speaks to a number of historically specific manifestations of concern about the identity, forms and roles of law—a practice at whose core is the generation of common meanings and standards—in a world disenchanted with the universalist imaginary. Yet it reproduces the problems it promises to address in the very gesture with which it purports to resolve them. Take the salient example of Dworkin's appeal to the "community of principle" which alone can generate the stable set of legal meanings which could give body to the idea(l) of "law as integrity". As Murphy puts it, a " 'community of principle' . . . is simply an intellectual fantasy, a vacuous abstraction whose only possible ground is the sociologically detached nature of the elite American university".[51] A single interpretive community identified on the basis of shared values could only look plausible on the basis of precisely the kind of pre-modern or romantic worldview which we saw as a feature of some versions of communitarianism: "The claim that national law represents the national community is as fictional as the assertion that the discourse of human rights represents the universal community".[52]

What Dworkin's idea in fact expresses is not so much a sociological naïvety as a return to universalism. All become members of the

---

[49] Cornell, Rosenfeld and Carlson (eds.) (1992); see also Cornell (1991), (1992), (1993): for further discussion, see Chapters 6 and 8.
[50] For an excellent discussion, see Gardbaum (1992).
[51] Murphy (1994) p. 29.
[52] Douzinas and Warrington (1994) p. 149.

interpretive community by the theorist's—or indeed the law's—definitional fiat, and questions about access to membership become not only unanswerable but also unaskable, because they are defined out of existence. The "Other" simply disappears, subsumed within the logic of identity—a process exemplified by the title of one of Dworkin's recent papers: "Equality, Democracy and the Constitution: We the People in Court".[53] As in political theory, questions of membership and power are quite simply not only the theoretical agenda. Their absence can not be regarded as politically innocent, but rather needs to be seen as part of the ideological apparatus central to modern law's legitimating function in relation to power.

Similar problems reproduce themselves in the more fragmented institutional practices associated with "community justice". Whilst the ideals which genuinely underpinned many such developments promised participation and the mobilisation of grass-roots communities in negotiated and non-hierarchical self-regulation, problem-solving and proactive trouble-avoidance, research suggests that the reality is very different. Actual practices of "community justice" are rather marked by another layer of hierarchies, often themselves controlled, positively or negatively, by the state or formal legal system; they imply the constitution of yet other excluded communities whose powerlessness is significantly increased by the invisibility entailed by inclusive communitarian rhetoric. Indeed, the very informality which promises to confound hierarchy can subtly reinforce the existing power inequalities with which participants enter the process. For example, the greater contextualisation of "problems"—in particular the tendency to "judge the whole person" rather than a circumscribed incident, which characterises forms of popular justice found in both socialist and fascist totalitarian political formations—has a distinctly repressive potential in the constitution of the abject identity of excluded Others.

As in the case of the role of appeals to community in political theory, however, the communitarian impulse in legal theory points up some important questions. For example, the purport of the critique of the individualism of the legal subject is far from clear. For if we give up the notion of the individual agent as claimant, we may deprive ourselves of a necessary component of one of the positive aspects of contemporary law: it can sometimes provide a forum for

[53] Dworkin (1990).

challenging dominant meanings and arrangements as well as for confirming and enforcing them. The challenge of reconstructing a notion of legal subjectivity or subjecthood adequate to critical legal practice is a central question for contemporary jurisprudence. Similarly, real questions arise about the possibility of extending law's communities—in terms both of access to powerful interpretive communities and of examining substantive questions about the meaning of membership of law's community as subject.[54] This in turn raises an issue about whether such questions can be addressed without appeal to the sort of substantive ethical conception at which discourses of community gesture.

BEYOND COMMUNITY?

In the light of what appears to be the inescapable obfuscation of discourses of community—their capacity, most importantly, to disguise the violent exclusions implicit in the constitution of the "we"—it is tempting simply to argue that we should avoid talk of community altogether, finding other language in which to express the analytical concepts and the ideals—empathy, mutual responsibility and so on— to which the idea of community can usefully alert us. This strategy certainly has some attractions. But it is rather different from the argument that we should walk away from the lessons that reflection on the salience of the metaphor of community can teach us about the state of law and legal theory. For better or worse, appeals to community are part of the currency of legal and political discourse. If we are to think about of how we might disarm the racism and other forms of identity-buttressing hatred which they may stand for, or build upon the democratic and egalitarian impulses which they sometimes undoubtedly express, we can do no better than to start by trying to estimate their existing meaning and value in those currencies. In the remainder of this chapter, I want to try to separate out a number of more general issues which underlie the debate about community. In particular, I shall map out the reemergence of an explicit concern with the ethical and with normative reconstruction in legal theory and consider the potential for a reconceptualisation of law in less violent, excluding and authoritarian terms.

[54] See Sarat (1990); Santos (1995).

The critical and the ethical

The tendency of contemporary critical legal theory to "deconstruct" or "trash" without "reconstructing" has been much remarked upon. In recent critical legal theory, however, there have begun to be signs of an attempt to resurrect a more vigorous conception of critically reflective subjectivity as a precondition of radical political agency, and moreover of an attempt to do so in terms which explicate a basis for utopian or reconstructive thinking as an inspiration for political practice. As Derrida puts it, these developments express:

> "a deconstruction that would like, in order to be consistent with itself, not to remain enclosed in purely speculative, theoretical, academic discourses but rather . . . to aspire to something more consequential, to *change* things and to intervene in an efficient and responsible, though always, of course, very mediated way, not only in the profession but also in what one calls the *cité*, the *polis* and more generally the world".[55]

I now want to examine some varied manifestations of this reconstructive utopian impulse within contemporary legal theory.

Attending to the Other

We have already seen that one of the main difficulties implicit in the normative appeal to community as a means of escaping the limitations of liberal individualism is the capacity of community to reinstitute an excluding universalism, and to do so in a particularly damaging way: the inclusive appeal of the "we" obfuscates its simultaneous repression of the excluded. In a series of articles and books, Drucilla Cornell has argued for a recognition of what she calls the "ethical moment" in deconstruction—an ethical moment which can escape the homogenising logic of the "we" because its very basis is the call to attend to the Other.[56] Drawing on an account of subjectivity as reciprocally constituted, a post-structuralist understanding of deconstruction, and Lacanian psychoanalysis, Cornell's account emphasises the openness of language. Notwithstanding the power of binary oppositions, a relational theory of language implies that

---

[55] Derrida (1992) pp. 8–9.
[56] Cornell (1991), (1992), (1993). For a more detailed discussion of Cornell, see Chapters 6 and 7.

language has an irreducibly open quality. Because meaning is constructed through the relations between linguistic counters, every linguistic utterance has its surmise—it entails an implicit reference to
what is suppressed. Combined with the inevitably metaphorical and
metonymic dimensions of language, and with the limitations of the
representational capacity of the symbolic order, which entails the split-
ting of subjectivity, this opens a space in which we can glimpse alternative possibilities. In the process of the reciprocal constitution of
subjectivity through linguistic encounters with others, the assertion of,
for example, objectivity or individuality inevitably evokes that which
is suppressed—subjectivity or collectivity. This means that the process
of deconstruction is not one which engages with closed linguistic
structures and which would therefore be limited only to unearthing
the repressed other *as conceived in terms of the dominant member of a
dichotomised pair*; it also presents possibilities of genuinely transformative understandings. By appealing to our capacity for "recollective
imagination"—the reconstruction of what might have been which is
inevitably referred to in the linguistic construction of the world—we
can find a space for the utopian, the ethical or the normative within
deconstructive critical legal theory: the question of justice, although
undecidable, is constantly on the agenda of legal interpretation.

A similar impulse underlies the genealogical approach to legal history represented in some of Peter Goodrich's work.[57] Goodrich
draws on Luce Irigaray's project of reconstructing a "feminine imaginary" as the basis for thinking other worlds—including legal
worlds—which have been suppressed in history but which might,
once imagined, hold out transformative possibilities and the imaginative base for concrete political struggles.[58] The figure of woman and
the location of legal "gynaetopias" operate both as the writing of a
(significantly) forgotten history—a politically important project in its
own right—and as powerful reminders of law's contingency and
hence as symbols not only of what might have been a different legal
practice but also of what such a practice might become. The figure
of woman stands here not for a biological entity but for the most consistently historically suppressed and excluded Other, and hence for
the most fertile source of different imaginings.[59] If courts administered by women and purporting legally to regulate that most

[57] Goodrich (1993b), (1997b).
[58] Irigaray (1991), (1992).
[59] Though the potentially essentialist implications of Irigaray's argument have been
widely debated: see Braidotti (1991) and Chapter 7.

quintessential component of the "private" sphere—love—can be rediscovered in twelfth century France,[60] what, one might ask, could possibly be the limitations of a reimagined law in the post-feminist era of the late twentieth century?

To take a third example, Costas Douzinas and Ronnie Warrington have drawn on Emmanuel Levinas's "ethics of alterity" to argue for the reinsertion of an ethical voice within post-modern jurisprudence.[61] Douzinas and Warrington locate their argument within the impoverishment of the ethical which is suggested as characterising the late modern world: the figures of rationality and self-mastery, of universality and formal equality, of the priority of the right over the good, which have entailed an "emptying out" of public discourse in relation to substantive values. This empty ethical quality of the modern imaginary, they argue, poses serious obstacles to meeting the moral and political challenge to develop an effective critique of contemporary realities such as the explosion of the content of legal regulation, the fragmentation of the legal form and the corruption of legal practice. They focus on Levinas's assertion of the call to responsibility implicit in the subject's face to face confrontation with the Other. This Other is conceived as irreducibly different—the stranger, the widow, the beggar—an irreducibility which is expressed by the unique qualities of a face. Yet the Other's personhood is understood in intersubjective terms—a feature which distinguishes Levinas's from Cornell's modified Hegelian notion of the reciprocal constitution of the subject. Douzinas and Warrington find a foothold for this ethical appeal in an idea central to the legal notion of fair adjudication—the *audi alteram partem* principle that a claimant has the right to be heard. With the judge as third party converting a face to face communication between the two parties into a public conversation, the trial turns out to be a model for ethical responsibility to the Other—a forum in which at least the promise of justice can be discerned and put to critical use.

The community of discourse

A rather different model for reinsertion of the ethical within the legal is that provided by the tradition of critical theory.[62] This position

[60] See Goodrich (1997b).
[61] Douzinas and Warrington (1994) Chs. 4, 5; Levinas (1969) sections III, IV.
[62] Habermas (1986).

seeks to reconstruct legal argumentation in terms of its potential as critical discussion, which could draw on the notion of discursive legitimation.[63] On this conception, the violent aspect of the legal as the assertion of will and power is legitimated (or perhaps effaced) in terms of procedural criteria based in a context-transcending conception of reason. One form of what has been called "dialogic communitarianism"[64] seeks to rescue and revive what is of value in the ideal of the rule of law: it fixes on what is sees as an inherent duality in legal practices, which not only represent the imposition of authority but also provide a space for challenge and debate. This space is once again, crucially, premised on the openness of language:

> "The value of concepts for critical discussion derives from their transcendent quality, their 'excess of meaning', which points beyond the positive reality to fuller social achievements and which enables us to disengage ourselves morally from positive reality and criticize it. Concepts like contract, rule of law, fair trial, human rights, democracy etc., lose their transcendent quality when they are reduced to their operational meaning."[65]

As applied to legal theory, the idea of discursive legitimation—in other words that a process of dialogue under conditions of ideal communication generates morally legitimate decisions—appears to promise a critical footing for projects of normative reconstruction which could realise themselves in changes in concrete institutional practices. Indeed, the resonance with the participatory and non-hierarchical ideals which informed the informal justice movement is very strong. In Dryzek's words;

> " 'Discursive design' [is] a social institution around which the expectations of a number of actors converge. It therefore has a place in their conscious awareness as a site for recurrent communicative interaction among them. Individuals should participate as citizens, not as representatives of the state or any other corporate and hierarchical body. No concerned individuals should be excluded . . . The focus of deliberations should include, but not be limited to, the individual or collective needs and interests of the individuals involved . . . Within discursive design, there should be no hierarchy of formal rules, though debate may be governed by informal canons of discourse. A decision rule of consensus should obtain. Finally, all the features I have enumerated should be redeemable within the discursive design itself.

[63] Peters (1986).
[64] Cornell (1987); cf. Frazer and Lacey (1993) Ch. 6.
[65] Peters (1986) pp. 270–1.

Participants should be free to reflectively and discursively override any or all of them."[66]

Critical theory occupies an interesting and somewhat ambiguous position on the spectrum of modernist and post-modernist approaches. On the one hand, its commitment to a transcendent conception of reason locates it within the philosophical discourse of modernity. On the other, its emphasis on the procedural and its refusal to avow substantive values entails an openness—an embrace of the contingency of just and ethical outcomes—which is resonant with post-modernist thought. Thus whilst there are certainly important differences between post-modern legal theories and those which are located within the tradition of discourse ethics, the status of the latter as a modernist position shorn of universalist illusions about the *substance* of ethical values and judgements entails some important connections between the two approaches. For critical theory construes questions about how we should live not as matters of objectively valid prescription or discovery but rather as the subject of decision, creation and commitment: democratic exchange becomes the paradigm of ethical practice.

Problems for critique

Legal theory developing ideas of both the community of discourse and the accommodation of difference offers, therefore, some important and connected imaginative resources for the reconstruction of legal practice. However, in the very moment which these contributions to critical legal theory suggest themselves as a source of ideas for institutional design, the difficulties inherent in realising their ideals in legal or quasi-legal institutional terms become apparent. Is it possible to imagine law without hierarchy or formal rules? What is to guarantee that subjects enter the discursive process sufficiently similarly situated to ensure anything like conditions of undistorted communication? And, whether in the case of law as critical discussion or of the trial as face to face encounter mediated by a judge, what or who is to determine the substantive standards on the basis of which decisions must be made in cases of intractable conflict between the parties?

Theoretically, these problems coalesce around a number of recurring questions. First, there is the notion of subjectivity. For Levinas,

[66] Dryzek (1990) p. 43.

and probably for Irigaray, there is no apparent tension between the assertion of intersubjectivity and respect for Otherness: for Cornell and, I would argue, for most propononents of discourse ethics, on the other hand, intersubjectivity would be seen as entailing the risk of the subsumption of difference—a threat which is all too present once one moves away, as political and legal institutions invariably do, from the face to face encounter. It is a danger which has found particularly forceful recognition in the work of feminist writers, many of whom have emphasised the need, given the historical shape of women's oppression, to reconstruct politically adequate notions of space, autonomy and privacy.[67] For positions deriving from discourse ethics, on the other hand, the reciprocity inherent in the constitution of subjectivity which derives from the necessary encounter with the Other represents a simultaneous recognition of *sameness and difference*—a refusal either to dichotomise self/other or to collapse one into the other. Leaving aside questions about the assumption of inter- and intra-subjective transparency and coherence which appear to be made by some of these arguments, we can see that once we put in question the relationship of "Otherness" to not only subjective identity but also values, any attempt to reinsert the ethical into the legal raises the problem of the "logic of identity"—the danger of suppressing difference in the process of abstraction, generalisation or identification.

This brings us to a second theoretical problem: that of the articulation and legitimation of substantive evaluative criteria. What are the ethics of the call to attend to Otherness where that Otherness consists in racist or fascist attachments? "Theorists of difference have not indicated where the line is to be drawn between forms of difference which foster democracy and forms of difference which reflect anti-democratic aspirations".[68] In both Cornell's work and the tradition of discourse ethics, there is a willingness to appeal to universal standards. For the position deriving from Levinas, too, what counts as a genuine institutional realisation of the "face to face" encounter—as being properly "heard"—presumably depends on the conditions of undistorted communication (articulacy, power, knowledge and so on) being met. Whereas with discourse ethics the puzzle remains how what are basically procedural criteria will necessarily give a substantial critical foothold in contentious cases, in Cornell's case the resort to the recollective imagination of the suppressed Other threat-

[67] See for example Benhabib (1992b); Nedelsky (1989).
[68] Benhabib (1994a) p. 6.

ens to amount to an act of faith in our ability to recognise and recol-
lect values which could generate effective critique. These are uncer-
tainties which the level of abstraction at which Cornell's argument
very often proceeds does little to dispel.

Conversely, any assertion of substantive context-transcending
criteria appears to raise once again the problem of the violent suppression of Otherness implicit in the imposition and reiteration of
standards which is arguably characteristic of legal practice. If the basic
values underlying the conditions of ideal communication or of attention to Otherness are substantive ones, it is not at all clear that this
can be avoided. Benhabib addresses this problem by distinguishing
between "integrationist" and "participationist" discursive models.[69]
In the former, the community of discourse is defined in terms of
shared values, and therefore both reproduces the logic of identity and
sacrifices what I identifed above as the post-modern impuse of critical theory, which construes ethical standards as open and based on
human commitment rather than on some transcendental ground. In
the latter, the discursive community is defined in terms of second-
order context-transcending commitments to a particular kind of
process. These commitments have to be accepted by all participants,
who are nonetheless free to challenge them from within the confines
of the game once they have accepted their limits. The question here
is whether these procedural criteria will turn out to have enough
teeth to generate the kind of critical practices which a genuine return
to the normative and ethical would seem to require. The point is well
expressed by Radin and Michelman:

> "From the poststructuralist vantage . . . dialogism's dilemma is that
> dialogue (insofar as it is not disguised coercion) presupposes commu-
> nity; but community is not, finally, a matter of will or sympathetic
> exertion but rather is a contingency of cognitive structures into which
> we are thrown."[70]

The problem of the logic of identity does not arise so explicitly in the
work of Douzinas and Warrington. This is because they do not
directly confront the question of context-transcendence in the way
in which Benhabib and Cornell, for example, do. But it is not clear
that it can be avoided if we are to give substance to the idea of what
constitutes a genuine or adequate hearing. If the trial judge has to
come to a conclusion, what guarantees that s/he can find terms

[69] Benhabib (1992b).
[70] Radin and Michelman (1991) p. 1041.

which are sufficiently acceptable to the parties to constitute a genuine expression of respect for the Other's irreducible Otherness? How are we to realise the metaphor of the face in institutional terms? The history of legal interpretations of the *audi alteram partem* rule seems a limited source of inspiration, especially given the way in which its gradually expanding scope has often led to a blunting of its substantive teeth.[71] The problems seem particularly acute when we consider the polycentricity of many legal issues. Ultimately, Levinas's striking combination of the assertion of intersubjectivity with the uniqueness of the Other appears to presage either a nostalgic romanticism with few concrete implications or a retreat into a rather extreme form of individualism which threatens to render conflicts among different human beings utterly intractable.[72]

Before moving on to think more concretely about the implications of these theoretical ideas for legal theory, it is worth pausing for a moment to consider some insights which might be offered by political theory. One of the strengths of the models for normative reconstruction in legal theory which I have sketched above is their willingness to engage in the project of reimagining concepts such as justice and equality which have constituted the central ideals held out by law to its subjects.[73] They also hold out the promise of productive reflection on the ways in which legal subjectivity might be reconstituted in less atomistic, competitive and more empathetic and solidaristic terms. However, one of the things which is puzzling about these approaches is that their normative preoccupation with justice and legal subjectivity is not matched by an equally fully realised project of developing a sophisticated conception of notions such as power, subordination and oppression. Yet these would seem to be essential not only to an adequate analysis of the social meaning of

[71] See Lacey (1992).

[72] This individualistic or atomistic reading of Levinas is perhaps supported by his account of erotic love. Love of this form entails, in his view, the lover's attachment to the image of himself in love. Thus Levinas describes erotic love as implying "a return to oneself": Levinas (1969) p. 266. Whilst this may be nicely suggestive of the structure of the erotic attachment of a judge like Robinson Gray to the law, I would be inclined to regard this rather depressing image of love as a form of narcissism as highly gendered (i.e. as masculine), and disinclined to regard the idea that my lover is motivated by the impulse to come to the assistance of my frailty as a satisfactory compensation (Levinas (1969) p. 256). Hence, notwithstanding the resonance of his emphasis on the touch and the caress as central to the expression of love with, for example, Irigaray's feminine imaginary, I think that any inclination of feminist theorists to, as it were, get into bed with Levinas is unlikely to lead to a very satisfactory climax . . . For further critical discussion, see Irigaray (1993b) pp. 185–217.

[73] See Chapter 8.

legal practices but also to any attempt to think how they might be reconstructed.

For example, it is now *de rigueur* in progressive legal theory to make some reference to the power of law in the discursive, Foucaultian sense (as well as, or sometimes (in my view mistakenly) instead of its sovereignty or property-like sense).[74] This focus on the "micro-politics of power" seems particularly apposite to any attempt to understand the dynamics of fragmented legal or quasi-legal practices such as institutions of informal justice. But critical legal theorists have given little attention to what might make this kind of power legitimate or illegitimate as opposed to merely productive. This is, of course, in keeping with Foucault's own approach, which eschewed the making of such normative judgements about the operations of power. But if we are to employ (as I think we can) Foucault's "practice" conception of power in critical legal theory, and if, like the writers I have discussed, we are concerned to reconstitute an ethical dimension to such theory, the question of legitimacy, and with it questions such as what count as oppressive exercises or manifestations of power, become absolutely central. The pursuit of such conceptual reconstruction is well beyond the scope of this chapter, but it is worth noting both its relevance to its theoretical concerns and that some important instances are already instantiated in feminist scholarship.[75]

RECONSTRUCTING LEGAL PRACTICES: REVALUING THE HORIZONTAL WITHOUT OBSCURING THE VERTICAL?

The problems encountered by the critical positions sketched in the previous section are not, however, merely theoretical. In this final section I want to consider the implications of these problems for reconstructive projects which seek to enhance the democratic and non-violent potential of legal institutions. I also want to argue that greater insight into both their shape and their potential resolution could be gained by a broader dialogue between critical legal theories and socio-legal studies. Furthermore, such a dialogue would also prompt some interesting questions about the conceptualisation of law and legal practices.

A central dilemma for legal politics which aspire to be transformative turns on the characteristic of law as a practice which makes

[74] Foucault (1980); Smart (1989); see further Chapter 3.
[75] Littleton (1987); Nedelsky (1989); Young (1990a).

determinations: state law has a top-down, vertical, authoritarian imposition of power as its central mode of operation. This is so notwithstanding the facts that in the reiterative form of precedent the
verticality and violence of the imposition is to some extent disguised,
and that law also draws on complementary bureaucratic and rhetorical modes of power.[76] In this moment of imposition, it seems, the
violence and excluding force of law is inevitable: the law-creating
subject and the subject of law's power are irreducibly divided, whilst
simultaneously being rejoined discursively in the name of the neutrality, objectivity and universality of legal judgment. For critical
approaches, therefore, a possible part of the reconstructive project
would seem to be to unearth and revalorise what Peters identifies as
the "other" aspect of law: its status as a forum for critical discussion,
for challenging established practices, for questioning prevailing definitions of the legal community and so on. Meagre though these
opportunities may be within and associated with the legal systems in
which we work, they constitute one of the few hopeful realities
which we can grasp. Critical legal theorists would, at the very least,
be contradicting their avowed affinities with radical legal practitioners if they were not quick to seize upon and try to think through the
institutional implications of this critical moment within legal argumentation.

Notwithstanding the power of established interpretive communities and the structural exclusions by which they are characterised, the
possibility of subversive interpretation is implicit in the recognition
of the discursive quality of legal texts: although we may recognise
that political and professional interpretive communities have the
power to impose certain meanings on a legal text, this very recognition is premised on the implicit recognition that an alternative meaning might have been constructed—that there is an "intrinsic
dialogue" within the text. This renders textual critique a genuine
form of political activism:

> "As a totality of discourses and practices the legal institution continu-
> ously strives to present the legal code as the symbolic representation
> of an ideal sociality, as a way of life and as the fundamental morality
> of belonging to the social whole. To challenge the values specifically
> established in legal texts and legal practices, to question the morality
> of the written symbols of justice, to refuse to accept passively the legal
> communities' doctrinal equation of law with reason—these positions
> are quite the opposite of the insignia of depair, they are the last

[76] Derrida (1992); Santos (1982).

vestiges of hope, the final flailing of historical consciousness and of political sensibility in the face of a pathological cynicism".[77]

But can this political resistance at the level of critical textual analysis be accompanied by any broader institutional practice? Can we make any progress towards a greater realisation of law as critical discussion, by experimenting with non-hierarchical or "feminine" legal forms, without risking disguising the irreducible violence of legal determinations? Can the analogy between political and legal dialogue be usefully pursued? One obvious possibility would be to focus on the development of alternative legal forms. One of the more sympathetic commentators on the emergence of appeals to "community" in legal theory touches on a central question about the transformative potential of such forms when he notes that:

> "[t]he community of discourse that emerges in the platonic dialogue is always *an alternative* to the state. The legitimate community of dialogue stands always against the coercive community of state authority."[78]

We should not be misled, in other words, into thinking that real conditions of discursive legitimacy obtain simply because we are dealing with *forms* of legal determination which are apparently closer to the ideal of discursive community. Nor should we assume that in the modern world it is easy to construct discursive communities whose power is genuinely autonomous from the state. Here the lessons of the various attempts to realise "popular", "community" or "informal" justice demand our attention, both as an imaginative resource and as a cautionary tale. Indeed, it is quite simply impossible to come to a sensible assessment of the recommendations of relevant critical legal theories without taking into account the lessons of socio-legal debates such as that about informal justice and alternative dispute resolution.

Crucially, it has *not* been the message of such research that these hitherto less visible, informal practices are necessarily less authoritarian, more consensus-oriented than, for example, the determinations of a formal court. Despite initial enthusiasm for alternative models of dispute resolution, socio-legal research has shown that the informalisation of justice can play into the hands of the powerful, whilst the more inflexible application of legal rules by courts can on occasion provide some protection to the powerless. Potential for inclusion in

---

[77] Goodrich (1986) p. 218; see also pp. 220–1.
[78] Kahn (1989) p. 83; emphasis added.

and exclusion from the legal community cannot therefore simply be equated with particular legal forms—just as the move towards greater contextualisation of legal issues will not necessarily work in favour of the powerless. At the end of the day, the configurations of the excluded and hated Other which underpin the fantasy structure of law's formal community are not so different from those which underpin the administration of "popular" justice. In each case we have to think through, both in institutional terms and in terms of general socio-theoretic propositions, how best to render that hatred as ineffective as possible.

On the other hand, particularly in terms of how we might realise a more horizontal or participatory approach to legal practice, socio-legal research undoubtedly generates certain insights or visions of difference: workplace participation in the development of codes of practice or rule-making; mediation schemes in certain areas; popular participation *not merely in the enforcement but also in the construction of the standards to be applied*. All of these have found (albeit imperfect) expression in a multiplicity of practices which socio-legal research has rightly reminded us are highly relevant to the social meaning of law. Indeed, if we have learnt anything from socio-legal scholarship, it is that an understanding of these broader interpretive and enforcement practices is indispensable to an appreciation of the deep meaning of the legal norms articulated more formally and at a more visible points in the legal hierarchy. It is therefore too soon to abandon entirely exploration of the implications of a more fragmented conception of the legal.[79] Even some of the fiercest critics of the informal justice movement are reluctant to surrender the transformative possibilities which informed the struggles of many of its practitioners: they point out the need for a differentiated analysis capable of distinguishing between genuinely liberal, radical or grass-roots community-based developments and those tending rather to a conservative neo-populism or covert state repression.[80] Whilst appreciating the intimate relations between them, we must continue to explore the different possibilities of violent, regulatory and persuasive/rhetorical modes of social regulation, and of the reconstruction of legal or quasi-legal practices in genuinely persuasive and inclusive terms.

[79] See Teubner (1986a); Teubner (ed.) 1986.

[80] As Santos puts it, if we "recognize that the basic political issue underlying community justice and legal pluralism is the possibility of an alternative legality as part and parcel of a progressive, emancipatory politics" then "[t]he need to discriminate among different forms of community organization and justice is probably the most urgent task confronting us": Santos (1992a) p. 141. See also Cain (1988); Fitzpatrick (1988); Harrington (1992).

Whilst we may recognise that goal of attaining justice through law is in principle impossible of achievement, it is unclear what other form a transformative legal politics could take.

It is also worth reflecting on the implications of the sort of *reconceptualisation* of law and the legal which a more thorough engagement between critical legal theory and socio-legal studies might engender. Many legal theorists have focused on the diversification and fragmentation of the legal form as one of the sources of the legitimation crisis of contemporary law.[81] In trying to attain a systematic understanding of this diversity, the intellectual resources of research within the law and society movement in the USA, the socio-legal studies movement in Britain and legal anthropology in both countries are particularly valuable. Scholars working within these traditions have cast their research nets well beyond the standard material of appeal court decisions and acts of legislation so as to consider as legally relevant bureaucratic, discretionary, administrative, informal practices such as the activities of tribunals, regulatory agencies, mediation officers, arbitrators, state and private police officers and security guards, prison officers, as well as the various institutional manifestations of informal justice purportedly independent of or ancillary to state justice. Given the implications of the interpretive activities of these "quasi-legal communities" for the impact and meaning of formal legal norms, it is a curiosity of contemporary legal theory that this accumulated body of socio-legal research has impinged almost not at all on either orthodox, or, even more surprisingly, critical conceptualisations of law and the legal. The "community" of those who combine an interest in both critical legal theory and theoretically informed sociological studies of law is bewilderingly small.[82] The nearest we have come to what Cotterrell has referred to as a "more pluralistic conceptualisation of law"—a conceptualisation which might open membership of the legal community more widely—has been the anthropological debate about legal pluralism. Yet legal pluralism has, perhaps not surprisingly, itself remained marginalised as "the Other" within the canon of jurisprudence. As Santos argues;

"The fact that legal pluralism and community justice challenge—how radically, it is questionable—liberal political and legal theory, has not been given due salience. As a result, the 'natural' interconnection

[81] Douzinas and Warrington (1994) Chapter 1; Teubner (ed.) (1986).
[82] Exceptions include Roger Cotterrell (1995); Alan Hunt (1993) (who retains a focus on "radical legal pluralism"; (see Ch. 13, especially pp. 326–30) and Boaventura de Sousa Santos (1987), (1992).

between these issues and issues such as the legitimacy of the state, forms of social power, the theory of legal subjectivity, socio-economic, racial or gender inequality, and forms of democracy, has not been elaborated on."[83]

In the textual outpourings of the critical legal industry, legal doctrine, legal discourse and legal practices remain those quintessential fetish objects of legal hierarchy—pieces of legislation and reports of the priesthood of the legal community, appeal court judges.

This scholarly habit of focusing on practices which present themselves in immediate textual form entails an unfortunate skewing of our critical attention. It threatens to blunt the edge of our political critique. This is true even of the more adventurous interpretive range of the genealogical project, which, in using (albeit forgotten) legal texts as the source of imaginative insight into difference, nonetheless rests the critical weight of its enterprise on a relatively narrow conceptualisation of precisely the institution which it seeks to imagine differently.[84] It is a constant danger of this as of other forms of "immanent critique" that it ends up by taking seriously, even by reproducing, some of the very features of law—its rule-governed nature, its pretensions to seriousness, its assertion of its own principled nature—which it was the original impulse of critical legal theory to question.[85]

In thinking about what a revitalised normative jurisprudence might actually deliver in terms of the promise of justice, we obviously need to avoid reproducing the sterile debate which characterised some marxist legal theory about whether pluralistic regulatory practices such as administrative rules, discretionary powers, codes of practice, mediation,—like the "administration of things" under communism—"are" legal or not. The serious question remains what the appropriate theoretical approach and political posture is in relation to the wide array of contemporary legal practices which are so powerful in allocating the benefits of membership and the brutalities of

[83] Santos (1992) p. 132.

[84] The paradigmatic conception of the legal also finds expression in the thought of Habermas, whose theory of communicative action has been influential in prompting the revival of a focus on the critically discursive aspects of law, yet whose analysis of the disintegrative development of modern societies has underpinned deep hostility to the increasing encroachment of the instrumental-legal.

[85] It is worth noting that one of the few serious attempts to reconceptualise law in more horizontal terms—Tove Stang Dahl's and the Oslo school's conception of "women's law": Stang Dahl (1986)—derives from a feminist tradition which has perhaps less of an investment in the *status quo* than do the predominantly white male critics speaking from the elite law schools of Britain and North America. See further Chapter 8.

exclusion. We may have to accept that the ethics of alterity would be killed in the moment of its institutionalisation, that justice can only ever be a promise in law and that, as Anne Barron argues, all attempts to capture the Other within a reconstructed, inclusive and more coherent notion of citizenship (or legal subjectivity) are fantasmatic:

> "The symptoms of desire . . . manifest themselves in the irruption of political subjectivities that cannot be captured by the category of the citizen . . . Yet to eradicate the symptom is an impossibility, for it is an inevitable expression of the antagonism that constitutes, sustains and finally limits the discursive field of the political. Lacanian psychoanalysis demands a constant awareness of this surplus of the real over every attempt at symbolisation; it requires a coming to terms with what remains always beyond accommodation; and it serves as a reminder that every description of the just society bears witness to the unpresentable. Justice, in short, has no guarantee; It 'remains to be attained: it is ahead of us'."[86]

But, as much critical legal theory shows, legal practices themselves provide a powerful source of inspiration and imagination in thinking ethically about law.

Given that this is the case, there is a powerful argument for broadening the horizons of critical legal theory beyond the rails of the formal legal order to encompass the tracks and sidings to which it has too often consigned the practices forming the object of socio-legal studies. This would allow critical legal theorists to encompass a wider conception of legally relevant practices in the search for glimpses of empathy for and recognition of the Other and hence for insight about how to weaken the arbitrary, excluding and hierarchical in the operations of legal power. It would also give us a more acute appreciation of the continuing exclusions inherent in institutional changes with rosy theoretical credentials. The call of the democratic project identified by Salecl—that of seeking to limit the effects of the exclusions and hatreds which inevitably structure the fantasy dimension of the legal and political community—remains a powerful one. The reconstruction of legal as much as of political institutions is surely at the heart of this project. In pursuing this project, an expanded horizon, to put it simply, provides a wider basis for engaging in recollective imagination, for glimpsing possibilities of genuine communication, and for exploiting the critical space opened up by the inclusive aspect

---

[86] Barron (1993) p. 83, quoting Lyotard (1985).

of the "we" of democratic legal systems, whilst constantly questioning its exclusions. The limits of the legal paradigm have to be transcended if critical legal politics are to have any relevance beyond the academy, and if the challenge of developing a genuinely transformative jurisprudence is to be met.

PART II

QUESTIONS OF METHOD IN FEMINIST LEGAL THEORY: WITHIN OR BEYOND CRITIQUE?

Closure and Critique in Feminist Jurisprudence:
Transcending the Dichotomy or a Foot in Both Camps?

The enterprise of feminist jurisprudence represents a distinctive test-ing ground for issues of method in legal theory. This is because the very possibility of feminist jurisprudence has been questioned, not just by anti-feminists, but also, and most powerfully, by feminist scholars themselves.[1] In this chapter, I shall reflect on why the issue of feminist jurisprudence is problematic for contemporary feminism. I shall argue that this debate touches on some deep sources of ambiva-lence in feminist thought, and that these sources raise fundamental theoretical questions which are related to the supposed dichotomy between closure and critique. Should feminism aspire to replace or reconstruct the framework of modern legal thought, or should it resist the desire for foundations in favour of a more resolutely critical stance? I shall begin by giving an outline of the cases for and against a feminist jurisprudence: I shall then move on to make some general comments on the debate and to identify a danger of theoretical slippage in discussions of some central problems of strategy and prin-ciple. In the final section of the chapter I shall draw some analogies between the debate about feminist jurisprudence and recent discus-sions in political and social theory. I shall suggest that whilst there are clear reasons for ambivalence about the appropriate location for fem-inist scholarship on the closure/critique axis, developments in social theory should lead us to question the idea of closure and critique as a dichotomy or a pair of mutually exclusive approaches to the analysis of social practices. In particular, I shall argue that the interpretive dimensions of the recent communitarian and "pragmatist" literature discussed in Chapter 5 can provide some useful tools for feminist thought in approaching if not resolving the question of the ground-ing for feminist critique.

Some preliminary remarks are called for about the notions of closure and critique around which my argument is structured. The idea of critique is widely used in legal and social theory, often with-out any great analytical precision. Indeed, the use of the description "critical" by those of us who see our work as politically radical has

---

[1] See Smart (1989); Thornton (1986).

sometimes caused resentment among those who, reasonably enough, point out that any self-respecting intellectual enterprise must see itself as critical.[2] In what follows, I shall be using the term critique broadly to identify projects within legal theory which are specifically concerned to go beyond the superficial appearance of legal practices and discourses, and to question, unsettle, expose to careful scrutiny not only current laws and their organisation but also the claims to authority and legitimacy which legal officials, law-makers, legal practices and theories implicitly express.

The idea of closure, on the other hand, implies claims of authority which are *grounded* in some way. I want to distinguish between legal closure on the one hand and philosophical closure on the other. By legal closure, I mean the claims to autonomy and specificity made by law or on law's behalf. The claims that there are right (legal) answers to questions of law, and that legal reasoning is a specific form of reasoning distinct from ethical or other forms of practical reasoning, would be good examples of ideas which presuppose legal closure. This is a rather different matter from the question of philosophical closure, which has been a particular preoccupation in ethics. Here, too, the issue is one of the *grounding* of claims, but the debate is at a more abstract level. Should we regard philosophical arguments as being grounded in, legitimated by, some transcendent order of truth or reality? Or are they grounded only in human practices and traditions which are historically specific and contingent? As we shall see, each of these kinds of closure raises questions to which feminist analysis can make a useful contribution. But they also raise important and difficult methodological questions for feminism. The closure/critique axis in legal and social theory is therefore a promising focus of inquiry from a feminist point of view.

ARGUMENTS FOR AND AGAINST A FEMINIST JURISPRUDENCE

Several arguments have been used to support the idea that feminist legal scholars should engage in the development of a feminist jurisprudence. Perhaps most obviously, it may be argued that feminist analysis and critique of laws and legal institutions is itself inevitably a theoretical enterprise which merits the denomination "jurisprudence". Furthermore, many of the "standard" jurispruden-

---

[2] See for example MacCormick (1993).

tial questions are of explicit or implicit relevance for feminist enter-prises. On the one hand, feminism poses certain distinctive theoreti-cal questions of and about law: why are women excluded from certain areas of law: what happens when women are included; how does law construct the female subject in language; how can law be changed better to reflect women's interests and experience? These explicitly feminist questions of legal theory are located within broader categories of legal theoretical enterprise: sociological jurisprudence, discourse theory, the analysis of law's ideological func-tions. More controversially, it could be argued that feminist legal theory inevitably begs questions about the definition of law and the legal sphere which have been the stuff of analytical jurisprudence. Feminisms which move beyond a liberal framework to develop a more radical critique generally reject and regard as theoretically flawed the very enterprises of "objective" analysis and of normative jurisprudence which claims to reflect the ethical "view from nowhere". These arguments detect, among other things, a strong tendency towards legal closure in orthodox constructions of the jurisprudential enterprise. Yet there are strong reasons to assert that jurisprudence encompasses critical and interpretive tasks which are quite in tune with feminist theoretical thinking.

A second reason for thinking that feminists should engage in jurisprudence has to do with the power of orthodox theoretical thinking about law and the legal sphere. For example, the traditional stance of analytical jurisprudence, with its common emphasis on legal closure—the autonomy of law—has been a crucially important focus for feminist critique of the pretended "objectivity" and "neutrality" of "the legal point of view". Yet feminist scholars have in fact engaged in rather little direct debate with traditional jurisprudence, perhaps out of a conviction that it is too antediluvian to merit explicit attention, or out of an anxiety that such a debate would inevitably be constructed in terms of an agenda set by orthodoxy.[3] This is unfor-tunate, given that many of the beliefs about neutrality and autonomy criticised by feminists are bolstered by the traditional jurisprudential texts which constitute the core of many jurisprudence courses. It also arguably weakens the feminist position by giving rise to a tendency to lump all "traditional jurisprudence" together, condemning it in undifferentiated terms as "positivist", "essentialist", "gender blind", "masculinist" or "objectivist". Traditional jurisprudence, of course,

---

[3] For two honourable exceptions, see Davies (1994) and Kerruish (1992).

encompasses a variety of theoretical projects and positions, which raise different kinds of problems from a feminist perspective, and not all of which are inevitably prone to either legal closure or gender-blindness. A critical feminist jurisprudence which took on particular jurisprudential doctrines and positions might well strengthen the case for the general propositions which feminists wish to assert.[4]

Thirdly, feminist legal scholarship's emphasis upon the importance of careful analysis and critique of particular legal practices could be read as contributing to a shift away from a monolithic, universalising conception of the jurisprudential project, centred around a number of abstract questions such as "what is law?" or "what is distinctive about legal reasoning?", towards a more concrete and particularistic conception of jurisprudence. Should we allow orthodox scholars to appropriate the concept of jurisprudence, marginalising the more "applied", political theoretical enterprises around law, or should we rather assert the status of this work as properly within the scope of jurisprudence?

Finally, the most straightforward way in which feminist legal scholarship may engage in jurisprudence is in terms of a liberal feminism mainly concerned to develop an "immanent critique" of laws and legal practices. In other words, this feminist approach takes jurisprudence and the legal sphere on their own terms, and then holds up their actuality to contrast them with their own professed standards and ideals. This is the kind of analysis which argues for formal legal equality and equality of opportunity for women in law, and which has met with a substantial degree of success in many legal systems in modern times.[5] Yet it is at precisely this point that ambivalence about feminist jurisprudence begins to surface. For the majority of feminist scholars working in this area today want to press beyond a liberal analysis to a more radical critique.[6]

---

[4] For example, natural law theory raises very different problems for feminism than does positivism; not all forms of analytical jurisprudence are either equally positivistic or equally committed to the autonomy of law; and much of the methodology of sociological jurisprudence is adaptable along feminist lines (see further Chapter 8).

[5] For further discussion see Chapter 7.

[6] The extent to which radical feminists such as Catharine MacKinnon (MacKinnon (1987), (1989)) can usefully exploit a quasi-liberal critique is just the kind of question which has given rise to the controversy which I shall analyse. The characterisation of MacKinnon's position as quasi-liberal is certainly not one which she herself would affirm: however, one could certainly argue that her law reform projects themselves take a paradigmatically liberal form, employing a concept of "harm" to women which might have been taken straight from John Stuart Mill. Her project could be also seen as engaging in the kind of philosophical closure implicit in much liberal discourse. For more detailed discussion, see Chapter 3.

The case against a feminist jurisprudence has been put most pow-erfully by Carol Smart. Smart notes the attractions of feminist jurisprudence:

> "The idea of a feminist jurisprudence is tantalizing in that it appears to hold out the promise of a fully integrated theoretical framework and political practice which will be transformative, unlike the partial or liberal measures of the past . . . It promises a general theory of law which has practical applications. Because it appears to offer the com-bination of theory and practice, and because it will be grounded in women's experience, the ideal of a feminist jurisprudence appears to be a way out of the impasse of liberal feminist theories of law reform".[7]

But she sees the idea as giving rise to two problems:

> "We should . . . consider whether the quest for a feminist jurispru-dence is not falling into the trap of . . . the 'androcentric standard' whereby feminists find they enter into a game whose rules are prede-termined by masculine requirements and a positivistic tradition. . . We need also to consider whether implicit in this quest is the tendency to place law far too much into the centre of our thinking."[8]

To take the latter point first, "grand" feminist theorising about law has, on this view, served women badly. Whilst Smart certainly does not reject theory itself, she is critical of the way in which the debate has too often remained at an abstract level, trapped within theoreti-cal dichotomies such as equality versus difference, public versus pri-vate, which are partly of its own creation. Such theory, she argues, contributes little to our understanding of the subtle, multiple and concrete ways in which legal practices construct and sustain women's oppression. This could be seen as an instrumentalist argument against feminists spending time and effort on a project which offers little hope of political gain or enlightenment.[9] Smart's other argument might be taken to suggest a more fundamental objection to "grand" theory. What are the "masculine requirements" which taint the very notion of feminist jurisprudence? One view could be that the very project of abstract theorisation is unsatisfactory and indeed to be regarded with suspicion by feminists and other radicals. For the move from concrete to abstract becomes a means of assimilating and hence

---

[7] Smart (1989) p. 66 ; Smart draws the notion of the "androcentric standard" from Thornton (1986).

[8] Smart (1989) pp. 67–8.

[9] Smart's main targets in this critique are MacKinnon (1987), (1989) and Gilligan (1982).

disguising the varied experiences of legal subjects: factors such as race and gender are rendered invisible by the move to abstraction; the voices of people of colour, poor people, women and other powerless groups are silenced. Theory may therefore serve precisely the mystifying objectification which it is a task of feminism to undermine and expose.

Smart wants to distinguish, however, between "grand" and "abstract" theory, her objection being to the former rather than the latter. On this view, "grand" theory is that which "totalises" or "universalises"—which claims to generate truths of general applicability. Any "total" theory of or about law may lead subtly to a "totalising" theory which represses difference, and even to "totalitarian" thinking and practice: any "normative" theory may lead towards "normalisation" and hence to repression. Alternatively, such "grand" theory may succeed only in offering accounts of the phenomena they purport to explain at so high a level of abstraction that they become banal or simplistic. I shall return below to the question of just what constitutes "grand" theory and whether "grandness" is distinct from "abstraction". Leaving that question aside for the moment, the main burden of Smart's argument is that legal theory as it traditionally conceives itself is ideological and hence effective in underpinning the very power of law:[10] its claims to truth, impartiality and objectivity, its place high up in the hierarchy of knowledges, which have been so damaging to women and other oppressed groups. Legal theory, in other words, participates in a strong form of legal closure which is inimical to a recognition of the politics of law.

INTERPRETING THE DEBATE

It would, of course, be possible to interpret the debate about feminist jurisprudence as a trivial disagreement which turns on semantics: can the term "jurisprudence" encompass critical and interpretive as opposed to analytic and prescriptive theoretical projects? To dismiss the debate in these terms would, I think, be a mistake. For it touches on a number of fundamental theoretical and political issues which are salient to contemporary feminism, and the very reason why the question of feminist jurisprudence is so problematic is connected to these deeper questions.

[10] Cf. Kerruish (1992).

Most obviously, there is the question of what kind of theoretical enterprise feminism should engage in, and how far it should concern itself with law in the first place. Is the very idea of a feminist theory of law one which implicitly acknowledges legal closure, the autonomy of the legal realm—a closure which is ultimately disempowering to feminism, whose main task is political critique? Is the idea of a feminist theory of law simply a contradiction in terms? Do we really have the power to construct the debate in our own terms—or is the jurisprudential enterprise inevitably loaded towards masculinist concepts and male interests, so that the construction of a feminist jurisprudence is, in Audre Lorde's famous phrase, a futile attempt to destroy the master's house with the master's tools?[11] Even worse, does the project of constructing a feminist theory of law commit the almost unmentionable sin of essentialism, participating in the idea that law has some fixed "essence", as opposed to being open to social and political reconstruction?[12] If legal theory does contain an irreducible core of essentialism, is this inevitable, or defensible on strategic grounds?[13]

Secondly, there is a set of questions about the place in feminism for normative, reconstructive or utopian thinking, as opposed to negatively critical or "deconstructive"[14] thinking. Does the idea of feminism as critique mean that we are always "trashing"—exposing sexism, bias, lack, absence—or is it the job of feminist legal scholars also to prescribe—to suggest legal reforms—or to imagine other possible legal worlds and processes, or indeed worlds without law? And if, as many feminists believe, there is this positive, reconstructive aspect to the feminist enterprise, does it need some kind of grounding or foundation?[15] This shades into a third important question, and brings the issue of philosophical closure into the argument. We must

[11] Lorde (1984).

[12] See Smart (1989) p. 69.

[13] For an excellent discussion of traces of essentialism within constructionist approaches, and of the case for strategic returns to essentialism, see Fuss (1989).

[14] The idea of deconstruction is now widely and somewhat loosely used in critical social theory. At Suzanne Shale's suggestion, I have tried to avoid using the term except where it is meant in the very specific sense developed by Jacques Derrida, with an emphasis on binary oppositions and on strategies of displacement and reversal, destabilising what is by confronting it with the Other which it excludes yet on which it depends. This sense of deconstruction has, of course, been influential in a wide range of literary, psychoanalytic and social theory. But, especially in Anglo-American work, the term "deconstruction" often refers to a much wider practice. I have referred to what I take to be this wider idea of "deconstruction" simply as "critique". For further discussion, see Chapters 5, 7 and 8.

[15] See Benhabib (1987); Fraser (1989); Nicholson (ed.) (1990).

ask whether feminist thought should continue to be located firmly in the post-enlightenment modernism in whose terms (rights, calls for equality and so on) we have become familiar with feminist claims being couched. Alternatively, it might be argued that the critical potential of modernism and liberalism have been exhausted, and must now give way to a post-modernist, resolutely critical mode which utterly rejects philosophical closure and opens up legal discourse to the "play of difference", to the multiple possibilities raised by deconstructive critique. Yet even this way of putting the question is misleading, for it suggests that deconstruction, discourse theory, post-modernist fragmentation and relativism necessarily go hand in hand. Whilst it is certainly true that this relationship is a familiar one, Drucilla Cornell has suggested that one can combine a deconstructive project with an ethical feminism significant aspects of which seem to belong firmly in the modernist tradition.[16] Ultimately, this brings us back to the question of what kind of theory feminism can and should engage in, refined in terms of possibly multiple combinations of modernist and post-modernist, critical and reconstructive, discourse-oriented and materialist, essentialist and social-constructionist projects. Should these dichotomies themselves be regarded as having any validity, and what combinations of project may be theoretically defensible or politically productive?

Fourthly, the questions already raised connect with a further important feminist preoccupation: that of the relationship between theory and practice. Feminism has generally been fiercely committed to the idea that theory and practice form inseparable parts of the political project: theory which is neither informed by the issues thrown up by practice nor likely to contribute to feminist praxis has been seen as an irrelevant and even elitist preoccupation, of no real theoretical or political validity. This commitment to the interrelation of theory and practice which feminism shares with many other radical discourses of course relates to feminist ambivalence about "grand"

[16] Cornell (1993) Ch. 4 (originally published in 1990). Cornell's more recent work continues to develop a distinctive blend of modernist and post-modernist orientations. In *Beyond Accommodation* (1991), Cornell aligns herself, with some reservations, with post-modernism; in *The Imaginary Domain* (1995) she defends a version of liberalism in the public sphere. This is, however, a liberalism which, though universalistic in its normative reach, resists any appeal to foundations. More generally, it would of course be a mistake to conflate the "textual turn" in contemporary social theory with a general post-modernist rejection of the possibility of coherent meta-narratives. For example, the work of Pierre Bourdieu (Bourdieu (1977)) combines a focus on discourse, social constructionism and a rejection of universalism with a decisive rejection of the post-modernism of other french social theorists such as Derrida and Lyotard.

and, in some feminisms, all abstract theory, and marks a tendency in feminist thought which is resistant to philosophical closure. But recent debates have thrown up, as I shall try to show, some intractable questions about the political and strategic defensibility of engaging in action informed by theory which falls short of feminist ideals: in Cornell's words, deciding to work for, for example, legal equality, whilst still knowing that this is something one will never be prepared to *settle for.*[17]

Fifth, the debate about feminist jurisprudence touches on important questions about the relationship of law to other institutions and structures of power. Is law a *relatively* autonomous field, change in which really holds out the hope of material gains for women? Or is law radically implicated with other powerful discourses and institutions in the social, political, cultural and economic realms? This question has a crucial bearing on the potential efficacy of feminist legal strategies. Finally, the debate about feminist jurisprudence raises questions about the relationship between feminism and other social critiques which present themselves as progressive—work in critical race theory, critical legal studies, marxist theory, post-structuralist and post-modernist analysis. In a sense, then, there is an important issue about closure within feminism—both in terms of how autonomous it is as a critical analysis, and in terms of how far it presupposes a foundationalist meta-ethics. The increasing recognition in modern feminist thought of the diversity and fragmentation of social experience and hence of the need to listen to the insights of women situated in a variety of locations relative to the many powerful sites of social oppression—class, race, sexuality—raises important questions about the power of a critique which draws on several sources of enlightenment and a common methodology. At the same time, the spectre of total fragmentation seems to threaten feminism's mission to speak in the voice of political outrage or advocacy[18]—a practice which at least superficially seems to pull feminism back in the direction of philosophical closure.

FEMINISM, LAW AND LEGAL THEORY

Some of the problems around which the debate about feminist jurisprudence has been centred seem as intractable as they do not just

[17] Cornell (1993) Ch. 4.
[18] For a thought-provoking analysis of the pitfalls of this aspect of feminism, see Brown (1995).

because of the complexity of the theoretical and political questions involved, but also because of a degree of slippage between those different questions. I shall illustrate this contention with some examples.

What is "grand theory"?

The debate about the problematic nature of "grand" theory seems to me to be under-developed, with the result that some versions of the argument are in danger of abandoning important feminist legal theoretical projects along with analytical jurisprudence, "viewpointless" normative jurisprudence and crudely monolithic feminist theories. It is open to feminists to construct the jurisprudential project in interpretive and critical ways which are friendly to feminism and certainly not "grand" in the relevant sense. Indeed, Carol Smart's critique of the "quest for a feminist jurisprudence" itself employs concepts such as "patriarchy" and "phallogocentrism" which are themselves highly theorised, just as much of her work shows a strong commitment to engage in theoretical tasks of conceptualisation and analysis. Foucaultian discourse theory and Derridean deconstruction could be said to be every bit as "grandly theoretical" as any jurisprudential theory so far attempted. They too are universalistic at least at the level of method, and to the extent that they seek our attention they inevitably claim a persuasiveness which participates in some kind of validity claim. Of course, we may well want to criticise critical theories as themselves unduly abstract, apolitical or inaccessible. But it seems unarguable that they have generated theoretical ideas which have been found to be powerful in developing feminist critiques of law.[19] This having been said, the question of just what makes a "grand theory" "grand" still needs clearer specification if we are to accept it as a generally negative denomination. And in seeking that clarification, we should be sensitive to the fact that, irrespective of the kinds of truth claims which they assert, the progressiveness and illuminating potential of theories is heavily context-dependent. For example, natural law theory's influence on liberation theology and positivism's basically constructionist stance and its critique of the authoritarian model of law and state implicit in some natural law theory constitute contributions with which many feminists would be sympathetic.

There are at least three elements to the idea of "grand" theory as a pejorative. The first objection is to theories which have pretensions

[19] See Rhode (1990).

to assert Truth (with a capital T!).[20] This may be "true" of all theories except for the most thoroughly deconstructive ones, but it is a
relatively trivial "truth". For comprehensive theories of law can
easily be reinterpreted as offering partial perspectives or insights—
interpretations rather than "truths". In other words, whilst theories
inevitably make an implicit claim to "truth" or "validity", it is up to
us, the critical audience, to reconstruct the status of their claims, and
in doing so to take on board such insights as they have rather than
rejecting them in a wholesale way. If the core of the idea of grand
theory lies in the status of its truth claims, this is perhaps something
which feminism need not fear in any general way. For it may be
argued that the very multiplicity of and controversy among "grand"
theories purporting to have access to Truth or to give us the last word
on reality are undermining to that status in a fairly effective way. The
interpretivist reconstruction of such theories does indeed seem to be
an important feminist move, but this should not rule out feminist
jurisprudence. Furthermore, while *law's* pretensions to Truth or
objective validity are clearly a central object of critique in feminist
theory, it is not clear that feminist *jurisprudence* necessarily has to
engage in the same pretensions. In this sense the burden of Smart's
argument concerns feminist engagement with *law* rather than with
legal theory.

The second theme which can be identified in the debate about
"grand" theory is an objection to theories which are monolithic in
the sense that they seek to reduce all aspects of women's oppression
to one or two basic factors such as sexuality or, as in the case of early
marxist feminism, a particular conception of class. This is indeed an
important defect of some theories, but it does not apply to all theories which purport to have a broad scope. The search for a "universal" theory of law does not necessarily imply that it must be
"universalising" or "totalising": it may in fact be eclectic, complex,
pluralistic. For example, Tove Stang Dahl interprets the feminist
jurisprudential project in a pluralistic and positive way, identifying a
number of sites and modes of legal subordination of women, and
engaging in a project of reconceptualisation of legal categories along
feminist lines.[21]

[20] Cf. Smart (1989) pp. 71–2, 85–6; for a philosophical defence of a similar position, see
Rorty (1991a).
[21] See Stang Dahl (1986). Her particular reconceptualisation is, I think, problematic, but
much of her methodology is instructive: for comment, see Lacey (1989); for discussion of
this genre of theory-building in social and political theory, see Nicholson (ed.) (1990);
Connell (1987); Walby (1990).

Finally, a third objection is to the (high) degree of abstraction of "grand" theories. Again, this seems to me to be an important objection given that the move from concrete to abstract can indeed serve as a cover for the marginalisation or suppression of varying perspectives: abstraction can indeed serve totalisation. Yet this must be a question of degree. *Any* use of theoretical terms inevitably involves conceptualisation and hence a degree of abstraction; indeed this is an inevitable feature of the use of language. As we have already seen, Smart and other feminist theorists themselves clearly affirm the necessity for legitimacy of abstraction in the theoretical enterprise. The three aspects of "grand" theory, then, need to be looked at separately in the case of any candidate for the category.

Against "grand" theory or against "centre-ing" law?

It seems to me that the central object of Carol Smart's critique is not so much the idea of grand theory but rather her second concern—the importance which the project of feminist jurisprudence implicitly accords to law as a site of women's oppression and, most importantly, for feminist activism and reform. Smart has powerful arguments about the limitations of law as a feminist strategy. To the extent that we accept them, these arguments give us powerful political reasons not to expend too much energy on reconstructive legal theory. This is a very different issue from that of the status of theory itself. But Smart's political argument can be questioned. Her explicit acceptance of the importance of the critical project implicitly recognises, as the title of her book suggests, the importance of law as a means of entrenching, expressing and maintaining women's oppression. If law can be powerful in these ways, does not legal critique and change hold out some prospect of progress for women, even if not a panacea? The view that law is a relatively unimportant site for feminist intervention, and that we should be cautious in engaging with it, is itself informed by a set of theoretical views about the relative significance of different sites and modes of power, among which Smart emphasises the importance of law's claims to Truth and its high position in the "hierarchy of knowledges".[22] But this argument is not in itself sufficient to support the "de-centre-ing" of law in feminist theory and practice; this conclusion only follows if it is clear that *other*

---

[22] Smart (1989) Ch. 1.

discourses or institutions exist or can be created which make a weaker claim to Truth than does law. Yet obvious possibilities such as institutions within the political sphere themselves engage in effective marginalising strategies which make them problematic in terms of feminist practice.[23]

The problem of induction from theory to practice

Whether or not it is appropriate to take a *general* position on the need for feminists to "de-centre" law in our approach to theory and practice, we need to avoid another potential slippage in the debate about feminist jurisprudence and legal reforms. This is a shift from a general argument about the need to "de-centre" law to a specific, and often powerful, critique of particular inductions from theory to practice in feminist legal scholarship. Perhaps the best example here is the debate around MacKinnon's and Dworkin's famous attempt to legislate against pornography by means of an ordinance which, among other things, sought to give individual women a civil right of action for the harms done to them by pornography as sex discrimination via the sexual objectification of women.[24] Smart, among others, has cogent criticisms of MacKinnon's induction from theory to practice.[25] Smart's critique has two dimensions: first, there is an argument about the kind of theory which MacKinnon develops—a monolithic, "grand" feminist jurisprudence which seeks to reduce all aspects of women's oppression to one dimension, and which treads dangerously close to a biologistic essentialism. The implication of this is something close to total hopelessness in terms of the prospects for feminist progress. On the other hand, there is a critique of

[23] Indeed, Richard Rorty (Rorty (1979)) has suggested that all human practices generate their own systems of truth which are relatively invulnerable to external critique. There are interesting resonances between such claims within discourse theory and pragmatism and those of systems theory: see Teubner (1993). In his engagement with feminist theory (Rorty (1991b)), Rorty discusses the sense in which the language of truth and right can still be meaningful in ethical and political debate even once the realist claim that such languages relates to an objective world independent of human practices is abandoned. He highlights the way in which we may speak "as if" things "really were" a particular way, and still be perfectly intelligible without being taken to be making a realist claim: see also Rorty (1989) Part 1. A similar position is defended in Chapter 8. For an assessment of the drawbacks of this kind of position for feminism, see Lovibond (1989).

[24] MacKinnon (1987) Part III; (1989) Chs. 7, 11. For a more detailed discussion, see Chapter 3.

[25] Smart (1989) Ch. 6.

MacKinnon's political strategy: even if we agreed with her analysis, would we want to affirm this particular kind of reformism?

Of course, this brings us back to the questions of the relation between theory and practice and between principle and strategy. The distinction which I have drawn between the two aspects of the critique of MacKinnon raises the converse possibility that even though we disagreed with her analysis, we might still see sense in her legal strategies. For example, despite its strategic dangers already discussed, one potential advantage of the anti-pornography campaign might well have been a contribution to opening up the legal process in a way which enables women to use it—both in the sense of having effective access to it, and in the sense of recognising the rights and claims it instantiates as responding to women's needs and therefore thinking of law as something which can be empowering to women as well as to men. More straightforwardly, I would argue that MacKinnon's campaign to have sexual harassment recognised as a legal wrong has been an important and in many ways effective feminist strategy.

I want to emphasise this distinction, because I think that it is most unlikely, given the centrally *political* impetus of feminism, that feminist lawyers will give up hope of the possibility of modest progress through legal change.[26] What is more, it would be very unfortunate if we did give it up. As Smart herself argues, it would be a mistake to regard all legal reformist strategies as equally flawed. What we need is not an abandonment of the legal and political project, but rather the development of more sophisticated understandings of legal practices, their strengths and well as their evident and important limitations. This would include a theoretical understanding of how law relates to other powerful institutions and discourses. Doubtless this is an inelegantly eclectic view, but I would contend that feminist politics around law have room not only for critical analysis of the *status quo* but also for both pragmatic/strategic and utopian thinking and action. If I am right, it follows that we must be alive to the differences between strategy and ideal, and of the different ways in which they must be assessed.

FEMINISM, LAW AND CRITIQUE

I have suggested that several of the problems which have surfaced in the debate about feminist jurisprudence have seemed more

[26] See further Chapters 1 and 8.

intractable than they need to because of a slippage in argument between questions of theory and those of practice and strategy. However, many of these points do not tell against a thoroughly critical stance which "de-centres" and even eschews not only the project of reconstruction via legal reform but also the very idea of feminism as concerned with political prescription or reconstruction. In her most recent work,[27] Carol Smart has followed through the implications of the rejection of abstract theorisation as totalising and potentially repressive. She has made a persuasive case for the position not only that feminism will be better served by a post-modernist critique, but also that this is the only theoretically sound position to be adopted. The relationship between feminism and post-modernism and of feminist attitudes to philosophical closure are, of course, among the most important questions of contemporary social theory. In the legal sphere, post-modernism and deconstruction raise crucial issues of theory and practice: given feminism's irreducibly political underpinning, can a radically critical project sustain the kind of politics, including the ideal of reconstruction, which has so long been accepted as a part of feminism?

As we saw in Chapter 5, Drucilla Cornell has recently argued that feminist legal scholars can and should combine a politically motivated deconstruction with an "ethical feminism" which argues for the reconstruction of the legal sphere.[28] Cornell's brand of deconstruction is rooted in psychoanalytic concepts which, she argues, escape the biological essentialism and strong social determinism which characterise many feminist theories. Cornell's position is particularly interesting in that we can see it as a vivid metaphor for what is perhaps the most difficult question for contemporary feminism: whether to break free of its modernist ties and step over into the kind of thorough post-modernism which Smart advocates, or whether to reject such a move as threatening a disintegration of feminism through the deconstruction of the very categories—woman, gender—which inform it. Doubtless this point should not be overplayed: feminist theory and practice has never taken the category "woman" as a given, but has struggled to reconstruct notions of femininity in ways which have changed the meaning of what it is to be a woman, and the possible ways of living femininity. In this sense, feminist reliance on the notion of woman may be seen as a necessary, strategic and non-dan-

---

[27] Smart (1995) Chs. 5, 11.
[28] See Cornell (1991), (1993). For further discussion of Cornell's work, see Chapters 5 and 7.

gerous form of weak essentialism.[29] Yet there is a sense in which the very feminist project assumes some degree of continuity among women's oppressions, and the rejection of this basic idea might be thought to threaten feminism with the spectre of disintegration. Does the kind of move which Smart advocates lead us towards exciting new possibilities, or to a politically frightening, or perhaps irresponsible, relativism? We could see Cornell's approach as "a foot in both camps"—or we may see it as a transcending of the modernism/post-modernism dichotomy. After all, many commentators have questioned just how far "post-modernism" represents a genuine rupture with enlightenment thinking, as opposed to one version or immanent critique of modernism.[30]

Cornell is certainly not alone in rejecting the idea that we must opt either for a thorough post-modern critique or a less radical modernist reconstructive project which participates in philosophical closure. Roberto Unger, for example, combines critique of legal doctrine with a commitment to utopian thinking about the possibilities for social reconstruction—for different social and legal practices and worlds.[31] We need not accept that the salvaging of the reconstructive project depends on a commitment to transcendent foundationalism. Indeed, this would be to resurrect rather than to undermine the closure-critique dichotomy. Arguably, Unger's utopianism, like the leaps of political imagination advocated by thoroughgoing social constructionists like Rorty, emphasises the opening up of different possibilities, of experimentation and the celebration of fluidity and variety, in a way which is more resonant with post-modern thinking than with the kind of transcendental normative ethics of modernist political, moral and legal philosophers. This appears to be much the kind of project envisaged by Cornell when she argues that we should be pointing to the possibility of "a new choreography of sexual difference". Indeed, Rorty argues that we lose nothing in embracing wholeheartedly contingency and an ironic attitude, since the promises of transcendental grounding have never been more than a chimera offered by abstract philosophy.[32] This need not lead us to abandon the use of normative language: it merely entails that we reconstruct the meaning of apparently realist/objectivist truth claims

---

[29] See Fuss (1989): the idea of "strategic essentialism" is criticised in Cornell (1991) pp. 179–83.

[30] See Fraser (1989); Nicholson (ed.) (1990); Wagner (1993); see also note 16.

[31] Unger (1983), (1987) Volume I.

[32] Rorty (1979), (1989), (1991b).

as statements made "as if" there were some independent reality to which we are appealing, rather than as making such claims.

As Susan Williams has suggested in a paper responding to Cornell's work,[33] the turn to communitarianism in recent social theory may offer something of a half-way house between the transcendental universalist approach and the radical relativism which seems to be embraced by some post-modernist theories and which arguably threatens to cut the political ground from under feminism's feet.[34] As we saw in Chapter 5, the definition of communitarianism is problematic, for the idea has emerged from a critique of liberalism developed by a number of theorists who have overlapping concerns but whose views are far from identical and who do not all identify themselves as communitarians.[35] Nonetheless, two main themes may be distinguished: a methodological, social-constructionist theme and a political, "value-communitarian" theme. For the purposes of this chapter, it is the first which is of interest. For it entails that communitarians reject the idea of political philosophy as an objective, non-socially-grounded project which proposes values and frameworks which are of universal validity. They replace this conception with a view of social theory as socially grounded and as interpretive. Emerging from this methodological stance communitarians have argued that both human identity and value are socially constructed. This exposes as a social construct the liberal idea of an abstract, disembodied individual who bears rights, needs and interests which are independent of any particular social situation. Moreover, the facts of human sociality and interdependence render the pre-social conception of individual personhood inappropriate as a starting point for political theory.[36] This kind of interpretivist methodology rejects a strong idea of philosophical closure, or one that is necessarily inimical to critique. Whilst communitarian political argument is clearly grounded in the sense of finding its foundation in certain concrete

[33] Susan Williams (1990); see also Cornell (1992) Ch. 2.

[34] On the need to resist the apparent dichotomy between a strong metaphysical realism and a radical subjectivism, see Nussbaum (1990) Chs. 8, 15; see particularly pp. 228–9.

[35] The main theorists in question are MacIntyre (1981), (1988), (1990), Sandel (1982), Taylor (1985), (1989), Unger (1987), and Walzer (1983), (1987); see also Chapter 2.

[36] For many of the communitarians, this kind of approach is exemplified in modern political philosophy by the work of John Rawls and in particular by his conception of the "original position" as a neo-contractarian legitimating device for his theory of justice: Rawls (1971). It is interesting to note that, whilst not accepting many of the arguments the communitarians have developed about his conception of the person, Rawls has made significant concessions, both methodologically and substantively, to communitarian ideas in his more recent work: see particularly Rawls (1980), (1985), reprinted in Rawls (1993).

social practices, it does not pretend to transcendent or objective foundations.

The interpretive method of communitarianism entails that political theory must find its critical foothold in our experience and understanding of prevailing cultural codes, conventions and discourses; our attempts to make sense of our lives and, crucially, to apply a critically reflexive attitude to our complex experiences. Feminist politics, like all politics, must be grounded in the insights which come from diverse, fragmented human experience of social life lived across a number of "interpretive communities". The attractions of this view are evident as a corrective to the kind of "grand" theory to which post-modernism objects: the trancendental claim to absolute truth which is monolithic and highly abstract, thus insensitive to the diversity of human experience. Could this be a way to explode the closure/critique, foundationalist/anti-foundationalist, modernist/post-modernist dichotomies in social theory? Certainly, it looks promising: communitarian interpretivism as a methodology for social theory at once spawns critique and engages in a weak form of closure (or even essentialism). The alternative critical discourses and strategies of resistance which it generates are located or "grounded" in human experience and consciousness and validated by the culture from which they emerge, rather than any transcendental pretension to ahistorical, asocial truth.

But, as the argument of Chapters 2 and 5 already implies, to acknowledge that interpretivist methodology in some sense transcends the dichotomy is not to say that it is unproblematic from the point of view of feminist politics. For one question which is absolutely central to feminist politics has yet to be addressed adequately by not only communitarianism but also other post-structuralist social theories which employ a similarly interpretivist, practice-oriented methodology. This is the question of how the critical insights which result from human experience attain the kind of status which accords political power. Interpretivism opens up the idea of a society in which different communities assert their competing or complementary points of view; it welcomes pluralism. But it leaves open the possibility (indeed the probability) that the perspectives which command assent, change or action are those emanating from the most powerful communities. It has little to say, as yet, about how marginalised groups are to attain political power. This may simply be an inevitable political problem, but we should guard against the danger that a communitarian interpretivism may translate into a rationalisation of the *status quo*—in other words, into conservatism.[37] This is particularly true of those forms of communitarianism such as MacIntyre's which have failed to emphasise the notion of critical reflexivity in the assessment of practices, and correspondingly less so of the work of writers like Taylor who give more thought to this question.[38] Clearly, further theoretical work needs to be done to relate the insights of the communitarians in political theory and developments in post-structuralist and other forms of critical social theory to the specific debates within feminist and other critical legal theory which we have been exploring in terms of the closure/ critique dichotomy. I hope that I have said enough here at least to demonstrate the potential fruitfulness of such work, and to suggest that holding to the closure/critique dichotomy may lead to an impoverished conception of the possibilities for feminist legal theory.

CONCLUDING THOUGHTS

If we were to think of law and theories of law as a species of game of whose structure and substance we are critical, we could think about the debate about feminist jurisprudence as torn between the options of trying to get into the team to have a better chance of changing the structure of the game or of engaging in strategic rule-breaking; of simply withdrawing to create and play a different game altogether; of watching on the sidelines and allowing ourselves the luxury of throwing the occasional rotten tomato from a safe distance; or some combination of these three. I have suggested that although the theoretically pure approach may well be the second, there will often be tactical and strategic reasons for engaging in the first and the third, and that we need a careful analysis in each case of just what the dangers and advantages of a pragmatic strategy are likely to be. The idea of "de-centre-ing" law is an attractive one to the extent either that there are other established practices, intervention in which would be likely to be more politically productive, or that the creation of

[37] See Chapters 2 and 5 for further discussion; see also Frazer and Lacey (1993); Moller Okin (1989) Ch. 3.

[38] By "critical reflexivity" I mean the capacity of persons to question, assess, reflect critically upon (even) those practices and beliefs which are dominant in their culture and which play a constitutive role in their identities and conceptions of the good. This involves the capacity to stand aside to some extent from the practices in question—but not to the extent needed to achieve the radically detached stance envisaged by much universalistic philosophy: see Passerin d'Entreves (1990) pp. 82–8; Walzer (1987).

alternative, autonomous practices offers, in the long run, the possibility of political progress as opposed to further marginalisation. But a combined strategy may often be less politically compromising than we fear. The development of alternative, resistant discourses is certainly a central project of feminism, but its political impetus must also lead feminists to engage with currently powerful discourses and institutions. It is far from clear that institutions such as politics, conventional morality, the family, religion are any more hospitable to feminist intervention, critique and reconstruction than is law. As feminist lawyers and legal scholars, it seems reasonable to assert that feminist theoretical projects around law, which need not amount to "grand theorising", will assume both an intellectual and political priority in our practice. In developing feminist approaches to law, we certainly have to be wary of a too hasty closure around the concept of law. But the recognition that contingent and constructed structures and institutions are nonetheless powerful means that the project must proceed.

On the questions of closure and critique, we must return to the distinction drawn early on in this chapter between legal and philosophical closure. As far as the former is concerned, any feminist theoretical project around law will inevitably reject the idea of law as an autonomous structure generating claims to truth which are insulated from political critique. Feminism, in common with other critical approaches in social theory, will always be concerned to undermine, to expose as false, law's pretended autonomy, objectivity and neutrality. As far as philosophical closure is concerned, however, we have to conclude that much feminist theory is still hovering over the alleged divide between modernist and post-modernist projects, uncertain whether to jump one way or another or to reject the dichotomy itself. Many feminists continue to fear that the move to post-modernism may cut our political ground from under us, may reduce our perspective to "just one view among others"—including that of sexism—and may deny us the basis for speaking in terms of anger and advocacy. We therefore hesitate on the boundary, fearful of the political consequences of fragmentation and relativism, and even sceptical of the emergence of post-modernism at just the moment when feminist modernist critiques seemed to be gaining some power. The temptation both to assert the moral high ground as our own, and simultaneously to cut it away from under ourselves as theoretically unsound, remain strong opposing tendencies in contemporary feminism. Ultimately, I would argue that the reasons for

resisting the closure/critique, modernism/post-modernism dichotomies in legal and social philosophy are strong ones. Feminist legal
theorists such as Carol Smart and Drucilla Cornell have asserted and
demonstrated in different ways the *political* power and status of critique,[39] and it seems highly unlikely that feminism will or should give
up its utopian and reconstructive dimension, whatever its epistemological basis is taken to be. In this context, the most persuasive
feminist work represents neither a real transcendence of the
closure/critique dichotomy, nor the unsatisfactory compromise suggested by the idea of a foot in both camps. It rather rejects the conceptual straightjacket which a rigid closure/critique dichotomy seeks
to impose, and questions the need to understand closure and critique
in strongly dichotomised terms. Perhaps the best lesson we can learn
from the debate about feminist jurisprudence is the importance of
feminism's power to question and reshape the categories of traditional theoretical debate. We should not abandon the concept of
jurisprudence to orthodoxy, but claim it for our own as part of a
transformative feminist practice.

[39] For an analogous argument in political theory, see Brown (1995); for further discussion, see Chapter 8.

7

Feminist Legal Theory Beyond Neutrality

"Le neutre est supposé représenter un ni-l'un-ni-l'autre. Avant que ce ni-l'un-ni-l'autre puisse se signifier, il importe que l'un et l'autre existent, que deux identités soient définies différement que comme pôles artificiellement opposés d'un modèle humain unique" (Luce Irigaray, *J'aime a toi* (Paris, Grasset, 1992), p. 198.)

The figure of neutrality stands in many ways as a powerful symbol for the challenges faced by contemporary feminist legal scholarship. For in questioning not only the reality but the very possibility of gender or sexual neutrality, feminism has pitched itself against both an ideal which lies at the heart of the ideological self-conception of a liberal legal order, and a key methodological tenet of what has been taken to be good scholarship. In this chapter, my focus will be on some supposed "double binds" which confront feminism as it appears to turn away from the neutrality which has a central place in the framework of modern thought and in the modern ideal of the rule of law.

I want to begin by sketching, in a necessarily caricatured way, the development of feminist legal thought from one position to another.[1] The first position—I shall call it "liberal feminism"—is one in which the analytic emphasis is on the implicit and explicit exclusion of women from the full status of legal subject, whilst the normative emphasis is on our inclusion via a strategy of sex-blind equality. The second, which I shall label "difference feminism", is one in which the analytic focus is on a problematic assimilation of women to a substantially male conception of legal subjectivity, and in which the nor-

---

[1] The characterisation is schematic and does not attempt to incorporate every position associated with feminist legal thought: it is designed rather to point up the particular trajectory which will be the main focus of my discussion. Similarly, the labels are used as a matter of expositional convenience: I do not mean to imply, for example, that all exponents of positions within the spectrum of "difference feminism" see themselves as moving beyond the ambit of liberal politics, broadly understood. Whilst some of the questions raised by difference feminism about liberalism and about the philosophical discourse of modernity are addressed indirectly later in the chapter, a full analysis of these issues runs well beyond its scope. For further discussion, see Chapters 5, 6 and 8 of this book.

mative emphasis is on the recognition and accommodation of difference. After colouring these sketches in, I shall go on to consider a number of apparent "double binds" which are thought to confront difference feminism. The particular questions which I want to address are these. First, what sort of feminist practice does difference feminism imply, and under what conditions can the practices which it engenders avoid reproducing images of sexual difference as, if not "essential", at least shaped in relatively intractable ways? Secondly, how does this issue affect the relationship between difference feminism and other critical theories, particularly those concerned with questions of class and race? And thirdly, how is the structure of these problems affected by the ways in which we conceptualise law or the legal? I shall think through these questions in relation to three current debates: first, a debate about how the legal subject is conceptualised; secondly, a debate about the place of psychoanalysis in feminist thought; and thirdly, a debate about the desirability of special rights for women.

FEMINIST LEGAL THEORY:
FROM THE AGE OF INNOCENCE TO THE COLOUR PURPLE?

The premises which informed liberal feminism and what might be called feminist legal theory's age of innocence are well known and can be very simply stated. In a variety of ways, implicitly and explicitly, women had been excluded from membership of the community of legal subjects. Whilst explicit discrimination such as the exclusion of women from political suffrage and from rights of ownership had largely been swept away by the time of feminism's rebirth in the 1960s, feminist lawyers pointed out a myriad of subtler and more indirect ways in which the constitution of legal rules and categories in fact excluded or disadvantaged women, and expressed a view of the world which reflected male interests.[2] This feminist analysis drew on a distinction between sex and gender, and, in doing so, sought to undermine received views about the importance of "natural" differences between the sexes. Since the ancient disadvantages and exclusions which had marked the legal status of women had generally been justified in terms of supposedly "natural" characteristics and incapacities, the interpretation of many, if not most, of these differences as

---

[2] For an example of this kind of work, see Atkins and Hoggett (1984).

social constructs—as matters of gender rather than of "given" sex—assumed a distinctive political importance. For if the social meanings of gender were contingent, albeit powerful, this entailed first, that they could no longer feature as counters in the justification for differential treatment; and secondly, that they could be changed by changing powerful social practices such as law. Notwithstanding references to biological differences such as reproductive capacities which would call for appropriately but exceptionally different treatment, sex difference per se was accorded little importance: what mattered to liberal feminism was the way the meaning of sex—i.e. gender—had been constructed. And if sex difference was unimportant, it could hardly be a barrier to a sexually universal—or neutral—conception of citizenship and legal subjecthood.

The task of constructing this feminist critique was, of course, a laborious one. It entailed an elaboration of the detailed ways in which the shape and enforcement of, for example, laws on rape, child custody, part-time work, or marital property, in fact had an adverse impact on women.[3] But the politics which informed the task was relatively unproblematic. For it was, in essence, the very same politics which informed the ideological self-conception of the liberal and democratic legal order which it took itself to be criticising. The argument was simply this: if, as a liberal society, you profess to accord women the full rights of citizenship, then you are logically committed to attending to the various ways in which your legal framework in fact falls short of this universalist ideal. Give women the same rights and entitlements as you give to men; treat women equally; dispense your justice even-handedly. Live up, in other words, to the ideal of neutrality between persons which is a central component of the modern imaginary. The clearest symbol of this brand of legal feminism's political achievement in Britain is probably therefore the Sex Discrimination Act 1975, which prohibits not discrimination against women, but rather discrimination *on grounds of sex*.[4]

---

[3] It also, crucially, entailed a careful analysis of the general patterns of legal intervention and non-intervention.

[4] It is interesting to note that this was, even formally, a commitment to sex neutrality but not, strictly speaking, to gender equality. For if gender is defined as that set of social practices and discourses which determine the *meaning* of a woman's or a man's sexed identity, it can hardly be doubted to include our sexual orientation. Yet the SDA 1975 does not straightforwardly encompass discrimination on grounds of sexuality as opposed to sex. Cf. Drucilla Cornell's argument for encompassing discrimination on grounds of sexual orientation within Title VII of the American Civil Rights Act (Cornell (1993) Ch. 6, also printed in Butler and Scott (eds.) (1992) p.280). For further discussion, see below at n. 63.

The position I have just described is often characterised in later feminist work as the call for formal as opposed to substantive equality.[5] This is something of a misdescription, because even this early liberal feminism went well beyond a call for formally equal status. For example, in deciding what would count as equal treatment, the present effects of past discrimination, which marked sexually the impact of sexually neutral rules, could be taken into account—as in the SDA's conception of indirect discrimination. And this concern not just with the formal surfaces of law but with its impact entailed a strong affinity between feminist scholarship and detailed socio-legal research which reached beyond the bounds of legal doctrine—cases and statutes—to comprehend enforcement practices, broadly understood.[6] This is an affinity which characterises feminist legal research to this day, and it is one which, as I shall argue in more detail later, we forget at our peril. Furthermore, the caricature of liberal equality as inevitably premised on "sameness" is an exaggeration: liberal theorists such as Ronald Dworkin, for example, have been concerned to emphasise the notion of equality as "treatment as an equal" rather than as "equal treatment".[7]

Nonetheless, it is clear that in several important respects liberal feminism contained the seeds of its own deconstruction, and these were quickly identified by difference feminism. The basic problems of liberal feminism were as intimately linked with its conceptual framework as the form/substance distinction which I have mentioned. One set of problems had to do with a particular configuration of the division between public and private, which feminists questioned in a way which began to take their feminism beyond the bounds of the liberalism which had given it birth.[8] This important subject has been analysed in Chapter 3 and I will not address it here.

The problem on which I do want to focus is the simple fact that liberal feminism's central ideal amounted to a strategy of assimilation of women to a standard set by and for men.[9] The rights assigned to men as legal subjects had to be made available to women wherever a comparison between the treatment of the two revealed a disparity:

[5] See for example O'Donovan (1985) Ch. 7; Smart (1989) pp. 82–5, 139–44.

[6] A good example is Smart (1984).

[7] Dworkin (1977) p. 227. This is not to imply that Dworkin's theory in general is satisfactory from a feminist point of view: see Frazer and Lacey (1993) pp. 53–77; Hunt and Kerruish (1992).

[8] See O'Donovan (1985); Olsen (1983) and Ch. 3.

[9] Lacey (1987); Cornell (1993) Ch. 6; O'Donovan (1985) Ch. 7; O'Donovan and Szyszczak (1988). See also Chapter 1.

but the equalisation was almost invariably in one direction—towards a male norm. The radical potential inherent in the idea of "treatment as an equal" was not realised, because the political debate issued in by liberal feminism was highly circumscribed. Far from engendering a substantial reconsideration of the way in which the world was organised, the public standards already in place were assumed to be valid, and the feminist conceptual tools of bias, discrimination, equal worth measured against them. To borrow Katherine O'Donovan's metaphor, the general tendency was simply to assume that "a woman could be more like a man". And even the occasionally converse strategy—that of "making a man more like a woman"—left in place prevailing views about sexual difference and, crucially, about its specific shape.[10] On the view emerging in the difference feminism which challenged liberal feminism, the SDA was toppled from its position at the summit of feminist achievement. With its symmetrical and comparative method and its sex-neutral conceptual framework, it became instead the symbol of the effacement of the feminine, of women, from legal discourse—an effacement which was all the more problematic because it was effected in the name of sexual equality.

The general shape of difference feminism entailed, of course, its own set of laborious and detailed analytic tasks. It brought with it a shift of emphasis beyond a concern with the differential impact of laws on subjects pre-formed as women and men to the recognition and explication of a more dynamic role for law in constructing and underpinning gender hierarchies.[11] It entailed the need to focus not just on law's construction of images of women and femininity but also its constitutions of men and masculinity. If the argument about the pitfalls of the liberal/comparative approach was to be made out, we had to substantiate the central claim that the legal subjecthood to which women had been assimilated was implicitly male, and possibly that the very methods of legal practices were masculine. Our focus shifted—in common with broader developments in critical legal theory—from the instrumental aspects of law to its symbolic aspects. The messages about women and men transmitted by law; the role of law as a discursive practice into which the material realities of women's and men's embodied lives are inserted, and in which the assumptions underlying law's conceptualisation of subjecthood are constructed as (T)ruths; the subtle role of law in categorising and dis-

[10] O'Donovan (1985) Chs. 7, 8.
[11] For a variety of work representing this kind of development, see Naffine (1990); Smart (1989), (1990), (1995) Ch. 5; Cornell (1991); Frug (1992).

ciplining its subjects: all these became the stuff of critical legal analysis, accompanying and sometimes displacing the more materialist focus of earlier critical traditions informed by Marxism.[12] As befitted the focus on discourse, the main emphasis of this feminist scholarship was on critical analysis. But an underlying normative commitment to the recognition of differently constituted subjectivities could be perceived from very early on, and has become both more insistent and more explicit with time. A new set of utopias began to emerge, and they were oriented to the construction or imagination of a more polyphonous and inclusive law, and to thinking beyond a law whose dominant mode is to fix its subjects' sexual or other identities within rigid categories.[13]

MORE ON THE SUBJECT OF SEX

I now want to give a somewhat more detailed account of just how the critique associated with difference feminism conceptualises the legal subject and argues for its maleness. The basic argument is that the paradigm legal subject has been constructed as an individual, and moreover as an individual abstracted from its social context, including the context of its own body, and of the dependence of its own identity on its relationship towards and affective ties with others.[14] The features of the subject to which legal rules and methods attach importance is characterised in terms of a number of distinctive capacities, foremost among which is reason: paradigm legal subjects are those who have the capacities for rational understanding, reflection and control of their own actions. It is this emphasis on reason and the capacity for self-control which underpins the equation of individual rational subjectivity with masculinity.

The argument depends on an assertion of the power of a number of binary oppositions within (and indeed prior to) modern Western thought. Important examples include reason and emotion, self and other, individual and community, mind and body, public and private, male and female. The feminist deployment of this argument depends on three assertions: first, that these oppositions are dichotomous—in

---

[12] See Collins (1982).

[13] See Chapters 5 and 8.

[14] See Naffine (1990), (1994); for analogous arguments in philosophy and political theory see Jaggar (1983) Chs. 3 and 7; Lloyd (1984): Frazer and Lacey (1993) Chs. 2, 3; Taylor, "Atomism", in Taylor (1985) pp. 187–210; Nedelsky (1993). See also Chapter 4.

other words that each member of the pair is defined in opposition to, and is hence inconsistent with, the other: secondly, that the dichotomies are marked by hierarchy—in other words, that one member of the pair has been privileged in modern Western thought and social practice; and thirdly, that the hierarchies are marked, among other things, by sex—in other words, that the feminine has been associated with the less valued members of each pair.[15] The feminine, and hence women, have been associated with emotion, the body, the private; masculinity, and hence men, with reason, the mind, the public. To the extent, then, that the conceptualisation of subjects within legal doctrine, and the insertion of embodied women and men into those frameworks via legal discourse, are genuinely marked by the features of reason and individuality and by the repression or forgetting of the body and affectivity, and to the extent that these hallmarks of subjecthood are elevated to the status of objectivity or universality, women will find themselves constructed as non-standard, as other.

This is not to say, however, that the female has no role to play within the legal construction of subjecthood. On the contrary, according to this argument woman's role as "other" is integral to man's constitution as "one": the woman as other acts as the support which gives back to man, in a mirror image, his sense of the integrity of his own identity. This function is poetically evoked by Luce Irigaray in the following passage from her letter to Nietzsche:

"Learn what was the foundation of everything you have built up. If you want to rise up once more, remember the earth you take flight from. For if she were to fail you, you would lose the very sensation of height.[16] . . .

And should you [here the addressee is female] stir even ever so slightly, that tightrope walker up there may fall into the abyss! That is how he manages to stay up there alone—if you don't remain the prisoner of his lack of freedom, he falls! And as (he) takes each next step, (he) suffers from the risk that it entails! And each time (he) plunges back into the depths of the flesh, her stillness exalts him and (he) thrills at the brilliance of his new exploit! As with her subterranean and submarine strength she keeps the rope secure for his glorious ascent."[17]

The point is made more directly by Ngaire Naffine:

---

[15] For an elegant statement of these arguments, see Olsen (1990).
[16] Irigaray (1991) p. 20
[17] Irigaray (1991) p. 24.

"Officially, the legal subject is potentially anyone, anywhere. And it is this any-personness of the legal person which is supposed to ensure that the law is at the disposal of us all, equally—without fear, favour or affection. This book, however, has found the legal subject to be someone with a quite specific set of distinguishing characteristics. But these characteristics do not sit easily together. On the one hand our man of law is assumed to be a freestanding, autonomous creature, rationally self-interested and hard-headed; on the other hand he is a being who is assumed both to have and to need access to the values of *Gemeinshaft*, the family values, though he must not display them in his public, legal *Gesellschaft* life. The legal person described here is thus essentially a paradox. . .

The argument of this volume has been that the law. . . assigns to women the job of holding the two worlds together. . . As the courts continue to tell us, the *Gemeinschaft* functions are vital and necessary ones, but they are most appropriately performed by dutiful wives and mothers—not by the man of law. Women's domestic labours sustain the paradox of the man of law."[18]

The unacknowledged feminine, then, operates as a necessary complement to the in fact partial constitution of the masculine subject of legal doctrine: its hidden existence is essential to the conjuring trick which sustains the illusion of the (masculine) subject's self-identity.

MAPPING THE (APPARENT) DOUBLE BINDS

I now want to sketch what are often thought to be double binds for difference feminism. I have already observed that one of the beauties of early liberal legal feminism was the relative simplicity of its politics: essentially, its politics were not oppositional, except at the level of challenging men's self-interest. Its analysis was the quintessential expression of the philosophical discourse of modernity; its ideology was liberal; and, on the assumption that that liberal ideology was widely shared, its strategy was simply to appeal to the good faith of those in political and legal power. Doubtless, given the strength of those interests and the short supply of good faith, this in itself was rarely an effective approach. But, in principle, there was an easy and

---

[18] Naffine (1990) pp. 148–9. The difference in written style of Naffine's and Irigaray's overlapping arguments is itself significant. Whilst Irigary speaks in the first person, Naffine's subjectivity is distanced by the use of the neutral, and hence, according to the logic of her own argument, masculine third person. I shall take up the question of written style and feminist theory in the final section of this chapter.

very direct inference from theory or analysis to policy or strategy.
And this was highly sympathetic for feminism, which has always
affirmed the intimacy of theory and practice.

With the move away from liberal feminism, this simplicity disap-
peared. And a more sophisticated and complex analysis seemed to
entail a far more complicated politics. This "loss of innocence" is
effectively evoked in Audre Lorde's famous metaphor: one cannot
use the master's tools to destroy the master's house.[19] Once law itself,
and indeed the very framework of liberal politics, had been argued to
be part of the problem, it no longer represented a straightforwardly
usable tool for feminist legal strategy.[20] But the problem was not
merely strategic: it was also conceptual. In the liberal feminist critique, feminists were able to draw on a rich set of normative and conceptual resources: the language of rights, justice and equality was
readily and unproblematically available as the medium for the articulation of feminist criticisms and claims. But since, according to later
feminism, these concepts too were marked by masculinity, they
could no longer be appealed to in the construction of feminist
utopias—or they could only be appealed to once they had been substantially reconstructed.[21] This seemed to locate an important part of
the feminist critical enterprise at the level of conceptual and hence
linguistic reconstruction. But here we seemed to be stuck in another
cul-de-sac—and, worse, one constructed by the very theories which
had helped us to form our feminist critique. For language, too, was
being reinterpreted as a social practice which itself reflects and reproduces gendered configurations of power.[22] This is the first double
bind which appears to confront difference feminism.

A further problem arose from the fact that the practices which we
sought to criticise had already developed to accommodate significant
elements of liberal feminism. Our successes in shifting the borders
between sex and gender—in interpreting more and more differences
between women's and men's lives as matters of constructed gender
rather than given sex—had drawn us into a politics which assumed
that the positing of gender neutrality would engender sexual equality. Persisting inequalities could be legitimated as determined by the
choices of autonomous liberal individuals. In law, this had made the

[19] Lorde (1984).
[20] This problem is most insistently expressed in Carol Smart's argument for the "decentring" of law: Smart (1989) Chs. 1, 4, 7, 8; see further Ch. 6.
[21] See Fudge (1989); Kingdom (1991); Smart (1989) Ch. 7. On reconstruction, see for
example Littleton (1987); Cornell (1991); Nedelsky (1989), (1993); and see Chapter 8.
[22] Cornell (1991) Ch. 2.

problem of sexual difference all but invisible, thus arguably engendering an even more difficult struggle—that to recover our sexed bodies, demand that they be taken notice of, and, most difficult of all, articulate that demand in terms which do not invite response in terms of the very stereotypes about women which we tried to overcome with the strategy of neutrality. The problem was simply that whilst gender—the social meaning of sex—was indeed contingent, the mapping of gender onto sexed bodies was, as a matter of history, distinctly patterned. Yet in tracing the ways in which laws and other social practices involved in imagining and discursively constructing reality consistently mapped certain configurations of gender onto particular sexed bodies, we appeared to be open to precisely the charge of sex essentialism which it had been the project of early feminism to deconstruct.[23] And here emerges a second, apparent, double bind.

THE SUBJECT OF CRIMINALISATION

Contextualisation as critique

I now want to take a closer look at difference feminism's critique of the legal subject by locating it within some specific debates in criminal law. I want to suggest that, although the supposed double binds which I have identified can indeed be loosened, our ability to do so has been hampered by a failure to distinguish between two different arguments. The first is a critical analysis of the conceptual framework of legal doctrine; the second is an argument about the basically extra-legal assumptions about masculinity and femininity which mark the insertion of women and men into that conceptual framework via legal discourse. I shall argue that we have sometimes been too quick to map a philosophical argument about the conceptual construction of subjecthood in legal doctrine onto a broader set of discourses whose assumptions about gendered subjecthood are in fact more

---

[23] For there was always a lurking question which our opponents wanted us to answer: if gender was constructed and contingent, why was the pattern so consistent? My point here is basically a tactical one. A politics which insists on *both* the contingency *and* the power and patterning of gender is engaged in something akin to a tightrope walk, in which its balance may easily be knocked by its opponents. For a thoughtful discussion of the problems confronting use of the sex/gender distinction, see Joan C. Williams (1989); on the re-emergence of "sex" in feminist legal theory, see Lacey (1997) and Ch. 4.

open and fragmented, and even less stable and consistent, than those of the doctrinal framework itself.

There is a striking affinity between the feminist argument about the contours of the legal subject and that developed within critical legal theory such as that in the criminal law sphere. Consider for a moment the standard conceptualisation of the responsible subject in criminal law, as encapsulated within H. L. A. Hart's influential theory.[24] The subject who is fairly held accountable for his actions is one who has standard cognitive and volitional capacities: only if he understands the nature of his action, and had a fair opportunity to act otherwise than he did, will it be appropriate to hold him responsible for it. In terms of legal doctrine, this theory issues in a paradigm conception of fault or "*mens rea*" as intention or subjective recklessness: choosing to do an act or bring about a consequence in so far as it is within your power to do so, or acting in awareness of the likely consequences of your actions. To the extent that objective forms of liability can be accommodated on this view, it is on the basis that the subject's normal capacities imply that he could have reached a "reasonable" standard of care of behaviour had he chosen to do so. The contortions undertaken by both judges and scholars to accommodate strict and more fully objective standards of liability within this essentially liberal account have been analysed at length elsewhere, and I shall not consider them here.[25] What I shall do is to sketch an influential critique—that of Alan Norrie—and to trace its continuities with the feminist argument that the legal subject is essentially male.

Norrie's argument is basically this.[26] The dominant mode of attributing responsibility in criminal law constructs the subject of criminalisation as an abstract individual judged outwith the broad parameters of his social context. The conditions of responsibility which legitimate the state's coercive response are essentially factual ones having to do with mental states contemporaneous with the commission of the offence. By decontextualising the judging process in this way, criminal law attempts to ensure its own legitimacy by insisting that it ascribes responsibility on fair terms, as is required by the punitive nature of its response, the general value ascribed to autonomy in liberal society, and the quasi-moral mode of judgment employed by criminalisation.[27] This decontextualised and formalised

---

[24] Hart (1968).

[25] See for example Lacey and Wells (1998), Ch. 1; Lacey (1985); Wells (1982).

[26] What follows is a schematic reconstruction of the argument of Norrie (1993a).

[27] I leave aside here the fact that criminal law often operates more as a bureaucratic/administrative system than as a quasi-moral one. I think that the diversity of modes of

mode of attribution serves to keep out of the courtroom the muddy-
ing social and political issues which are in fact deeply implicated in a
broader understanding of how behaviour comes to be defined as
criminal: it keeps out of sight those facts which produce the embarrassing truth that criminalising power in fact disciplines a sector of the
population vividly marked by socio-economic status, by race or
ethnicity, and by sex. It constructs legal justice, in other words, in a
way which keeps it relatively insulated from broader notions of social
justice.

But the strategy is highly unstable. This is because the imperative
for criminal law to legitimate itself within a liberal framework constantly leads to doctrinal concessions which in fact reveal the broader
relevance of the subject's social context.[28] For example, the defences
of necessity, provocation, self-defence or duress shift the time-frame
of the law's inquiry away from the moment of the commission of the
"*actus reus*" to encompass as relevant a wider set of antecedents.[29]
Debates about "reasonableness" inevitably raise ethical and political
questions. And at the sentencing stage, the defendant's action is even
more fully contextualised, with the production of social inquiry
reports which, even within a "just deserts" approach to punishment,
envisage a degree of discretionary individualisation—of particular
rather than standardised justice—which is at odds with paradigm legal
method.[30] Of course, within doctrine, criminal law has a number of
strategies geared to containing these concessions within narrow limits—for example by constructing defences as excuses which go to
"factual" aspects of the defendant's responsibility rather than as justi-
fications which embody a more "at large" questioning of the actual
standard being applied.[31] But the fluidity of the conceptual categories
of legal doctrine which these "exceptional" concessions reveal itself
unsettles the commonsensical givenness of the "normal" mode of
attributing responsibility. The careful delineation of the departures of
legal doctrine from its own standard method is therefore an effective
critical strategy for exposing the politics of criminal law.

It should be fairly obvious even from this brief sketch that there
are strong continuities between this critique of the contours of the

criminalisation in fact adds strength to the argument which follows, but it complicates it in
a way which reaches beyond the scope of this chapter. For further discussion see Farmer
(1997) Chs. 1, 2.

[28] Cf. the argument made by Naffine in the passage quoted above.
[29] Cf. Kelman (1981).
[30] Cf. the broader argument made by Daly (1989).
[31] See for example Lacey and Wells (1998) Chapter 1.II.d. and 3.II.f.

subject of criminal law and the feminist argument about the masculinity of the legal subject.[32] A central aspect of the argument in both difference feminism and critical criminal law is a strategy of what we might call recontextualisation *as critique*. In Norrie's account, subjects of criminalisation are recontextualised within a political and socio-economic world whose conditions help to explain the substantially different chances which differently situated subjects have to keep within the norms of criminal law as interpreted by enforcement agencies.[33] This argument is used in turn to undermine the supposed legitimacy of liberal systems of criminal law, and to reveal the ideological operations within doctrine which sustain that image of legitimacy. Feminist theory also recontextualises the subject—for example the woman who has killed her husband within the long-term context of his violence towards her, or within more general gendered imbalances of power. And this is used as a discursive strategy to reveal the substantive sexual injustice of the application of the criminal law's usually circumscribed focus. By seeing how criminal law excludes certain features of context which are extra-legally crucial to the shape of women's lives, we can reveal how women (and indeed non-"normally" situated men) are silenced. For they are made to tell their stories within a framework which, by assuming a particular image of "normal" subjecthood, systematically excludes certain features of experience and keeps difficult political issues about imbalances of power out of the courtroom.[34] This is an argument which of course reveals law's method not so much as a decontextualisation but rather as itself a specific and politically problematic contextualisation: abstraction is an ideology as much as a fact, and what matters is what gets abstracted and how.

[32] This is not to say, however, that critical criminal lawyers have been quick to make the connection. My own book on punishment, (Lacey 1988) which employs a similar argument about liberal individualism in a critical analysis of theories of punishment, is one whose pages are peopled by feminine pronouns but not by embodied women, whose substantive voices are perhaps all the more firmly silenced through the grammatical tokens which I used. In the index of Norrie's book we find white collar crime but not women; serial murder, but not sex; jack the ripper, but not gender (Norrie 1993a).

[33] These should be broadly understood to include not only official agencies such as police and courts but also, for example, news media and ordinary citizens, whose reports to the police are the main initiators of the criminal process.

[34] On this point, see Chapter 4.

Contexualisation as feminist strategy

In some of its forms, however, the feminist argument builds on its critical recontextualisation to make a further and significantly different set of normative and strategic points. It asserts that the recognition and realisation of intersubjectivity and connection—what we might call the relational aspect of subjectivity—has itself been of greater importance in women's than in men's lives. Furthermore, it has been marked as feminine in our culture and correspondingly disvalued. One important source of this kind of argument is Carol Gilligan's book *In a Different Voice*,[35] which drew a distinction between an individualistic, rights or justice-based mode of constructing moral questions and a holistic, responsibility-based, relational or caring model. Debate has raged about how we should understand Gilligan's association of the caring voice with women: whether this is a replay of damaging gender essentialism; whether the caring voice is, rather than something to be valued and celebrated, in fact the voice of the oppressed; and what Gilligan's argument implies for the critique and reconstruction of law and legal method. Here I merely want to point out the way in which arguments like Gilligan's have sometimes been taken to provide an ethical mandate for a set of institutional *strategies* which seek to relocate the legal subject within a broader bodily, psychological and relational context. This has taken the well-known shape, for example, of arguments for specific defences such as that based on pre-menstrual syndrome or battered women's syndrome, or, perhaps less problematically, the reconstruction of existing defences such as provocation, diminished responsibility or self-defence in terms which take account of broader features of a woman's situation which are relevant to the behaviour in question.[36] I want to consider this feminist leaning towards strategies of contextualisation, which I think entails certain confusions and complexities which have sometimes gone unnoticed.

What are we to make of the idea that a legal method which contextualised subjects more broadly—attending to their bodies, their relationships and responsibilities—would in itself be favourable to women?[37] Clearly, the question of how we recognise and accommodate all subjects' interdependence, how we recognise the relational,

[35] Gilligan (1982): for critical discussion, see Benhabib (1992a) Chs. 5, 6; Larrabee (ed.) (1993); Frug (1992) Ch. 3.
[36] O'Donovan (1991); McColgan (1993).
[37] Cf. Minow (1987); Minow and Spelman (1990).

embodied and affective aspects of lived experience within institutions whose method is to judge, fix, categorise (indeed whether these features of legal method could go unreconstructed) is crucially important. But the notion that we could make any progress to its solution by an introduction of increased "contextualisation" of the conceptual framework of legal subjecthood strikes me as somewhat naive.[38] For the idea that contextualisation within a broader set of relationships could in itself be progressive seems to depend on the idea that the broader social relationships within which we might locate a reconceptualised legal subject (for example by modifying rules of evidence to encompass the subject's location within the practices of the family, of the labour market, of the political sphere) and the non-legal discourses of femininity and masculinity which might thereby be invoked, can be assumed, on average, to be less excluding of women, less limiting and less strongly marked by stereotyped assumptions about sex difference than are legal discourse and legal practice. It assumes, in other words, that these other social practices are less implicated in the cultural production of a particular masculinity and femininity than is law.

It may well be that local instances afford opportunities of progressive recontextualisation. The weakening of the immediacy requirement in self-defence cases strikes me as one possible example, although unless carefully handled it might well play into the interests of the stronger rather than the weaker party in any conflict. But other instances may rather reproduce and indeed institutionalise the assumptions about femininity and masculinity which we want to question. Is it appropriate, for example, to allow a man accused of rape to contextualise his misrecognition of the woman's "no" as "yes" within the cultural context of prevailing ideas about women's sexuality? Another troubling example is the development of the notion of "battered women's syndrome", which contextualises the effects of violence to women within what amounts to a psychiatric pathology which can be comprehended by the diminished responsibility defence.[39] As an individual strategy for a defence lawyer concerned to protect to the best possible degree her or his client's interests, this is of course impeccable. But our diagnosis of the broader discursive implications of what is effectively a deepening construction of diminished responsibility as the feminine and of provocation as the masculine defence must be more ambiguous.

---

[38] I have discussed this point in more detail in Chapter 5.
[39] As argued for example in the case of *Ahluwalia* [1992] 4 All ER 889.

The politics of contextualisation, then, cannot be assumed to go in one direction only. Indeed, as experience with more radical changes such as those represented by institutions of informal justice and mediation has shown, dispute-resolving frameworks which seek to emphasise and build upon pre-existing relationships and responsibilities sometimes reproduce the power relationships with which the parties arrive at the decision-making forum even more starkly than do more formal arrangements.[40] Before we assert the value of contextualising the doctrinal subject in terms of her being and her relating rather than of her having certain powers or capacities, therefore, we need to think about the broader assumptions which will inform the ensuing judgements about who we are and how we live. For it is these assumptions which will determine how real people—with differently sexed bodies, of different races, ages, religions, nationalities, with different sexual orientations—will be inserted into the legal framework. We need to focus not just on the structure of legal doctrine but on criminalisation, understood as a broad social practice whose shape is determined in many places other than legislatures or indeed courtrooms.[41] For the patterns which mark the path of criminalising power are informed not just by assumptions about what *capacities* characterise a "normal" subject but also about what kinds of characteristics and ways of life are acceptable, both at large, and in relation to people with particular kinds of bodies. As soon as we begin to think, for example, about how people are selected for prosecution, or what form of sentence is selected for particular types of offender, we have to acknowledge that the sum effect of criminalisation, far from being to judge abstract legal subjects, is to target problem populations, to label suspect communities, to stigmatise certain forms of relationship, to disqualify certain ways of life. We have tended to lose sight of real ways in which criminal justice, among other legal practices, *already* contextualises its subjects and indeed instantiates something approaching relational ethic—often in ways which are oppressive to women among others.[42] The strategy of recontextualisation, in other words, could only promise progress if it were preceded by a more differentiated and inclusive acceptance of varying ways of life.

[40] For critical analysis of the contextualising aspects of institutions of informal justice, see Abel (ed.) (1982); Matthews (ed.) (1988); Santos (ed.) (1992). For further discussion see also Chapter 5 and 8.

[41] For examples of feminist research on broad practices of criminalisation, see Eaton (1986); Allen (1987); Carlen (1983).

[42] For a persuasive analysis along these lines, see Daly (1989).

This argument entails that the primary focus of feminist critique has to be not legal doctrine or law at all but rather the broader assumptions about masculinity and femininity which have marked the insertion of sexed bodies into the doctrinal framework. Focusing for a moment on those broader assumptions, it seems to me that there has been a tendency in feminist work to lose sight of the contradictions which we know to characterise prevailing views about women and men, and to narrate legal discourses of subjectivity as ones of seamless sexism which construe men as the active, rational, responsible subjects and women as passive, emotional and victimised. In other words, we have been too ready to map our argument about the gendered conceptualisation of legal subjectivity onto what is really a broader critical analysis of legal and social discourse.[43] Of course, these images are not without their doctrinal confirmations.[44] I cannot resist the temptation to allude to my favourite legislative instance: the definition of incest, which penalises a man for "having" sexual intercourse with one of his female relatives and a woman for "permitting" (graciously, one presumes) one of her male relatives "to have" intercourse with her.[45] But once we focus on the broader assumptions about femininity and masculinity which inform judicial discourse, it becomes apparent that one of our main critical tools is feminist rhetoric. And at a rhetorical level, the recapitulation of discourses of victimised and passive feminine identity is ultimately disempowering. It is a much more effective strategy to instance, with as much irreverent humour as possible, the extraordinary contradictions in the ways in which legal discourse constructs men and women, femininity and masculinity, in the process of "applying the law to the facts"—placing real women and men within doctrinal categories which themselves turn out to be extraordinarily little constrained by the gendered assumptions which have been argued to shape them. We could recall, for example, that the powerful and sexually aggressive man who rapes a woman is also the vulnerable creature who is so susceptible to the influence of feminine wiles that he loses control of his volitional capacities at the mere sight of a woman out on her own at night, and who is so far from being in command of his cognitive capacities that he sometimes cannot tell the difference between that apparently rather straightforward dichotomy, yes and

---

[43] The movement between these two levels of analysis is exemplified by the passage by Naffine quoted above.

[44] We can take many examples from Kennedy (1992).

[45] Sexual Offences Act 1956, ss 10, 11.

no. Conversely the passive female victim of men's sexual aggression is equally the calculating seductress, the deceptive woman; the pathologised "single mother" whom we have heard so much about recently is equally that paragon of rationality who controls even her reproductive faculties so as to maximise her chances of council housing. One of the avoidable double binds that we have sometimes been caught in, then, is a reassertion of the very stereotypes we are challenging. By getting seduced by the explanatory power of our doctrinal critique, and in our enthusiasm to deconstruct the oppositions which it has exposed, we see them where they may already have been dislodged; we construct them as more seamless than they are. We confirm the stories we say legal doctrine has told, and even begin to believe that they are as powerful as the most sexist man could wish.

RECONCEIVING FEMINIST POLITICS

A hierarchy of differences?

I now want to to consider the continuities between difference feminism and other critical positions which interpret the legal subject as marked not only by sex but also by other axes of social differentiation such as class and race.[46] Among these various socially important and ethically problematic "differences", should that based on sex be accorded any particular status? This may seem an old-fashioned question. After all, the association of non-standard subjects with the body, with affectivity and with the private can easily be extended beyond the category of sex. For example, recent work on post-colonialism suggests that the role of the "racial" other in giving back its identity to the white subject is structurally similar to that of woman in relation to man.[47] The most obvious way to construe the broad critical project is therefore as one which seeks to expose all the varied politically problematic axes of differentiation which mark the construction of the legal practices. It is a project which will raise many different questions and which may entail different sets of critical strategies. But it does not imply a need to accord priority to any one among relevant differences.[48]

[46] One way of reading Norrie's argument, of course, is as a construction of the criminal legal subject as marked by class.

[47] In the legal sphere, see Fitzpatrick (1992a), (1995b).

[48] The identification of just what those "other" differences are requires substantial argument. For the purposes of this chapter, I shall simply assume that class, race or ethnicity and

The idea that sex difference is *the* basic difference has, of course, played a role in what has been known as radical or cultural feminism, in much the same way as class difference has had theoretical and political primacy in marxist thought.[49] But in recent feminist theory there has emerged a new set of arguments which appear to suggest a primacy—or at least a particular status—for sex difference. The arguments are based on a complex and sometimes unpalatable cocktail of psychoanalysis and deconstruction. I shall try to reconstruct this cocktail in a simplified way—something which I think can be done without much violence to its substance and with some improvement to its flavour. I want to give it some attention, because I think it represents us with the recurring dilemma about sexual essentialism which has plagued radical feminism and which continues, as I have argued, to trouble "difference" feminism. This new development is of particular concern because it is voiced by some of the most intellectually sophisticated and rhetorically gifted exponents of contemporary legal feminism.

The argument finds its most vivid and articulate expression in the work of Drucilla Cornell.[50] It takes off from a standard psychoanalytic account of the early Oedipal drama, and in particular the child's separation from its mother, which structures the acquisition of its identity in a sexually differentiated way. In gaining its own identity, a child also experiences a loss of connection. The male child will react to his loss by taking comfort in his possession of the penis, which promises to "bring the mother back" because it is the means of satisfying her desire. The female child, on the other hand, has no such strategy available to her.[51] This basic story is given a distinctive

---

sexual orientation are obvious candidates for inclusion. For an excellent discussion of the challenge posed by this kind of integrated approach, see Harris (1990). For useful general discussion of problems of essentialism in social theory, see Fuss (1989), and Spelman (1989).

[49] For further discussion see Jaggar (1983) Chs. 5, 9.

[50] Cornell (1991), (1992), (1993). Cornell's work is also discussed in Chapters 4–6.

[51] Although, as feminist critics and psychoanalysts have pointed out, the moment of separation itself has a different configuration for the female child. Her acquisition of identity is in relation to a subject to whom she is in an important respect similar—thus the need for differentiation, and the trauma it entails, may well be less acute. In different veins, see Nancy Chodorow (1978) (whose object-relations theory is the subject of critique in Cornell (1991) at pp. 50–51); Mitchell (1974); Mitchell and Rose (1982). Cf. Irigaray (1994) at p. 18: "Woman's subjective identity is not at all the same as a man's. She does not have to distance herself from her mother as he does—by a yes but especially a no, a near or a far, an inside opposed to an outside—to discover her sex. She is faced with a different problem entirely. She must be able to identify with her mother as a woman to realise her own sexuality. But her mother is the same as she. She cannot reduce or manipulate her as an object in the way

twist by Lacan's reinterpretation of Freud. In Lacanian thought, the subject's birth is marked by its acceptance of the Law of the Father through its entry into the symbolic order of language. Whilst the male child's desire for the mother is repressed and becomes part of the unspeakable Real, language becomes the medium through which he seeks symbols to express and fulfill that repressed desire. And because language attempts to fill the lack experienced on the birth of the subject, the sexual differentiation implicit in children's acquisition of identity becomes encoded in the role of the phallus as the "transcendental signifier" which underpins the construction of meaning. It is the metaphor for what could bring the mother back, and hence the ultimate symbol for the power of the word. This is what is meant by the claim that language is "phallogocentric".

Lacan insists that the penis and the phallus are not the same—the first belongs to the imaginary order, the second to the symbolic. But in the masculine imagination, the operative fantasy is that having the penis is the same as having the phallus: hence language itself is a symbolic order in which the possessor of the phallus is subject and she who does not possess the phallus is defined in terms of lack. Furthermore, this castrated other—Irigaray's "sex which is not one"[52]—has a special relationship to the pre-linguistic fantasy world. For the realms of fantasy and desire which are repressed on the entry into language are associated with the feminine, which is not properly a subject of the symbolic order; conversely the symbolic order is associated with the masculine. As Cornell puts it,

> "Woman is assimilated as the necessary basis for the illusion of the ego's self-sufficiency.[53]

> Women can appropriate the phallus—and who better to know how this is done than a woman law professor—but the phallus remains the very symbol of potency and of power. Put simply, to enter into the masculine world, women must take up the masculine position".[54]

When I attempted—in a practical deconstruction of the public/private distinction—to sketch this theory over breakfast one morning, my husband, after listening patiently, replied: "Only a man

a little boy or a man does". See also Irigaray (1992) pp. 167, 212–13. For further discussion of psychoanalysis and feminist legal theory, see Chapters 4 and 5.

[52] Irigaray (1985b); Irigaray's title also plays on the idea that the feminine genre is less implicated in the illusion of unitary identity and self-sufficiency than is the masculine.

[53] Cornell (1992) p. 177.

[54] Cornell (1992) p. 175.

could have thought such a theory up (as it were)". His wry turn of phrase, funnily enough, expresses exactly why Lacan has had such a fascination for feminists. For Cornell's interpretation of Lacan fixes precisely upon the sense in which the phallus is *thought* up. Since Lacan affirms that the equation of the penis and the phallus is imaginary, it is merely a metaphor for what the mother desires. The masculine privilege which Lacan argues to be encoded in language is based on a fantasy—albeit a fantasy which has acquired a social "reality". As long as we recognise the susceptibility of language to reinterpretation, the possibility of its imaginative reconstruction, we can begin, linguistically, to change the metaphor, to displace the association, and to deflate the currency (or perhaps the erection) of the male subject of language. The specifically feminist deployment of this argument therefore locates feminist politics primarily at the level of linguistic reconstruction: political action may itself be constituted by rhetorical strategies.

Thus even if linguistic structures are marked by sexually specific dynamics, those structures are not fixed, and their concepts can be re-imagined, reconstructed. Since linguistic signs always get their meaning by reference to and through differentiation from other signs, that meaning is never closed: language has an irreducibly performative aspect. In any linguistic utterance there is an implicit reference both to what is unspoken and to what might have been spoken, and this gives rise to what Cornell calls the "utopian moment" in the deconstruction which she derives from the philosophy of Jacques Derrida.[55] Far from simply representing or reflecting the world in an unproblematic way, language can never completely capture lived (or psychic) experience: all linguistic usage is in a sense metaphorical, and meaning is constructed by means of a dynamic process of deferral and differentiation evoked by the term "*différance*". The feminist project, then, is the gradual construction or recovery in language of a specifically feminine imaginary which can end women's silence or exclusion from audible speech. In Cornell's words, this is a project of "recollective imagination" geared to the writing of a "new choreography of sexual difference": the recovery of repressed or unheard meanings within institutional speech such as legal discourse.[56] It is aimed at opening up our sense of the contingency of current legal arrangements: its intention is to locate gaps and spaces within which

[55] For Derrida's own reflections on law, see Derrida (1992).
[56] For an instance of a similar method applied to the recovery of forgotten legal histories, see Goodrich (1993b).

meanings sympathetic to currently subordinated ways of life can gain an institutional foothold.

I want to question certain aspects of Cornell's reliance on Lacanian psychoanalysis by tracing some of its implications for the effectiveness of the linguistic strategies for which she argues. Without feeling qualified to add much to the extensive feminist literature on the topic, I am unconvinced that Lacan's account of the sexual structure of the originary drama can be rescued for feminist use. For the story of the dynamics of the acquisition of identity are told from a male point of view, in the sense that it is the boy's trauma which determines the way in which that trauma is fixed in language and psychically managed in the public world.[57] In a sense, Lacan's theory is simply a replay of the standard sexist account of the public/private distinction, of masculinity and femininity, of reason and emotion. Far from needing sophisticated psychoanalytic theories to explain to us how to think beyond the phallic framework, it seems to me that we already do so.[58] Indeed the phallus is a dangerous toy for contemporary feminism. We may take comfort, however, in the thought that this particular toy is much like a balloon: if we simply let it go, its power is lost; it is automatically deflated. If any feminist engagement with this aspect of Lacan's work is called for, it is probably one of satire: a strategy of talking the phallus down, like a balloon, by sending it up.[59]

I want to make two specific points about the political implications of a feminist espousal of the Lacanian view of language. First, it is easily read (even if this is a misreading) as an alliance which entails the privileging of sexual differentiation over other axes of social oppression. It may therefore inhibit the development of our understanding of how those different "othernesses" intersect and affect one another—the development, in other words, of an integrated critique which acknowledges the marginalisation of dialects other than the feminine in prevailing discursive practices. And in weakening those links, it may reinforce the hold of the double bind of essentialism. For

[57] Similar points are made by some of the critics cited at n. 51.

[58] One excellent example is provided by the strategies against rape canvassed by Marcus (1992). These include articulating the insight of "the fragility of erections and the vulnerability of male genitalia" (p.400) (!). Feminist satire provides yet another instance.

[59] Cornell would certainly reject this interpretation of Lacan. She insists that we can read him historically, and that we should recognise that his account of sexual difference is specific to the "era of the ego"—i.e. modernity. This seems unconvincing, given that sexual difference also characterised the ancient societies whose dialogic philosophical method it is currently fashionable to celebrate as a style less implicated in the idea of self-identity.

this double bind is, I would argue, more threatening to feminism
than to other critical positions, because the idea of sex difference as
fixed or structural is still seen as more plausible than the analogous
arguments in relation to class, race or even sexual orientation. Whilst
the Lacanian account in principle interprets sex difference as a construct, it is a construct which is so basic, so deeply embedded in the
structures of identity-acquisition and language, that it may well seem
the functional equivalent of an "essential" difference. Secondly, it
seems to me that, at a rhetorical level, the assumption of the power
of the phallus and the diagnosis of femininity as, in essence, a condition of pathology—of abnormality, abjection, and silence—echoes
through and taints many of the arguments of and images deployed by
this kind of feminist critique, as it is relentlessly mapped back on to
women's speaking bodies. This is particularly so in the case of some
of Irigaray's recent work, as I shall try to illustrate in the final section
of this chapter.

But is the psychoanalytic theory detachable from the rest of
Cornell's account?[60] Her really important insight, it seems to me, is
her location of a utopian moment within deconstruction.[61]
Certainly, this depends on the assumption that configurations of
power become reflected in linguistic structures, thus depriving
women (among others) of access to an authentic or audible means of
expression in the public world. This would explain the experience
vividly reproduced in female ethnographies of being silenced, of the
marginalisation of women's speech in a myriad institutional contexts,
including the legal. But we need hardly look to Lacan for the insight
that language is gendered. We can find plenty of explications of the
power structures of language, in socio-linguistics for example, and in
other disciplines which attempt to develop more concrete institutional accounts of how social practices—language among them—
come to reflect and reproduce prevailing frameworks of power.[62] We
should not turn our back on these broader intellectual resources,
which may be less resonant with a closed and structural view of the
gender of language—a view belied by a host of textual and oral man-

[60] I am tempted to frame this question in terms of whether Cornell's argument can be
detached from the phallus without being castrated in the process. But this, of course, would
be to replay the very assumption which I am criticising: that lack of the phallus necessarily
implies lack of power.

[61] I shall leave aside the further question of whether Cornell needs a specifically
Derridean theoretical framework to effect the reconstructive projects which she recom-
mends.

[62] See for example Cameron (1985), and (ed.) (1990).

ifestations challenging the gender hierarchy; feminist scholarship to name but one. Cornell's contribution is in suggesting how we may think beyond language marked by power. She has developed a persuasive critical analysis of law's mode of fixing meanings, categories, identities, and of the fragility and instability of this mode. But when, for example, she constructs an argument for encompassing discrimination against homosexuals within the concept of sex discrimination, she needs not the phallus but the merely a simpler conceptual toy. This is the idea of gender—including sexual orientation—as social construct yet as powerful determinant of the realities of men's and women's lives.[63] What Cornell's account does lack, however, is an institutional theory capable of illuminating the circumstances in which particular rhetorical strategies are likely to be effective rather than ineffective or even dangerous. If rhetoric is a form of political action, then some assessment of the political implications of that rhetoric must form a part of the theory which underlies it.[64]

I should conclude this section by emphasising that I do not meant to imply that no toys from the psychoanalytic playbox are relevant to feminism. For example, the notion of repression, particularly as applied to affectivity and the body, and the split subjectivity which this entails, strike me as important, as does the idea that the rhetorical power of language is sometimes to be explained in terms of its subliminal appeal to psychic needs which cannot directly be recovered in language.[65] But these ideas need not be based on a sexually invariant and primarily sexual originary story—a story which threatens broader alliances which we have both intellectual and political reason for keeping intact.

Politics, rhetoric and misrecognition

I want, finally, to give a particular illustration of the pitfalls of versions of difference feminism which accord a priority to sexual difference. I argued earlier that the simple inference from theory to practice implicit in liberal feminism was rendered problematic by the transition to more complex, discourse-oriented interpretations; and,

[63] See Cornell (1993) Ch. 6. One way of explaining the appeal of psychoanalysis for feminism is precisely its promise to answer the question of *why* gender hierarchy has been so consistently mapped onto sexed bodies (see n. 23).

[64] I sketch a framework for such assessments in Chapter 8.

[65] For an imaginative use of the idea of repression in critical legal analysis, see Goodrich (1994). The subliminal power of "political signifiers" is discussed in Chapter 5.

secondly, that the feminist commitment to translating theoretical analysis into political practice has sometimes led to unjustified inferences from theory to practice. Put simply, difference feminism has issued in a set of *rhetorical* strategies of critique which are themselves a form of political practice. Yet there is a constant danger they will be misrecognised as prescribing an instrumental political practice—and that feminist strategies may reinscribe discourses such as the legal and legally relevant with images of woman which perpetuate rather than challenge stereotyped and disempowering notions of the feminine. In some sense these difference feminisms are committed to reasserting the symmetry of male and female subjecthood—a "strange" symmetry based upon the recognition of different but equally worthy forms of human subjectivity, and one in which the idea of neutrality can perhaps be resurrected in a sense which would not repress but respect difference.[66] Can they be any more successful in escaping conventional stereotypes than the policy of contextualisation which I have already criticised?

A particularly imaginative example of the discursive politics intrinsic to difference feminism is Luce Irigaray's distinctive *"écriture féminine"* which seeks to recover the repressed feminine, the unacknowledged body, and give them a place within language—albeit a language rather different from the analytic expressions of the symbolic order which generally characterise intellectual discourse. Irigaray's *"écriture féminine"* is self-consciously poetic and elliptical, often dialogic in form, and evocative rather than analytic in style.[67] It was therefore something of a surprise to many of her readers when she formulated an apparently institutional argument for special or sexuate rights. I want to focus on this aspect of Irigaray's work both because it is particularly susceptible of a very dangerous misreading and because it exemplifies the echoes of femininity as pathology which I identified as one of the dangers of the psychoanalytic framework which also informs her work.[68] I shall sketch her argument and

[66] For example, Irigaray (1992) argues that ethical relations between persons must be premised on the existence of two different genres of human subjectivity—the masculine and the feminine: only once women as well as men have access to a recognised culture which underpins their subject status can relations between the sexes amount to genuine reciprocity or intersubjectivity as distinct from object-relations based on the notion of the other as property: see also the quotation with which this chapter begins.

[67] Irigaray's distinctive style is perhaps most vividly exemplified in Irigaray (1991); see also Irigaray (1993b). It is interesting to draw an analogy with Richard Rorty's argument (1989) that the crucial political project of extending human empathy is often best effected by novels and poetry rather than by political and moral philosophy.

[68] This is not to imply that Irigaray is uncritical of Lacan: see n. 51.

then go on to ask two sets of questions about it: first, to what extent, judged as a rhetorical strategy of re-imagining the feminine, is it successful in evoking a powerful and different image of subjectivity? Secondly, how are we to interpret the fact that Irigaray's argument is couched in the language of institutional reform?

In *Thinking the Difference*—a set of essays originally written for meetings convened by the Italian Communist Party—Irigaray recapitulates a critique of the capacity-based and contractual notion of the subject as rights-bearer which we saw to be an important aspect of difference feminism:

> "Redefining the right to civil identity is one of the urgent tasks of our time, not only for the sake of living women and men, but for the sake of a possible future for the national and international community. Today, rights are increasing almost exclusively in the sphere of rights to ownership of property, benefits, various types of capital, etc. These new rights are greatly concerned with having (property) but little concerned with being(s)—women and men—and little with relationships amongst individuals based on this notion of free, responsible human identity.[69]

> As long as women have no civil identity of their own, it is to be expected, unfortunately, that they will conform to the only existing models, supposedly neutral, but in fact male. Hence the need to redefine the objective content of civil rights as they apply to men and women—since the neutral individual is nothing but a cultural fiction—and to attempt to establish the legal bases of possible reciprocity between the sexes".[70]

In imagining an ethical world which moves beyond liberal notions of neutrality, then, part of Irigaray's imaginative paintbox is a set of "special rights". These include the right to human dignity, which encompasses stopping the commercial use of womens' bodies and the right to valid representations of women in actions, words and images in all public places; and a right to human identity which encompasses the legal encodification of virginity as a component of female identity that is not reducible to money, and not cash-convertible by the family, the state or religious bodies.[71] They also include—less

[69] Irigaray, *Thinking the Difference* (1994) p. xvii. Irigaray's original title was *Le Temps de la Différence: Pour une révolution pacifique*.

[70] Irigaray (1994) p. 75.

[71] Irigaray (1993a) p. 86–7. It is interesting to note the resonance between Irigaray's specification of the right to dignity and Catharine MacKinnon's emphasis on pornography as a fundamental means of women's subordination: see MacKinnon (1989) Ch. 11. For critical comment see Frazer and Lacey (1993) pp. 92–5. Like MacKinnon's and Andrea Dworkin's

problematically, I think—the right to equivalence in systems of exchange such as the linguistic, and representation in equal numbers in all civil and religious decision-making bodies.[72]

Irigaray's assertion of these special rights or women's laws moves between two very different voices or styles.[73] First is an evidently imaginary and speculative voice. Examples include her injunction to "question the origins of the law currently in force, particularly in relation to the time when women really were civil persons, a time misleadingly termed Prehistory".[74] The speculative voice is also expressed in her depiction of a past female law as characterised by features such as respect for local places and divinities, a higher morality based upon love and peace, and "a community of all members of humankind".[75] At other moments she borrows the language of an institutional programme for legal and political reform. In response to an interviewer's question about her interest in law, she replies:

> "Why deal with legal questions more concretely? Because . . . I have regularly worked with women or groups of women who belong to liberation movements, and in these I've observed problems or impasses that can't be resolved except through the establishment of an equitable legal system for both sexes".[76]

And speaking of one particular problem—that of incest—she argues:

> "Faced by [this form] of men's lack of civility . . . practising real incest within the family—legal recourse is necessary. I propose that the right to virginity as belonging to the girl, and not to her father, brother or future husband, should be enshrined in law. In other words, I think that the right to virginity should be part of girls' civil identity as a right to respect for their physical and moral integrity".[77]

---

anti-pornography ordinance, Irigaray's argument envisages the civil rather than the penal enforcement of rights in this area.

[72] Irigaray (1993a) p. 89.

[73] For a thoughtful meditation on Irigaray's apparently contrasting projects, see Pottage (1994).

[74] Irigaray (1993a) p. 92.

[75] Irigaray (1993a) p. 90. The reference to community is problematic given the logic of identity built into many understandings of community: see Benhabib (1992a); Young (1990b) Chs. 4, 6; and Ch. 5.

[76] Irigaray (1993a) p. 82.

[77] Irigaray (1993a) p. 74; cf. (1994) p. xvi: "civil law must be changed to give both sexes their identities as citizens"; see also p. 60. In somewhat more philosophical mode, see also Irigaray (1992) pp. 18–19; 42–3; 90–100; 205–10.

What should we make of Irigaray's argument as a feminist politics? It may be that her movement between speculative and institutional languages is itself a rhetorical strategy designed to underline the point that current constructions of the legal are contingent—could be otherwise than they are. And perhaps there is no real danger that her proposals will be read at their institutional face value. But even judged as a rhetorical strategy, it is worth noting that many of the images which she invokes—virginity, motherhood, peace, the integrity of the planet and women's special feeling for this—resonate with conventional stereotypes of femininity, and would, if institutionalised in public speech as much as in law, have the effect of fixing women within identities which it is surely Irigaray's political strategy to question and unsettle. Indeed some of her comments are virtually indistinguishable from the images of femininity in the most sexist discourse:

> "Men are uncivil as a result of too many rights and too few duties, and women as a result of too few rights and too many duties, for which they compensate by impulsiveness and subjectivity without social bounds, in the form of either persistent childish behaviour or maternal authoritarianism extending into the social sphere".[78]

I am inclined to regard this as an almost compulsive repetition of the notion of femininity as a condition of disorder, abnormality and pathology which is embodied in Lacanian psychoanalysis. It is a condition which Irigaray's own lyrical meditations and evocations in her *ecriture feminine* serve practically and concretely to undermine.[79] Yet its reiteration in aspects of her argument for civil rights can hardly be doubted to have adverse rhetorical effects from a feminist point of view. Irigaray's defenders have been quick to assert that hers is "no separatist politics".[80] But as a woman who hates housework, has no nostalgia for virginity, is not a (biological) mother, and who would like to be able to behave impulsively without being accused of being "a typical woman", I find it hard to identify with a politics whose central components include rights "to virginity, motherhood by choice, preferential guardianship of children and caring for the

---

[78] Irigaray (1994) p. 78: see also her comment on p. 82 about women's lack of public responsibilities leaving us (significantly, she says "them") "mired in instability, dissatisfaction, criticism".

[79] Indeed this discourse of Irigaray's tempts me to think that she has not learned the lesson she attributes, beautifully, to Nietzsche: "when the other does not hear you it is better to be silent. By doing violence to the ear, one loses the music": Irigaray (1991) p. 39.

[80] Spivak (1992) pp. 74–5.

home".[81] Whilst it is true that Irigaray is most easily (mis)taken for an essentialist when her readers ignore the "aggressive role of rhetoricity in her prose", her framing of that rhetoric within a language of institutional reform seems to come so close to rewriting woman as other *as defined in dominant discourse* that one needs to be a highly qualified philosopher to see the difference. A rhetoric which calls for such close reading can hardly count as an effective contribution to feminist politics.

There is, however, a really important issue underlying Irigaray's argument for special rights. This is the claim that it is not merely the substance but rather the very structure of civil rights which needs to be reconstructed.[82] In Irigaray's view, the questions of form and substance are inextricably linked. The core of her argument is that rights need to be reconstructed so as to recognise not just object or property relations but also intransitive relations between different kinds of subjects—a genuine intersubjectivity which moves between, and which can only be premised on the mutual recognition of the existence of, (at least?) two irreducibly different genres. This point appears to speak to the form of rights, but in the distinctive configuration of her argument it also entails a separation of the subject matter of rights according to the specificities of two sexually differentiated cultures or ways of life. Only if the substantive interests, concerns and values appropriate to feminine culture are instantiated juridically can the promise of relational and intersubjective as opposed to competitive and proprietary legal and ethical relations be realised.

Two interesting interpretive questions may be raised about Irigaray's argument. First, I have suggested that her delineation of the content of some of the special rights for women recapitulates stereotyped and disempowering visions of femininity, and fixes women within "a feminine culture" as valued and defined by men in a heterosexist world. To the extent that this critique is persuasive, can Irigaray's argument about substance—about feminine culture—either be detached from the argument about the form of rights, or reimagined in a way which is both less stereotypical and which avoids

---

[81] Irigaray (1994) p. 81. Some aspects of Irigaray's argument—for example that on virginity—also suggest a lack of familiarity both with legal reforms already widely effected and with the socio-legal insight that legislative inscription is far from being the same as practical instantiation.

[82] This argument is most fully developed in *J'aime a toi* (1992), a book whose title evokes the intransitivity of genuinely ethical relations which are premised on the recognition of irreducibly different being(s). I analyse this aspect of Irigaray's position more closely in Chapter 8.

the obvious problem of fixing women and men within particular sexed identities? Secondly, is it possible to escape the essentialist resonance of Irigaray's argument, and all the problems which this entails, by re-reading her analysis of the role of sexual difference as a metaphor for difference more generally—for example, for difference based on race or sexual orientation? If the liberating power of her theory is its capacity to escape the imperialistic illusion of self-identity and to express the imperative of attention to difference—an insight encapsulated in the idea that " *'Je suis sexué(e)" implique 'je ne suis pas tout(e)' "*—can it be re-read as entailing that, for example, "I am white" also implies "I am not everything"?[83] If the appeal of her ideas lies in their capacity to address the issue which I raised in my earlier discussion of criminalisation—that of how we should go about ensuring the acceptance of varying ways of life as a precondition for a meaningful politics of recontextualisation—then why should this accommodation of difference be confined to two distinctive cultures?

A number of difficulties immediately confront such an interpretation. The most obvious objections to it include the actual centrality of sexual difference to Irigaray's texts, and theoretical problems, given the structure of her argument, about the possibility of extending her analysis to differences which are not binary in the way in which she understands sexual difference to be. It is nonetheless, I would argue, in the possibility of such a re-interpretation that the full political potential of Irigaray's project might be fully imagined. Without such a re-reading, the expositional vividness of the particular content of her special rights overwhelms her subtler argument about their form. The composite argument therefore risks being read as an invitation to institutionalise stereotyped visions of the feminine within a conceptual form currently marked, as Irigaray herself recognises, by a property-based, competitive and individualistic view of the world. The having of rights is based on the having of capacities, and geared to entitlements to goods on a contractual model: the language of rights is quintessentially the masculine language of performance, measurement, control. Irigaray's comments on the need for rights to reflect "being" rather than "having", and on the relational aspects of rights *"entre nous"*, are suggestive: yet they become submerged in her discourses on the substance of special rights. A more radical project of conceptual reconstruction than she has so far attempted is implied by the broad framework of her argument.

[83] Irigaray (1992) p. 91.

In short, Irigaray is more persuasive in her poetic and speculative than in her political–institutional mode. In a sense her argument for special rights falls between two stools. Whereas Cornell, staying within the analytic mode, focuses to some extent on a concrete and detailed project of showing how the specificities of legal discourse can afford opportunities for questioning and reconstructing legal rules and categories along different lines, and whereas Irigaray's *écriture féminine* provides a powerful poetic source of the imagination of a differently configured world, Irigaray's argument for special rights provides neither a compelling image of difference nor a comprehensible political strategy.

IN CONCLUSION

Appropriately enough to a chapter which promised to glimpse the loosening of double binds, I must leave many threads untied. Some threads can, however, be drawn together. The "difference feminism" which I have described is premised on a complicated and differentiated view of the power of law: it acknowledges what Santos has usefully distinguished as the violent or coercive, the bureaucratic or regulatory, and the rhetorical or persuasive aspects of law's power.[84] Each of these aspects calls for critical analysis. And each engenders a different relation between theory and practice—or perhaps I should say, a different conception *of* political practice. Strategies which seek to mitigate the injustice of particular instances of law's coercive power as it applies to women will always be an important part of the feminist project, particularly for practitioners. But there is a need for realism about just how much can be changed by legal means. Furthermore, I have argued that it is only if we conceptualise the legal or the legally relevant in an inclusive way that we can come to a sensible appreciation of the real role of law in underpinning gender hierarchy. Ultimately, it is only by understanding at an institutional level how legal and other practices interact and sustain each other that we can make any realistic assessment of the scope for change.

The critical projects of exposing the gendered nature of law's power and of trying to imagine how this might be differently configured are of equal importance to feminist legal scholars. With the move in critical legal theory towards an understanding of law's

---

[84] Santos (1982).

discursive, rhetorical power, rhetorical counter-strategies have themselves been revealed as an important part of feminist politics. But they can only be effective if they are recognised as such, and not mistranslated directly into instrumental political and legal interventions which speak rather to the coercive or bureaucratic aspects of law's power.

Much work, practical and theoretical, analytical and imaginative, needs to be done if the notions of neutrality, rights, equality and justice are to be understood in their racially, sexually and otherwise oppressively patterned reality, and if they are to be reconstructed in a way which promises the genuine accommodation of different forms of life, different subjectivities. For feminism, there is always a deep pitfall to be avoided here. For without an elusive mix of courage and caution, of audacity and subtlety, it may be that in seeking to imagine difference, in pursuit of its ultimate inclusion or recognition, we may not so much make a difference, as reproduce, as it were, the same difference. In doing so, we inevitably lend weight to its misinterpretation as fixed. Only if we are constantly aware of this double pitfall will we have any hope of developing strategies for stepping around it.

The breadth of my frame has necessarily entailed a somewhat impressionistic tapestry. But I have taken my cue here from a very powerful female role model: George Eliot. In *The Mill on the Floss*, she explains how Mr. Tulliver's general sense of the "complicated, puzzling nature of human affairs" meshes with his apparently contradictory "tendency to act promptly under the influence of a strong feeling"—one of perhaps rather few composite dispositions which he might be taken to share with feminist legal theorists. George Eliot remarks: "I have observed that for getting a strong impression that a skein is tangled, there is nothing like snatching hastily at a single thread". Her observation tunes with a general point which I hope to have made: that in our diagnosis and analysis of double binds supposedly facing feminist thought, our tendency to focus on single threads, or groups of threads, rather than on the larger practices of which they are part, has sometimes accentuated our sense of impasse. And our narrow focus can blind us to larger problems which we may be creating in trying to loose a single strand which is invariably connected to others. It is an irony, given my theme, that the social conditions of Victorian England dictated that George Eliot had to assume the nominal subject position of a man in order publicly to address her readers. Yet, notwithstanding the masculine veil with which she wrapped, or perhaps pretended to wrap herself, we—women and men—now read her as a woman. This is, I suggest, a nice metaphor for the possibility of recognising the sexually differentiated positions which we occupy as social subjects without denying the power of a woman's voice.

8

Normative Reconstruction in Socio-Legal Theory

In this chapter, I address in greater depth an interesting and (in my view) salutary development in contemporary legal theory already mentioned in Chapter 5. This is the emergence of a distinctive concern for ethical questions, and a particular orientation towards those questions. Taking this issue up where Chapter 5 left it, I want to map out the implications of this revival for the relationship between a number of different enterprises in contemporary legal studies, paying particular attention to the contributions of feminist scholarship. I shall begin by sketching what I think this development signifies, and what I take the shape of its ethical orientation to be. I shall then go on to trace the relevance of the renewed and distinctive concern with ethical questions for socio-legal studies and for the relevance of socio-legal research to feminist and other critical legal theory. I shall do this by clarifying the relationship between a number of distinct yet overlapping theoretical tasks: the critique of existing legal and social arrangements; the imagination of different ethical values, relationships and institutions; and the design of political strategies which seek to change current legal-institutional arrangements. The idea of "normative reconstruction" attempts to capture something of each of these tasks, whilst leaving open the delineation of important differences between them.[1]

It will be useful to set out from a preliminary characterisation of the areas of scholarship relevant to my project. I shall take *critical legal*

[1] In using the term "reconstruction" I do not mean to imply any simple antinomy between reconstruction and deconstruction, but rather to play upon the ambiguity of "reconstruction" as between "rebuilding" and "reinterpretation". My argument assumes that critique is itself a form of political action, albeit not the *only* form of political action which is relevant within the academy (cf. Benhabib (1994a). I should also like to note certain unsatisfactory implications of the term "socio-legal", in particular its suggestion that its two constituent elements—the social and the legal—each constitutes a coherent and relatively discrete entity. The notions of both "socio-legal" and "law in context" seem to me at once to take the interpenetration of "context" and "law" insufficiently seriously, and to leave "law" unquestioned in its autonomy and power. For further discussion see Fitzpatrick (1995a).

theory to be that portion of normative legal theory which is specifically concerned to dig beneath the surface of legal doctrines and practices; to go beyond a project of explication and rationalisation and to interrogate the deeper political, historical and philosophical logics which underpin the power of law. Conceived in this way, critical legal theory encompasses a variety of traditions including marxist legal theory, American critical legal studies, feminist legal theory, critical race theory and post-modern jurisprudence. *Socio-legal studies* I take to be a similarly diverse body of scholarship which is united by two concerns. First, socio-legal scholarship locates legal practices within the context of the other social practices which constitute their immediate environment. Thus it comprehends a complex of administrative, commercial, economic, medical, psychiatric and other disciplinary practices, wherever they impinge upon or interact with law. Secondly, socio-legal studies subject legal practices to a (broadly speaking) empirical inquiry which scrutinises not merely the legal articulation of the relevant rules and processes but the meaning and effects of those rules and processes as interpreted and enforced, and as experienced by their subjects.

This characterisation raises the question of the relationship between socio-legal studies and the broader sociological and social-theoretic frameworks which inform (or ought to inform) socio-legal research. Of particular relevance is the *sociology of law*, which I understand as any systematic attempt to explicate the nature of law within specific social formations, as a part of the social framework, for example as a (symbolic and instrumental) mode of constituting and representing social order.[2] Sociological approaches to law are therefore diverse, but are related by their espousal of an "external", non-lawyer's perspective on the practices which they address; by their concern "to understand legal doctrine and legal institutions in terms of their social, economic and political environment; and to design inquiries so as to contribute to a deeper understanding of legal doctrine and legal institutions in general in the variety of societies and social settings in which legal phenomena exist".[3] As such, sociology of law is one region of *social theory*, conceived as the broader, trans-disciplinary enterprise of conceptualising the shape of and the rela-

---

[2] In his recent work, Roger Cotterrell provides an account of some of the most important traditions within the sociology of law and, in his conception of law as "institutionalised doctrine", establishes a basis for mapping the relationship between the sociology of law and normative legal theory. See in particular Cotterrell (1995a) Chs. 2, 3.

[3] Cotterrell (1995a) p. 77 and Ch. 2 generally.

tionships between the diverse array of practices—language, religion, magic, political and economic power, disciplines such as medicine and psychiatry, institutions such as the family—which constitute particular social worlds.

Two motivations inform my project. The first speaks to the question of the relationship between socio-legal studies and its most obvious theoretical resource, the sociology of law. To what extent has socio-legal scholarship been informed by an adequate understanding of the nature and significance of legal practices of particular kinds in particular times and places? To the extent that socio-legal studies have been relatively "untheorised" (which is to say, not informed by any *explicit* attachment to particular paradigms within the sociology of law or social theory), what have the implications been for the assumptions underlying, and the intellectual strength or practical effectiveness of socio-legal research? And how does this bear upon the (at first sight puzzling) lack of dialogue between legal theory and socio-legal studies? Secondly, what has been the implication of the fact that much socio-legal research has been less than explicit about its ethical or political orientations? How should one interpret the "scientific" or value-free self-conception of a significant portion of socio-legal research, or the technocratic instrumentalism of "policy-oriented" studies? What scope is there for a more explicit self-reflection within the socio-legal enterprise on its ethical orientations?

In addressing these questions by way of mapping the relationships between different theoretical enterprises bearing upon them, it will be evident that I have a particular audience in mind. It consists in those who, like myself, set out from a position sympathetic to the contextual and interdisciplinary orientation implicit in socio-legal studies, but who find themselves disoriented in the journey across a landscape whose theoretical underpinnings often seem to slip away in marshy ground, and whose ethical orientations are sometimes obscured by a fog of quasi-scientific or technocratic discourse. Implicit in my call for "normative reconstruction" is the judgment that a more theoretically self-reflective socio-legal studies, at the level of both method and values, would provide a chart for more interesting and illuminating journeys in contemporary legal scholarship.

THE RENEWED CONCERN WITH THE ETHICAL
IN LEGAL THEORY

Mapping the development

To speak in terms of renewal of concern with the ethical in legal theory is, of course, to presuppose the existence of a period in which legal
theorists have turned their attention away from normative or ethical
questions. The existence of a plentiful normative-political literature in
liberal legal theory—indeed of a movement within liberal legal theory which has progressively questioned the integrity of the boundaries
between legal and political or moral philosophy—puts this assumption
in doubt.[4] So I should make it clear that my main focus here is on
what might broadly be called "critical legal theory".[5] A specific focus
on critical legal theory is justified for at least two reasons. First, some
of the questions raised within critical legal theory are of particular relevance to my project. These include a certain genre of scepticism
about ethics, values and normative prescription and certain reservations about reformism which seeks to institutionalise the insights of
critique. Secondly, there has always been, and arguably increasingly is,
a professional overlap between socio-legal scholarship and legal theory which attempts to reach beyond the conventional philosophical
methodology which has informed both analytical jurisprudence and
liberal normative legal theory. The development of socio-legal
research has (implicitly though not often explicitly) posed a deep challenge to the conventional understanding of legal theory. For the
implication of much socio-legal research is that we need to extend the
ambit of our analysis, and that we have to put sociological and social
theory questions on the agenda of legal theory. To the extent that legal
theorists have taken up this challenge, they have generally been theorists working in critical legal theory and the sociology of law, and
hence outside the orthodoxy of analytical jurisprudence.[6]

   Why, then, has much critical legal theory tended to be sceptical
about or relatively uninterested in any overt engagement with ethical questions and (at least outside the academy) the institutionalisation

---

   [4] See for example Dworkin (1977), (1986).
   [5] My specific focus over the next few pages is American critical legal studies as represented by the work of writers such as Duncan Kennedy, Robert Gordon and Mark Kelman.
See for examples Hutchinson (ed.) (1989); Boyle (ed.) (1994).
   [6] See for example Cotterrell (1992),(1995a); Fitzpatrick (1992a); Santos (1987), (1992a),
(1995); Smart (1989).

of change? The key to understanding this lies, I think, in two related concerns. The first has to do with what might be called *the primacy of critique:* the idea that the primary theoretical task is the critical understanding of current social institutions and relationships. Whilst the instrinsic importance of this search for critical understanding is evident, the notion of its primacy needs to be explained in terms of three specific objections to normative, prescriptive or utopian thinking. First, it is argued that the dreaming up of blueprints and utopias *with a view to their realisation* proceeds from a totalising impulse to fix meanings, to control the world.[7] Secondly, a real understanding of the dynamic process of social construction entails that the imagination of utopias or blueprints is unrealistic. For their shape can not be adequately grounded in an understanding of the full complexity of the institutional and other conditions of existence of more just or ethical arrangements.[8] Finally, the imposition of blueprints is undemocratic, in that it is premised upon (often unarticulated and generally unjustified) assumptions about the validity or indeed "objectivity" of the viewpoints from which the blueprints proceed. This last concern connects with a question about the status of ethical judgements—one which has always been debated in terms of cognitivism and non-cognitivism, objectivism and relativism in ethics, but which has found a distinctive expression within the contemporary debate about post-modernism.[9] For both intellectual and democratic reasons, then, critical legal theory has primarily been concerned with immanent critique and with deconstruction rather than with imagining or attempting to institutionalise alternative social arrangements.[10]

Whilst this analysis identifies an intellectual basis for a particular kind of scepticism or perhaps tentativeness towards the normative dimension of legal theory, it would be a mistake to read the history of even American critical legal theory as one of indifference to the political or ethical.[11] Within the early work of Duncan Kennedy, for example, it is possible to identify an inchoate communitarian politics which has perhaps found its most vivid expression in the work of Roberto Unger.[12] And critical legal studies has shown an insistent

[7] Norrie (ed.) (1993) Chs. 1, 11; Smart (1989) Chs. 1, 4.
[8] Frazer and Lacey (1993) Ch. 1; Cotterrell (1995a) Ch. 10, especially pp. 213–14.
[9] Bauman (1993); see Chapters 5 and 6.
[10] See MacCormick (1993); Norrie (1993b).
[11] Cf. Bauman (1988).
[12] See Unger (1983); cf. Kennedy (1976). For further discussion of the relationship between different aspects of critical legal studies, see Gabel and Kennedy (1984); Gordon (1984); Cotterrell (1995a) pp. 16–17 and Ch. 10; see also Chapter 5.

concern with the institutional reconstruction of legal education and of the legal academy. A yet more vivid counter to this general characterisation is feminist legal theory, which has always been inclined to speak in a moral voice, to construct or imagine utopias, and to concern itself, both critically and imaginatively, with the conceptual terms—rights, justice, equality—within which such ideals might be framed. Interestingly, feminist scholarship has generally been characterised by a less radical divide between theoretical and socio-legal concerns than has non-feminist legal theory. In identifying deficiencies in the analysis of conventional legal scholarship, feminist legal theorists have been centrally concerned with the impact of laws and the meaning of their existence and enforcement or non-enforcement for their subjects.[13] Feminist scholars have always recognised the need to look beyond legislatures and courtrooms, and have addressed a broad set of legally relevant social institutions—the family, a variety of regulatory agencies, the welfare state, medical and psychiatric practice (though, somewhat puzzlingly, far less frequently the economy).

Whilst legal theorists (including critical legal theorists) have been slow to respond to the challenge to their own, primarily doctrinal, conceptualisation of law and the legal which socio-legal scholarship undoubtedly poses, recent work in critical legal theory has begun to concern itself more explicitly with the values and ideals which emerge from critique of legal practices and institutions. Evidence of this renewed and distinctive utopian or ethical voice can be found in the work of a number of feminist writers. As we saw in Chapters 5 and 7, examples include Drucilla Cornell's "ethical feminism", which insists on the ethical dimension of Derridean deconstruction, and Luce Irigaray's argument for a reconstruction of rights.[14]

The source and shape of this emerging ethical voice can be traced to a broader set of developments in philosophy and social theory. Central among these is a re-understanding of the very notion of the ethical. The main source of this re-understanding is work which identifies itself as interpretive or post-modernist, and which reconstructs the normative project as one of interpretation and persuasion.[15] Here the insights of a thoroughgoing social constructionism

---

[13] O'Donovan (1985); Smart (1989).

[14] Cornell (1991); Irigaray (1992), (1993a). It is also evident in Jacques Derrida's interventions in legal theory (Derrida 1992).

[15] Examples would include the philosophical writings of Richard Rorty (1989), (1991a) and Charles Taylor (1985), (1989). Whilst Rorty's view on this is undoubtedly more radical, more post-modern, than is Taylor's, both see values as emerging from social practices, and

are digested without a collapse into the sort of relativism which would make ethical discourse meaningless.[16] A graphic example is Zygmunt Bauman's idea of *Postmodern Ethics* (1993). According to Bauman, these contemporary debates about the status of ethical judgements should be understood as expressing not so much the condition of post-modernity but rather that of modernity without illusions—the illusions in question being those of a transcendent, objective foundation for ethical beliefs. Once this fantasy is abandoned, it is possible to "re-enchant" the world. For one can recognise that the undertaking of commitments—the attachment to as well as critical reflection on values, the attempt to persuade others of their worth and even to realise them in social practices—far from being meaningless or an exercise in aesthetics, is in fact one of the centrally important projects of humanity. Ethics, then, proceed from human practice, and the abandonment of debate about and critical reflection on values would be a genuinely dehumanising process. This view entails an intimate relationship between ethics and democratic politics: if alternative ethical visions are not to be constructed and imposed in ways as coercive as the current arrangements which are subject to critique, those alternatives must emerge within a process which is democratically legitimated.[17] Furthermore, the notion of ethical values as the product of an ongoing process of dialogue, rather than as already existing and awaiting "discovery", suggests a resolution of the objection to utopian thinking as either totalitarian or undemocratic. For it evokes a somewhat different conception of the utopian—a conception which, as I shall illustrate below, is now finding expression in legal theory.

Far from associating a loss of interest in ethical questions with postmodernism, then, the theoretical position I have sketched interprets the abandonment of the ethical project as the product of certain defining features of modernity. The development of modern thought and social practice is seen as being marked by a formal, atomistic conception of the citizen, a technocratic and managerial approach to governance, a circumscribed conception of the public sphere and of the proper objects of political debate, and an increasingly insistent separation of the right from the good. These features have brought

---

hence as being subject to critical debate and reconstruction within human discourse. For a more detailed discussion, see Chapter 5.

[16] Cf. Bernstein (1983).

[17] The relationship between the ethical and the political is perhaps most vividly captured within the tradition of discourse ethics: (Benhabib (1994b); Habermas (1981)).

with them a tendency towards the juridification of an ever broader range of social relations, in the quest for standards and judgements which may be regarded as valid.[18] The modern world is one which has progressively evacuated the questions of the moral, the good, the virtuous from political life.[19] This argument expresses a sense of loss and nostalgia which informs work as diverse as post-modern social theory, civic republicanism in constitutional theory, American philosophical pragmatism, critical theory of the Frankfurt school and communitarian political theory. Such nostalgia is undoubtedly one of the things which has helped to engender the current revival of concern with the ethical in critical legal theory.

Another is the sense that the textual, doctrinal critique which has been central to critical legal studies and which has been so valuable in directing our attention to the rhetorical and discursive aspects of law's power has nonetheless entailed a certain cost. For in celebrating the diversity of interpretive possibilities, it has sometimes appeared to slip into a disempowering relativism.[20] This has doubtless accentuated the impact of the other factors enumerated above in impeding a fuller articulation of critical legal theory's implicit ethical and political commitments. Moreover, it has undoubtedly tended to shift our attention (contrary to the insights of socio-legal scholarship) away from legal practices which do not primarily announce themselves in textual form, and whose direct and coercive impact on people's lives seems to call for a reconstructive critique.[21] Hence there is an emerging recognition of the need to attempt to understand how powerful social practices such as law are implicated in the establishment of some and suppression of other values and ways of life, *both* at the level

[18] In this sense the concern with the values and principles immanent within law which characterises liberal legal theory such as that of Ronald Dworkin may be seen as precisely an expression of the moral impoverishment of late modernity: there is nowhere but law to look for valid standards. On this view, normative legal philosophy may also be seen as playing a particular ideological role, in obscuring what is of value in the positivist insight that modern law is a distinctively institutionalised system of power. There is perhaps a certain paradox in the fact that the diagnosis of the juridification of the social in some critical legal theory is nonetheless itself accompanied by a relatively optimistic prognosis for tracing the just and the ethical within the legal: see, in different ways, Cornell (1991) and Douzinas and Warrington (1994).

[19] I do not mean to imply that I agree with this analysis in its entirety. Whilst its substantive account is persuasive, it seems to me that the diagnosis of an evacuation of the ethical from the public sphere is somewhat misconceived: rather, I would see the problem in terms of the growing inscription of a particular (and impoverished) conception of ethics—that of utilitarianism—in public discourse.

[20] See Sandland (1995).

[21] See Cain (1995).

of meaning *and* at that of physical and economic coercion. There is also a growing impulse to consider how such practices might be reinterpreted or otherwise reconstructed so as to imagine or realise alternatives. The various institutional and rhetorical means which might be employed in such reconstruction form the object of later sections of this chapter.

Identifying the ethical conception

The specific shape of these emerging ethical conceptions is also marked by some shared central themes. The development of feminist legal scholarship beyond the liberalism with which it has been associated[22] provides a useful illustration of some of these common ideas. In the emerging critique of the limitations of liberal feminism, theorists traced the ways in which the apparently neutral, universally inclusive concepts on which liberalism came to be based—the subject, citizenship, rights, equality and so on—were in fact structured so as to express and reproduce certain assumptions of normality and hence to exclude from full membership of the liberal legal community those, such as women, whose lives or bodies did not match up to the hidden assumptions. Furthermore, underlying the apparently neutral conception of subjecthood lay suppressed values and ways of life which were in fact necessary sources of the subject's pretended identity and stability.[23] Behind the formal structure of liberal subjecthood lay not so much an ethical vacuum as a whole cluster of unexamined ethical assumptions. The project was therefore to unearth these and to subject them to critical examination. One of the main trajectories of the ensuing critique traced the ways in which, beneath the liberal veil of neutrality, there lay a normalising political practice—a practice which insisted that subjects assimilate themselves to a particular norm, or else suffer exclusion. So whilst the central project of both feminist and critical race theory's work in this area was to map the shape of excluded differences, there was always an implicit normative concern with the recognition and acceptance of difference, and with the imagination of a more polyphonous and inclusive

[22] This is not to imply that feminism emerged from liberalism. For discussion of the independence of early feminist writers from any overarching political tradition, see Pateman (1994).
[23] See Naffine (1990); Smart (1989); for further discussion, see Chapter 7.

legal and political practice which might attenuate the subordination and repression of difference.[24]

The conclusion which which seems to have been reached—albeit reached by a variety of routes and articulated with different inflections—is that there is a need for commitment to practices which express values and attachments; that those values themselves proceed from social practices which are open to critique and reconstruction; and that, substantively, one of the most urgent ethical questions has to do with how diverse peoples, subjectivities, cultures, values, ways of life, can be recognised without abandoning the recognition of a common humanity, of interdependence, of the necessity of living together within a variety of co-ordinating institutions such as the legal. Hence issues concerning multiculturalism and law have come to occupy a central place in contemporary debate, encompassing concrete matters such as the scope and limits of a "cultural defence" in criminal law;[25] the reconstruction of anti-discrimination law in terms which move beyond the model of comparison with a white male norm;[26] and the reinterpretation of contract law in terms capable of accommodating ongoing relationships as much as negotiated rights.[27]

These concerns ought to lie at the heart of socio-legal studies. They should do so for at least three reasons. First, the legally relevant social practices with which socio-legal studies are concerned are themselves sources of values, commitments, ethical understandings. Secondly, the ability to recognise the exclusions and injustices implicit in legal practices often come from socio-legal research— research which reveals the meaning of those practices for subjects.[28] And third, the complexity of the social world, the interconnections between a wide range of social practices and institutions, dictate that any understanding of how a less excluding legal practice might be realised must be premised on a broader set of institutions than those encompassed within traditional legal scholarship or legal theory, be it orthodox or critical. Yet whilst socio-legal scholarship has certainly fed a critical understanding of law, it has often been unreflective about both its socio-theoretic underpinnings and its ethical orientations. For example, funded research cast within a framework of policy-orientation typically engages in only a circumscribed appraisal

---

[24] See further Chapter 5.
[25] See Volpp (1994).
[26] See Crenshaw (1989), and Chapter 1.
[27] See Collins (1997); Frug (1992).
[28] See for example McBarnet (1981); Carlen (1983); Eaton (1986).

of the wider policy framework, and basically incorporates an instrumentalist conception of the relationship between law and social change. The promise which socio-legal studies should hold out to critical legal theory—that of generating insights not only about the deep meaning of legal practices but also about how such practices might be reconstructed—is blocked wherever it takes up a quasi-scientific stance which distances evaluative or political questions and wherever it fails to take a sophisticated approach to the complexity of interactions between legal and extra-legal practices. These failings unfortunately give critical legal theorists the excuse for "writing off" socio-legal work as theoretically and politically naive, and hence have the effect of fencing off the ground for a potentially productive dialogue.

CRITIQUE, UTOPIANISM AND REFORMISM

Distinguishing the projects

I now want to suggest a distinction between three different kinds of projects—projects which, for expositional convenience, I shall label "critique", "utopianism" and "reformism". Each of them is, I shall argue, important to the theoretical concerns underpinning socio-legal research, and each of them raises ethical questions, albeit in different ways. I shall then go on to make some suggestions about how the projects relate to one another, and about the further theoretical questions raised by an attempt to comprehend their interrelationship.

The first project I want to consider is that of *critique*—something I have already identified as the central concern of critical legal studies. Here the enterprise is often characterised as one of immanent or internal critique: the method is to scrutinise the discourses or practices in question in terms of their own realisation of the values by which they profess to be informed. Critique comes in more or less radical, searching forms. Liberal feminism might be regarded as a paradigm of a modest version—what I shall call internal critique: it held liberal legal systems up to scrutiny in terms of the standards which they professed to instantiate universally, by showing how aspects of legal and political practice systematically failed to accord rights or dispense justice even-handedly across different groups of citizens. The movement from liberal to "difference" feminism, discussed in the previous chapter, exemplifies the ways in which an initially

sympathetic internal critique can map a path towards a deeper, immanent critique which radically shifts understanding in ways which
moves beyond the normative framework with which the internal critique was sympathetic. For as feminist critique developed beyond an
engagement with the surface level of practices or their impact, and
began to scrutinise the conceptual framework on which liberal politics was based, self-contradictions and instabilities within that framework were gradually revealed. The classic example of this is probably
the critique of the public/private distinction, which showed how a
division fundamental to liberalism logically excluded the delivery of
liberalism's own universalistic promise.[29] As critique bit deeper and
deeper into conceptual framework, focusing on the various oppositions on which liberal and modern thought was premised, the instability and fragility of that thought was progressively revealed. Values,
ways of life, practices which were unacknowledged yet which were
central to the maintenance of liberal legal order—women's domestic
work and sexual subordination to take important examples—were
revealed not only as hidden but also as "dangerous supplements" to
the dominant understandings.[30]

   The project of unearthing these dangerous supplements revealed
the contingency of current arrangements, and, crucially, the role of
various sorts of power in sustaining sets of arrangements which were
themselves being interpreted as ethically problematic. Ethical and
political issues were shown to be inextricably linked. Though the
notion of critique has had greatest salience in relation to legal doctrine, the importance of critique applied to broader discursive practices—as feminist work exemplifies—was clear. Hence adequately
theorised socio-legal studies as much as critical legal theory fed this
particular critical enterprise. And whilst critique rather than reconstruction had a primacy in this work, ethics was never far away.
Notwithstanding the iconoclastic and polemical self-presentation of
"trashing", there was always a concern with how things could have
been, and might be, different. It wasn't just an irresponsible, existen-
tial enjoyment in shaking up the world. In its serious form the mapping of existing configurations of power and their interpretation as
contingent was part of a political and ethical project.[31]

   [29] See Chapter 3.
   [30] Fitzpatrick (ed.) (1991).
   [31] Conversely, the reflexive demands of critical method may be argued to be equally
important to the two other projects which I shall delineate: Cotterrell (1995a) pp. 212–13.
For examples of the political motivation of critical legal scholarship, see Kennedy (1976);
Olsen (1983); Unger (1983); Gabel and Kennedy (1984); Gordon (1984).

It is the impulse further to develop this implicit ethical project which is now being articulated, and which forms *utopianism*—the second of the theoretical tasks which I want to delineate. The "utopian moment within deconstruction" has been forcefully articulated by Drucilla Cornell. Like Derridean deconstruction, Cornell's critique is premised on a particular (post-structuralist) view of the openness of language.[32] Language does not operate simply by reflecting objects in the world in a directly representational way. Rather, it has an invariably performative or constructive aspect. Hence language always in a sense operates at a metaphorical level. And because linguistic signs get their meaning not by any simple correspondence with the world but also by reference to (through a process of difference in relation to) other signs, there is an irreducible reference in all linguistic utterances to what was not but might have been said. Meaning, in other words, is never closed. It is in discursive opennesses and gaps that the possibility of other meanings, of other worlds, may be discerned through a process which Cornell terms "recollective imagination". Implicit in this analysis is the idea that those worlds in some sense exist in the very moment in which they are repressed.

Whilst Cornell is willing to use the word "utopian" in relation to her project,[33] this is not so of all exponents of this second kind of imaginative ethical thought. Luce Irigaray, for example, has recently argued for the imagination of a distinctive feminine law: she explicitly repudiates the idea of utopias, and speaks rather in terms of the imagination of the impossible—wanting what is not yet as the only possibility for the future.[34] Whilst this may appear mere semantic quibbling, the disagreement about the propriety of the term "utopia" touches on a substantive issue about what it means to engage in this kind of imaginative thought. Far from attempting the design of complete and idealised blueprints—a project which encounters, as we have seen, democratic as well as intellectual objections—this form of utopianism is engaged in the "impossible" task of thinking beyond the conceptual limits of the present. The utopianism itself consists in the ongoing project of (re)imagination—a process which would arguably be killed in the very moment of its institutionalisation in law. As I shall argue, however, it is a mistake to conclude that this

[32] See Cornell (1991), (1992), (1993); for more detailed discussion of Cornell's theory, see Chapters 4–6.
[33] See for example Cornell (1991) pp. 168–72.
[34] Irigaray (1992) p. 26.

imaginative and non-prescriptive utopianism has nothing to do with reconstructive politics.

What is distinctive about projects such as those of Irigaray and Cornell is that they operate first and foremost at an imaginative and rhetorical level. They build on the importance of critique's insight about contingency, by insisting that we can imagine the world differently, and that the normative concepts in terms of which we shape our world—rights, justice, equality—can be reimagined, reconstructed in radically different ways. Significantly, these kinds of projects are primarily interested in the shape and dynamics of the institution of language. They seek to break out of what might have appeared as a double bind for discourse-oriented critique in relation to radical politics. This is the fact that language is itself marked by socially predominant configurations of power, and therefore our normative conceptual framework is, for example, marked by gendered and racialised exclusions. Hence it might be thought that there is no way forward from critique: the insights of critique seem to engender silence. The important message that critique is not so silenced is exemplified by these imaginative post-structuralist feminisms, which engage in the impossible project of speaking that which, according to their own analysis, cannot be spoken.

Different again is the third and final task which I shall delineate. This is the *reformist* project of thinking, at a concrete and institutional level, how ideas generated at the level of critique or idealistic imagination might be approached or even realised in practice. This has evidently been an important project within feminist and socio-legal scholarship, much of which has argued directly for policy changes of one kind or another. It is also a project which raises very difficult questions of professional ethics. Funding for socio-legal research may be premised on the funding agency's prior political commitment to a particular outcome.[35] Reformist policy prescription also encounters practical problems. These are usually taken to involve the ways in which researchers' analyses and recommendations get distorted or attenuated in the executive and legislative process, as political compromises are reached, or adequate funds found to be wanting.

However, a focus on these political problems of reformism may obscure our view of another more central, and intellectually com-

---

[35] This is of particular importance given the current move towards using policy relevance as an explicit criterion in the allocation of research funding in Britain. For a perceptive discussion of the "policy-science" and "socio-technics" conceptions of sociology, see Cotterrell (1995a) pp. 58–68.

pelling, set of problems—problems to which conventional socio-legal research has been less sensitive. These problems lie in the fact that the institutions which reformist interventions seek to change are themselves interwoven with and dependent upon a complex network of other institutions. Interventions within one set of practices all too often have unseen and adverse implications for others. And a concrete and specific attempt to redress, for example, an imbalance of power in one area of social practice is unlikely to be successful if the configurations of power which it tries to reshape in fact characterise all or most of the social institutions which go to make up the relevant environment. This is depressingly obviously true of configurations of power patterned around race, ethnicity, gender, to mention just a few examples.

But this is not a recipe for pessimism and passivity. Rather, it poses us with a challenge. The challenge is to try to understand how social institutions interact with each other, which are the most open to change, and which means of changing them are likely, in particular contexts, to be least dangerous or most successful. For the institutional complexity of the world—the ways in which lives are lived across different practices, and move between different subjectivities—itself presents possibilities for, as much as barriers to, change. These possibilities can only be approached if socio-legal research is informed by an adequate sociology of law—indeed by adequate general social theoretic understandings, including an appreciation of the importance of critical method.

Relating the projects

So far I have been concerned to emphasise the differences between the three projects of critique, utopian thinking and reformism or policy prescription. This is because there has sometimes been a tendency to assume that we can straightforwardly "read off" institutional strategies from critical or utopian theories. Andrea Dworkin's and Catharine MacKinnon's anti-pornography ordinance is one example[36] and, as I shall argue below, Luce Irigaray's argument for special rights risks being misunderstood as another. Beyond feminist work, the debate about institutions of informal or popular justice exemplifies the same problem. Reforms which attempt to realise a

---

[36] MacKinnon (1987) Ch. 11: for discussion of the ordinance, see Chapter 3.

critique of the violence and inefficiency of formalised state-run practices in terms of an alternative set of institutions may be marked by the
same configurations of power which sullied the formal model.[37] This
constitutes another important instructive failure. I want to argue,
however, that whilst the distinctness of the critical, utopian and
reformist projects is important in the sense that they presuppose rather
different kinds of knowledge or understanding, and whilst as scholars
we therefore have to be aware of our own movements between them,
they are, at another level, closely related. Furthermore, their relationship is itself a product of the ethical stance which informs (persuasive
versions of) all three enterprises. I therefore now want to provide a
remapping of the relationship between the three projects, as a means
of locating the specific arguments to be addressed in the last section of
the chapter, and to prepare the ground for a particular understanding
of what I have called "normative reconstruction".

The relationship between the enterprises of critique, utopianism
and reformist policy prescription can be expressed schematically in a
number of ways. We might say, for example, that the understanding
of the power of contingent social arrangements to which critique
works is generally motivated by a commitment to changing the
world. This depends in turn upon the vision of a substantially different world imagined in utopian thought. And it has the ultimate (perhaps very distant) project of approaching that vision through the
process of developing practices and institutions *via* reformism—the
process and shape of reform itself in turn having rhetorical aspects and
generating further ground for critique and reimagination.

Two crucially important features of this interdependence make it
far more complex and fragile than the schematic statement implies.
First, the sort of rhetorical politics which is imagined in utopian
thought will, if directly institutionalised, have effects very different
from those ideally envisioned. This is simply because, by definition,
they are realised within a very different kind of world. Utopias cannot be reached: rather they provide horizons towards which we
attempt to move.[38] Hence, secondly, the movement towards such
utopias depends on a dynamic and general process of social transformation to which the consciousness of contingency and the discursive
construction of difference are only *preconditions*. For the institutionalisation of such imagined worlds without a more general change
would—as in many experiments with informal justice—merely

[37] See Abel (ed.) (1982); Santos (ed.) (1992).
[38] For further discussion, see Chapters 4 and 5.

reproduce the violence, the anti-democratic totalisation, resistance to which underpinned the primacy of critique.

To argue that the coordination of utopian understandings is merely a precondition to social change is not to deny their crucial importance. To take a perhaps unsympathetic example, Margaret Thatcher's political rhetoric unsettled existing understandings of the propriety of Keynesian management of the economy and articulated a vision of an economy run on neo-classical principles and a society built on an "enterprise culture". There can be no doubt that the rhetorical power of these arguments was a precondition for the radical change which her Government's policies engendered. Changing people's *ideas of the possible* is a crucial element in reformism. The question is, how far can we attain any general understandings which will help us to chart the path from precondition to change?

In order to take utopian rhetorical strategies further, as well as to understand how the ethical visions emerging from critical legal theory relate to reformism, at least two other projects also have to be advanced. First, rhetorical strategies beg a conception of what would constitute an adequate democratic practice—an understanding of how a genuine dialogue about visions of difference might be engendered. Secondly, they presuppose an understanding of how particular human societies operate and develop, of how discursive and material practices and changes interact, of how power flows through the social body. In other words, the legitimacy as well as the power of rhetoric as politics depends upon the development of institutionally oriented social theoretic insights. Without this, the critique and the imaginative rhetoric of the first two projects, which themselves justifiably claim the status of distinctive political action or engagement, can not move beyond their current (often limited) audience. Nor can they attain any understanding of what their effects may be. A politics which denies the relevance of its own effects may fairly be accused of some degree of irresponsibility.

It is therefore unfortunate that there is relatively little dialogue between much critical legal theory and socio-legal research on the one hand and the sociology of law or other theoretical frameworks in the social sciences on the other.[39] Furthermore, this silence

---

[39] For honourable exceptions, see Cotterrell (1995a); Murphy (1977); Santos (1995). The exceptions tend, however, to be partial ones. For example, Cotterrell's orientation to general questions of social theory and legal sociology, combined with his emphasis on the link between sociology of law and normative legal theory via the conception of law as institutionalised doctrine, inhibits his capacity to pursue the links with grounded socio-legal research to which he gestures in the later chapters of his recent book.

maintains a seemingly unbridgeable gap between critique and utopianism on the one hand and reformism on the other, and hence
between critical legal theory and socio-legal studies. Perhaps the lack
of dialogue is due to the fact that social theory takes lawyers furthest
from our own discipline—though the participation of many sociolo-
gists in socio-legal research makes this an incomplete explanation.
The explanation is further undermined by the growing willingness of
legal scholars to acquaint themselves with a range of disciplinary
resources beyond the legal. A more powerful explanation probably
has to do with a fact mentioned earlier: that policy-oriented research
is often funded by the body interested in the policy in question. This
means that, almost by definition, it is framed within a circumscribed
and instrumentalist conception of the law/society relation. Moreover, the failures of reforms inspired or informed by socio-legal
research are all too easily explained away as failures of implementation rather than of conception.[40] Such partial explanations consistently divert our attention from the more difficult social-theoretic
questions in terms of which a proper explanation would need to be
framed.[41]

   To sum up: I do not reject the idea that socio-legal research often
is, and generally should be, geared to effecting social change—to
making the world a better place. Indeed I think this is the central ethical impulse of such research. But its approach to policy change has
all too often been premised on both a poorly theorised account of
social institutions and an insufficient attention to the democratic
legitimacy of proposed changes. Inadequately theorised and contextualised socio-legal research, in other words, ignores relevant questions raised by the three projects which I have delineated. It proceeds
from an insufficiently thorough critique of existing legal institutional
forms: indeed its critique risks amounting to a view of the inefficiency or impracticality of legal arrangements received from the
funding body. The range of practices within its purview is similarly
circumscribed. Its imaginative scope is blunted by the fact that it is
framed by the funder's own policy or ethical orientation. And it is
unduly limited in its assessment of the potential effects of its own
implementation. These failings have provided an unfortunate basis

---

[40] For a perceptive discussion of this kind of problem in the sphere of criminal justice,
see Cohen (1985).
[41] For examples of broadly theorised socio-legal research, see Teubner (ed.) (1986);
Santos (ed.) (1992). For a wide-ranging review of sociological theories of law, see Cotterrell
(1993).

for critical legal theorists to ignore the relevance of socio-legal research to their own projects.

Normative reconstruction: moving between the projects

I now want to illustrate the potential interaction of the projects of critique, utopianism and reformism within an adequately theorised practice of socio-legal research. I shall do so by mapping out a schematic set of arguments which engage from a feminist perspective in what I shall call the normative reconstruction of some central legal and ethical concepts; by drawing attention to some of the limitations of conventional socio-legal approaches to these questions; and by pointing out the sort of analysis for which a further development of the arguments would call. I shall focus on two concepts which have been of particular importance to each of the projects I have delineated. These are the ideas of rights and of equality. I shall sketch a feminist critique of the shape of these concepts and the place which they have in current legal and political practice, and go on to consider the potential for reimagining these concepts in ways which meet objections to their current contours. I shall then make some suggestions about how one might understand both the possibilities and the limits which these reconstructed conceptions present for the project of institutional change, in the light of some of the questions raised by a broad social-theoretic framework of the kind which I have argued is often lacking.

The role of the ideas of rights and of equality within both the institutional framework and the ideological self-conception of a liberal legal order is obvious and requires no substantial description here. It is equally obvious that they have played a central role in attempts to reform law in a direction sympathetic to feminism and other radical politics—for example, in the legal institutionalisation of a particular idea of sexual equality of opportunity in the Sex Discrimination or Equal Pay Acts, or in the recognition of a woman's right to terminate a pregnancy. The ideas of equality and rights, furthermore, continue to play a part in the conceptual framework of critical feminisms which move beyond the constraints of liberalism. Notwithstanding feminist critique of the assumptions underlying liberal understandings and institutionalisations of equality and rights, there is a need for some language in which to express our critical and alternative ideas. Since there is, by definition, no language unmarked by gendered configurations of power, the project of normative reconstruction of available languages, as well as of working towards a socio-theoretic understanding of what may give such reconstructed languages a foothold in more broadly co-ordinated understandings and, ultimately, practices, is a centrally important one for feminism.[42]

A necessary prelude to conceptual reconstruction is, of course, a searching critique of the current understandings and implications of the concepts in question. It is worth rehearsing the main features of the relevant feminist critique. In the case of equality, it has been argued that liberal notions of equality are fundamentally premised on the idea of sameness: equal treatment is due to all who are similarly situated to the full liberal subject. Hence, if that subject is implicitly marked as masculine—is understood in terms of bodily and psychic characteristics which have been culturally understood to be associated with men—then the strategy of equality amounts to the assimilation of women to a norm set by and for men.[43] This problem about the underlying view of the equal subject also muddies liberal conceptions of equality which move beyond formal equality as sameness. For example, the dynamic, processual idea of equality of opportunity also fails women and other non-standard subjects in so far as the conception of a normal life—a life, for example, lived in the full-time labour market—itself goes unreconstructed: unequal outcomes can simply be explained away, legitimated in terms of the choices of different autonomous liberal individuals. Even the yet more substantial notions of equality of welfare or equality of resources are inadequate to the extent that the ambit of their critical reconstruction is limited. For what constitutes meaningful well-being, what count as important resources, what is seen as of equal or equivalent value, are themselves understood in ways which systematically, if not invariably, favour men. Feminist reconstructions of the notion of equality seek to realise the progressive potential in the idea of "treatment as an equal" by questioning the deepest structures, the most powerful (and often most hidden) processes whereby what it is argued should be equally

[42] This is not to say, of course, that rights and equality are the only important candidates for conceptual reconstruction: others include, for example, autonomy, justice, trust, courage, honesty, empathy and subjecthood itself: see Frazer, Hornsby and Lovibond (eds.) (1992) pp. 1–18. Furthermore, these different concepts are themselves interlinked in important ways. However, the centrality of the ideas of rights and of equality to both dominant and critical legal theoretical discourse justifies my taking them as examples. For instructive examples of feminist reconstruction of key political and ethical concepts, see Nedelsky (1989), (1993); Littleton (1987).

[43] See Chapters 1 and 7.

valued has been constructed. They argue for the equivalent worth of, for example, rights, to differently situated subjects; for rights to an "imaginary domain" within which all subjects can conceive themselves as whole persons, worthy of respect and capable of self-respect; or for "equality as acceptance"—a notion which seeks to escape the hidden reliance on the normalisation and valuation of some ways of life and not others.[44]

It is evident, then, that an important approach has been made towards a critical understanding of not only the limits of equality as currently institutionalised but also what a reconstructed equality might look like. It is equally evident, however, that this is very far from amounting to an understanding of how "real" equality might be realised. This is not to say that feminist analysis does not have some grasp of the conditions of existence of genuine equality. On the contrary, it is well understood that this has to do with broad distributions and flows of social power. Moreover, it has been argued that we can find imaginative resources within (often socially disapproved or marginalised) local relationships which are relatively insulated from some of the more important vectors of power which generally inhibit the realisation of an equality which is worth having. This is one of the interests, for example, of gay and lesbian culture.[45] It is also one of the distinctive themes of critical race theory, which gives prominence to practices and ways of life which have been suppressed yet which generate alternative visions of not only relationships but also rationalities, decision-making processes and other important social practices.[46] Feminist scholarship has generated a pretty good idea of why legal strategies of equality do not work. It also has a sense of the limits of some such strategies to which it is nonetheless committed. A good example here is the criminalisation of marital rape, which undoubtedly at some level changes the nature of the marital relationship in a genuinely more equal direction—removing as it does a blatant difference in the valuation of women's and men's sexual integrity. Equally clearly, the formal criminalisation of marital rape will not engender sexual equality in marriage; and this is because of all sorts of other flows of power—economic power being significant among them—which cannot be affected except by very radical social change which cannot be engendered directly by legal means.

---

[44] Cornell (1993) Ch. 6, (1995); Littleton (1987).
[45] See Moran (1996); Butler (1990).
[46] See Hill Collins (1990); Williams (1991), (1995).

What is unusual about the reform of marital rape law, however, is that it is relatively unproblematic in the sense that it has no obviously negative counter-effects. The legal institutionalisation of a particular vision of equality within the Sex Discrimination Act is a far more complex and, unfortunately, a far more typical example, and one which illustrates vividly the limitations of policy change which fails to engage with the insights of critique. For whilst the economic and political gains which women have had from the SDA are modest in the extreme, the problems set up by the establishment of an unsatisfactory, impoverished equality are immense. These include the politically problematic fact that those in power can now say that women have equality, and that call for the repeal of the SDA would itself be an impossible strategy for feminism. Such double binds set up by feminist reformism are numerous: another example lies in the implications of a more sexually neutral approach to child custody in a world in which women still disproportionately care for children.

On the view which emphasises the totalising tendencies of a too-ready normativism, incremental change may, in some cases, be all that, democratically, we ought to seek. What I am arguing therefore is not that the reformism which appears to proceed from our normative reconstruction should be rejected, but rather that it is important to be very clear-headed about its limits, and very cautious about the negative implications of legal reform in advance of cultural or political change.[47] The history of anti-pornography legislation in the USA strikes me as an instance which is particularly instructive both in illustrating the distinction between critique and reformist strategy and in underlining the dangers inherent in inferring the latter from the former.[48] Law is only one among interrelated social frameworks within which dominant understandings of the value of different ways of life are instantiated. Legal change which ignores this, and which takes a narrow view of the rhetorical and expressive as well as the instrumental aspects of reformism itself, will be at best ineffective and at worst counter-productive.

Let me now turn to the concept of rights. Like equality, rights are in liberal discourse salient markers, supposed guarantees, of universal citizenship and legal subjecthood. And feminist theory has subjected

---

[47] In this respect I am sympathetic to Carol Smart's position: Smart (1989), although, like Sandland (1995), I reject the idea that it implies the irrelevance of critique to legal reform, or indeed a general rejection of legal reformism: see Chapter 6.

[48] See Chapter 3.

them to a similarly pungent critique.[49] This critique has traced the ways in which rights presuppose a particular view of the subject and of that subject's place in the world. The rights bearer is an individual who is defined in terms of certain powers and capacities: in a sense this subject is alienated even from himself, in that he stands in a relationship of ownership to his defining characteristics. Furthermore, his relation to the world and to other subjects is, when mediated in terms of rights, essentially that of subject to object: the having of rights is the having of a form of property, for which one competes with others, which one asserts or defends competitively as against others, and which are enforced coercively against others. As in the case of equality, the liberal discourse of rights has been far more concerned with the formal having of rights than with their substantive worth to differently situated subjects. And just as liberalism has been blind to patterned configurations of power which determine that rights are of systematically lower value to certain social groups, it has also ignored their resonance with a mode of governance which operates managerially by recording, measuring, categorising. The impact of these critical arguments on the development of socio-legal reform-oriented research has, however, been patchy.

How, then, might rights be reconceived so as to escape their competitive individualism, their construction of object relations, their proprietary nature, and their dependence on coercive state structures of enforcement? Not all feminists think this possible, and undoubtedly some of the reconstructive models which have been attempted—such as the expansion of rights to encompass the interests and identities of groups rather than merely of individuals—merely reproduce many of the difficulties of liberal concepts of rights.[50] But to think that rights are not susceptible of re-imagination, and that reconstructed rights might not have some progressive political potential *at least in certain contexts*, seems itself an odd form of conceptual essentialism.[51] If a social constructionist critique of language is accepted, there is no reason to think that any concepts are (in principle) beyond reconstruction. And in her recent work, Luce Irigaray has composed an intriguing and radical argument for intersubjective

[49] See Fudge (1989); Kingdom (1991); Smart (1989) Ch. 7; though cf. hesitations about a rejection of rights in critical race theory: Delgado (1987), (1995); Williams (1991); and cf. critique of rights in marxist and socialist thought: Campbell (1983).

[50] See Chapter 1.

[51] For an example of socio-legal work which is critical of prevailing ideas of rights yet which escapes this kind of essentialism, see Herman (1994). For a persuasive reconceptualisation of rights "as relationship", see Nedelsky (1993).

rights which express and confirm genuine relations among persons rather than property relations—rights, as she puts it, of being rather than of having.[52]

Irigaray's analysis goes to the core of the problematic way in which dominant liberal discourse represses difference, and in particular of the way in which it excludes the feminine from subject status. Her argument is that a relational conception of rights would have to be premised on the recognition of irreducibly different subjectivities which relate in an instransitive way to one another. Until women, in other words, are recognised as full subjects, those of us with female bodies will never be either citizens or rights-bearers. Conversely, the masculine illusion of self-identity which the cultural repression of the feminine sustains implies that men too have no access to genuinely intersubjective relations. Men's inability to recognise intersubjective dependence entails that their relationships proceed on the assumption of the object status of the other.

Irigaray maps this subtle argument about the deep structure of rights onto an argument about feminine and masculine culture. Her view is that only if women are given access to a distinctive culture which is socially recognised and valued will we achieve the subject status which is currently denied us. This analysis leads Irigaray to weave an argument for substantively different, special rights for women into her critique of the form of rights. The institutionalisation of special rights might provide a conceptual framework which would be capable of cultivating an "idiom of admiration" (i.e. of intransitive, intersubjective relations) and a law which could act as a "symbolic repertoire through which feminine selves might be engendered". [53] If, she argues, women were accorded special rights appropriate to the feminine genre—and these include such things as rights to virginity and motherhood, to guardianship of the home, as well as rights to equal institutional representation and access to economic resources—this would itself represent a recognition of our subjectivity, which would in turn change the nature of our possible relations with men and with one another.

---

[52] Irigaray (1992) pp. 18–19, 42–3, 90–100, 205–10; (1993a) Chs. 9, 10; (1994) Ch. 3. Irigaray's analysis informs Cornell's recent argument for a reconceptualisation of rights in terms capable of accommodating the embodied and pscyhic aspects of human being. Cornell argues in particular for the right to an imaginary domain in which women could conceive themselves as whole persons, worthy of respect, as a precondition to any meaningful instantiation of standard liberal rights based on autonomy: Cornell (1995). For further discussion, see Chapter 4.

[53] Pottage (1995) p. 1195.

I want to discuss two difficulties with this integration of an argument for substantively special rights with the critique of the form of rights. The first problem, which I have already canvassed in Chapter 7, has to do with the implications of reinscribing within the argument both an essentialist view of woman—a view reinforced by some of the visions of femininity from which Irigaray's list of rights proceeds—and a difference-repressing logic of identity. One way of understanding Irigaray's argument is that it replaces one universalism—a universalism which has been effectively deconstructed as totalising and excluding—with two. These two are mapped onto the masculine and the feminine. They take no account of the many other differences which structure subjectivity and the experience of the material world. The root of this difficulty lies in a certain set of psychoanalytic arguments which are important to Irigaray's feminism and which threaten to unsettle important intellectual and political alliances between difference feminism and other critical traditions. There is a liberatory potential in Irigaray's thought that "*je suis sexué(e)*" implies "*je ne suis pas tout(e)*". But this depends on our reading her analysis of sexual difference as a metaphor for difference more generally. We need, in other words, to resist the binarism which her analysis of sexual difference as fundamental reasserts, and to locate the ethical impulse to attend to otherness not just within the vector of sexual difference but within those of racial, ethnic, national, class and other differences too.

There is a second difficulty with Irigaray's argument for special rights, and one which nicely illustrates a problem converse to that of reform-oriented socio-legal scholarship failing to attend to the theoretical projects of critique and utopianism via an adequately complex social theory or sociology of law. This is that in constructing an argument which is a blend of critique and utopianism, Irigaray borrows (unusually within her work) the language of the third project—that of institutional reform. In doing so, she espouses a curiously naive and apparently instrumental optimism about legal reform and takes up a position which appears to assume the very autonomy of law which has been revealed as problematic by the sociology of law.[54] She also appears to invite a policy response which, in the current political, economic and legal conditions of either France or Britain, would be retrogressive. Understood as political rhetoric, the replay of sexual stereotypes is already problematic. Understood as a programme for reform, it is potentially disastrous.

[54] See Cotterrell (1995a) Ch. 5.

In developing this critique of Irigaray's work, I am at risk of doing violence to the specificity of her project.[55] I want to linger on this point for a moment, because it links up with a question which I glossed over: that of the implication of the post-structuralist critique of language that the repressed or the different is literally unspeakable. In engaging in the (logically) impossible project of speaking the unspeakable, post-structuralist feminisms have engaged in a number of stylistic and substantive ploys, an important one of which has been to write in overtly metaphorical, poetic and elliptical styles. These writings are often dialogic and oblique rather than monologic and linear in form.[56] This is certainly true of much of Irigaray's work, and it suggests that she is seeking to operate at a different level of discourse—one which appeals to capacities of imagination, to body as much as to mind, to what might be called "the passions of the soul" (Pottage (1995) p. 1174). Hence a literal reading of her as sociologically naive is, to put it kindly, a very thin one. Read and felt imaginatively, one might receive Irigaray's reversion to the language of institutional reform as itself a metaphor, an emancipatory vision of a world in which women had as much power as do men to shape the content of powerful social institutions. In this vein, Pottage suggests that Irigaray's deployment of "nature" in her depiction of the feminine genre is "at once a naive appeal and a rhetorical motif which renders ironic the very notion of the naive".[57]

Yet just as there is a responsibility to read and interpret texts from a position which seeks genuinely to engage with the author's project, there is arguably a converse responsibility on the writer to attend to readers and context. I would suggest that Irigary's particular argument for special rights fails to attend to this latter form of political responsibility. If imaginative rhetorical strategies are a political way forward (a position with which I am in agreement) then the question of whether particular rhetorics *can* move us forward is a relevant question, and one whose analysis raises questions about the relationships between different social institutions. It is indeed a form of conceptual essentialism to think that rights cannot be normatively re-imagined. But to the extent that the feminist critique of rights has identified reasons for thinking that, at a

---

[55] Pottage (1994), (1995).

[56] Irigaray (1992) and, particularly, (1991); cf., in relation to critical analysis of issues of race, the allegorical and poetic style of Patricia J. Williams (Williams (1991)).

[57] Pottage (1995) p. 1189.

strategic level (both institutionally and rhetorically) rights as currently understood pose some distinctive and particularly intractable political problems, these problems have to be confronted by those who employ the framework of (albeit reconstructed) rights at the rhetorical level.

The relevant problems have not only to do with the analysis of rights as individualistic and competitive—an analysis to which Irigaray's conceptual reconstruction speaks directly and effectively. They have also to do with the power of a particular form of rights discourse in the world as we know it, and with the capacity of rhetorical strategies to dislodge the dominant conception once they move from argument to legal institutionalisation. We have only to think of actual instances of "special rights" for women—those surrounding pregnancy are the best example—to see their adverse implications for women in a world in which activities such as child-rearing have not been effectively economically or culturally valued.[58] It is at this level—the cultural and economic, the struggle for the extension of tolerance, respect and empathy, for human beings to comprehend the worth of lives lived differently—that the reconstructive project, broadly conceived, must proceed. Until we have got further with that, our reformist programmes must be cautious. Our utopianism and our rhetoric, on the other hand, must indeed be audacious, albeit not naive about their own political implications. They must resist an indulgence in the fantasy of a direct legal institutionalisation which contradicts some of the deepest premises on which they are themselves based.

CONCLUDING THOUGHTS

It is something of a truism that justice can generally only be glimpsed in law, and that when law delivers justice, this is often as much by accident as by design. Law's operation in terms of relatively fixed categories, its generally dispositive method, its delineation and imposition of standard "solutions", inevitably make it a blunt and sometimes a violent instrument. The ideal of a just sensitivity to all relevant

---

[58] As Carole Pateman notes, there is an important irony in the very fact that such measures for women, even though directed to an egalitarian goal, are conceptualised in terms of "protection" and "special" rights, whereas the historically pervasive special rights enjoyed by men—rights which cannot plausibly be brought within a liberal-egalitarian framework—have never been so marked: Pateman (1995).

differences and particularities is impossible to incorporate in legal
frameworks: it remains outside, as a legitimating ideology which
resonates with law's implicit promise, and which acts as the residual
conscience of reasonably democratic legal orders. But the hope of
approaching justice (however (re)conceived) in law—the hope of
law, legal practices, legal methods—which are less distant from
ethical ideals, will always be a focus for critical and socio-legal
theory. Whilst the idea of an ethical law may be impossible—
utopian in the deep sense—the idea that there are ethical arguments
which bear on law and its reform, and indeed that law could be less
unjust and unethical than it is, remains central to progressive legal
scholarship.

If this progressive journey is to be undertaken, its travellers will
need a map which is informed by the different theoretical projects
which I have argued are relevant to the terrain. Legal scholarship
involves analysis, critique, imagination, persuasion. It also involves
the attempt to understand the complex social networks of power of
which law—as feminist and socio-legal scholars have sometimes been
quicker to notice than their critical legal colleagues—is only one
expression. We cannot yet imagine what law would look like in a
genuinely equal world peopled by relational subjects connected to
each other by mutual respect for each other's irreducible difference.
And we make a large mistake when we think that by changing, for
example, dispute-settling processes within the current world in an
attempt to make them less excluding, less authoritarian, more democratic, we *necessarily* make progress. This can only be straightforwardly so where the practice in question is relatively insulated—a
very rare thing for important social practices to be.

The idea that law, any more than rights, is unreconstructible is
contradicted by the constructionism to which most legal theory is
now committed. But, as marxists saw, the reconstruction of the legal
has to be premised on the reconstruction of economic, social, political relations: on massive changes in the configuration of social power
at every level. Only if both the distinctness of and the interrelation-
ships between the projects of critiqe, utopianism and reformism are
recognised will intellectual practices—feminist, socio-legal or otherwise—move any closer to the ethical ideals which, implicitly or
explicitly, they espouse. Only by constructing a more consistent dialogue between the three projects, and by locating this dialogue
within the broad understandings of the sociology of law and social
theory, can the curious and intellectually stultifying "gap" between

so-called critical legal theory and so-called socio-legal studies be filled, and the potentially fruitful opening up of interdisciplinary legal studies be realised. This is, in my view, the most important project in contemporary legal theory. It is one to which feminist legal scholarship will continue to make a vital contribution.

Bibliography

ABEL, RICHARD (ed.) (1982) *The Politics of Informal Justice*, vols i and ii (New York, Academic Press)
—— (1982a) "The contraditions of informal justice", in Abel (ed.) vol. 2 p. 267
ACKERMAN, BRUCE (1980) *Social Justice in the Liberal State* (New Haven, Yale University Press)
ALLEN, HILARY (1987) *Justice Unbalanced* (Milton Keynes, Open University Press)
ANDERSON, BENEDICT (1983) *Imagined Communities: Reflections on the Origin and Spread of Nationalism* (London, Verso)
ASHWORTH, ANDREW (1995) *Principles of Criminal Law* (2nd edn) (Oxford, Clarendon Press)
ATKINS, SUSAN and HOGGETT, BRENDA (1984) *Women and the Law* (Oxford, Basil Blackwell)
BARBER, BENJAMIN (1984) *Strong Democracy* (Berkeley, University of California Press)
BARRON, ANNE (1993) "The Illusions of the 'I': Citizenship and the Politics of Identity", in Norrie (ed.) p. 80
BARRY, BRIAN (1965) *Political Argument* (London, Routledge and Kegan Paul)
—— (1973) *The Liberal Theory of Justice* (Oxford, Clarendon Press)
—— (1989) *Theories of Justice: A Treatise on Social Justice*, vol I (Oxford University Press)
BAUMAN, RICHARD (1988) "The Communitarian Vision of Critical Legal Studies" (1988) 33 *McGill Law Journal* 295
BAUMAN, ZYGMUNT (1993) *Postmodern Ethics* (Oxford, Basil Blackwell)
BELL, DERRICK A. JR. (1987) *And We Are Not Saved: The Elusive Quest for Racial Justice* (New York, Basic Books)
—— (1992) *Race, Racism and American Law*, 3rd ed. (Boston, Little Brown)
BENHABIB, SEYLA (1987) "The Generalised and the Concrete Other", in Benhabib and Cornell (eds.) p. 77, and in Benhabib (1992a) p. 148.
—— (1992a) *Situating the Self; Gender, Community and Postmodernism in Contemporary Ethics* (Oxford, Polity)
—— (1992b) "Autonomy, modernity and community", in Benhabib (1992a) p. 68.
—— (1994a) "Democracy and difference: Reflections on Rationality, Democracy and Postmodernism", unpublished manuscript: shorter version published as "Democracy and Difference: Reflections on the Metapolitics of Lyotard and Derrida" (1994) 2 *Journal of Political Philosophy*

BENHABIB, SEYLA (1994b) "Deliberative Rationality and Models of Democratic Legitimacy" (1994) 1 *Constellations* no.1

—— and CORNELL, DRUCILLA (eds.) (1987) *Feminism as Critique* (Oxford, Polity Press)

BERLIN, ISAIAH (1989) *Four Essays on Liberty* (Oxford University Press)

BERNSTEIN, RICHARD (1983) *Beyond Objectivism and Relativism* (Oxford, Basil Blackwell)

BOTTOMLEY, ANNE (ed.) (1996), *Feminist Perspectives on the Foundational Subjects of Law* (London, Cavendish Publishing)

—— and CONAGHAN, JOANNE (eds.) (1993) *Feminist Theory and Legal Strategy* (Oxford, Basil Blackwell)

BOURDIEU, PIERRE (1977) *Outline of a Theory of Practice* transl. Richard Nice (Cambridge University Press)

BOYLE, JAMES (ed.) (1994) *Critical Legal Studies* (New York University Press)

BOX, STEVEN (1987) *Recession, Crime and Punishment* (London, Macmillan)

BRAIDOTTI, ROSI (1991) *Patterns of Dissonance* (Oxford, Polity Press)

BRAITHWAITE, JOHN (1993) "Shame and Modernity", (1993) 33 *British Journal of Criminology* 1

BREST, PAUL (1988) "Further beyond the Republican Ideal" (1988) 97 *Yale Law Journal* 1623

BRISON, SUSAN J. (1997) "Outliving Oneself: Trauma, Memory and Personal Identity" in Meyers (ed.) p. 12

BRONNIT, SIMON (1994) "The Direction of Rape Law in Australia: Toward a Positive Consent Standard" (1994) *Criminal Law Journal* 249

BROWN, BEVERLEY, BURMAN, MICHELE and JAMIESON, LYNN (1993) *Sex Crimes on Trial* (Edinburgh University Press)

BROWN, WENDY (1995) *States of Injury* (Princeton University Press)

BUTLER, JUDITH (1990) *Gender Trouble* (New York, Routledge)

—— (1993) *Bodies that Matter: On the Discursive Limits of "Sex"* (New York, Routledge)

—— (1997) *Excitable Speech* (New York, Routledge)

—— and SCOTT, JOAN W. (eds.) (1992) *Feminists Theorise the Political* (New York, Routledge)

CAIN, MAUREEN (1988) "Beyond Informal Justice", in Matthews (ed.), p. 51

—— (1995) "Horatio's Mistake: Notes on Some Spaces in an Old Text" (1995) 22 *Journal of Law and Society* 68

CAMERON, DEBORAH (1985) *Feminism and Linguistic Theory* (London, Macmillan)

—— (1990) *The Feminist Critique of Language: A Reader* (London, Routledge)

—— and FRAZER, ELIZABETH (1987) *The Lust to Kill: a feminist investigation of sexual murder* (Oxford, Polity Press)

CAMPBELL, BEATRIX (1993) *Goliath: Britain's Dangerous Places* (London, Methuen)

CAMPBELL, TOM (1983) *The Left and Rights* (London, Routledge and Kegan Paul)

CARLEN, PAT (1983) *Women's Imprisonment* (London, Routledge and Kegan Paul)

CHAMBERS, G. and MILLAR, A. (1987) "Proving Sexual Assault: Prosecuting the Offender or Persecuting the Victim?" in P. Carlen and A. Worrall (eds.), *Gender, Crime and Justice* (Milton Keynes, Open University Press)

CHAPMAN, JOHN W. and SHAPIRO, IAN (eds) (1991) *Democratic Community*, NOMOS XXXXV (New York University Press)

CHAYES, A. (1976) "The role of the judge in public law litigation" (1976) 89 *Harvard Law Review* 1281

CHEAH, PHENG, FRASER, DAVID and GRBICH, JUDITH (eds.) (1996) *Thinking Through the Body of the Law* (New York University Press)

CHODOROW, NANCY (1978) *The Reproduction of Mothering* (University of California Press)

CHURCH, JENNIFER (1997) "Ownership and the Body", in Meyers (ed.) p. 85

COHEN, STANLEY (1985) *Visions of Social Control* (Oxford, Polity Press)

COLLINS, HUGH (1982) *Marxism and Law*, Oxford, Clarendon Press)

—— (1997) *The Law of Contract* 3rd edn (London, Butterworths)

COMMISSION FOR RACIAL EQUALITY (1983) *Time for a Change?* (London, CRE)

—— (1985) *Review of the Race Relations Act 1976: Proposals for Change* (London, CRE)

CONNELL, R.W. (1987) *Gender and Power* (Oxford, Polity Press)

CORNELL, DRUCILLA (1987) "Beyond Tragedy and Complacency" (1987) 81 *Northwestern University Law Review* 693

—— (1991) *Beyond Accommodation: Ethical Feminism, Deconstruction and the Law* (London and New York, Routledge)

—— (1992) *The Philosophy of the Limit* (London and New York, Routledge)

—— (1992a) "The 'Postmodern Challenge to the Ideal of Community'", in Cornell (1992) p. 39

—— (1993) *Transformations: Recollective Imagination and Sexual Difference* (London and New York, Routledge)

—— (1995) *The Imaginary Domain* (London and New York, Routledge)

——, ROSENFELD, MICHEL and GRAY CARLSON, DAVID (eds.) (1992) *Deconstruction and the Possibility of Justice* (New York, Routledge)

COTTERRELL, ROGER (1981) "The Impact of Sex Discrimination Legislation" (1981) *Public Law* 469

—— (1989) *The Politics of Jurisprudence* (London, Butterworths)

—— (1992) "Law's Community: Legal Theory and the Image of Legality", (1992) 19 *Journal of Law and Society* 405

COTTERRELL, ROGER (1993) *The Sociology of Law: An Introduction*, 2nd edn (London, Butterworths)

COTTERRELL, ROGER (1995a) *Law's Community* (Oxford, Clarendon Press)
—— (1995b) "Socio-Legal Studies: Between Policy and Community"; in Cotterrell (1995a) p. 296
COWARD, ROSALIND (1984) *Female Desire* (London, Paladin)
CRENSHAW, KIMBERLE W. (1988) "Race, Reform and Retrenchment: Transformation and Legitimation in Anti-discrimination Law" (1988) 101 *Harvard Law Review* 1331
—— (1989) "Demarginalising the Intersection between Race and Sex" (1989) *University of Chicago Legal Forum* 139
DALE, J. and FOSTER, P. (1986) *Feminists and the Welfare State* (London, Routledge and Kegan Paul)
DALY, KATHLEEN (1989) "Criminal Justice Ideologies and Practices in Different Voices: Some Feminist Questions about Justice" (1989) 17 *International Journal of the Sociology of Law* 1
DANIELS, NORMAN (ed.) (1975) *Reading Rawls* (Oxford, Blackwell)
DAVIES, MARGARET (1994) *Asking the Law Question* (Sydney, Law Book Company)
—— (1996) *Delimiting the Law* (London, Pluto Press)
DELGADO, RICHARD (1987) "The Ethereal Scholar: Does Critical Legal Studies Have What Ethnic Minorities Want?" (1987) 22 *Harvard Civil Rights-Civil Liberties Law Review* 301
—— (1995) *The Rodrigo Chronicles: Conversations about America and Race* (New York University Press)
DERRIDA, JACQUES (1990) "Force of Law: The 'Mystical Foundation of Authority'" 11, *Cardozo Law Review*, also in Cornell *et al* (eds.) (1992), p. 3
DIPROSE, ROSALYN (1996) "The gift, sexed body property and the law", in Cheah *et al* (eds.) p. 120
DONZELOT, JACQUES (1979) *Policing the Family: Welfare Versus the State* (London, Hutchinson)
DOUGLAS, MARY (1966) *Purity and Danger* (London, Routledge and Kegan Paul)
DOUZINAS, COSTAS and WARRINGTON, RONNIE with SEAN MCVEIGH (1991) *Postmodern Jurisprudence: The Law of Texts in the Texts of Law* (London, Routledge)
—— and —— (1994) *Justice Miscarried: Ethics and Aesthetics in Law* (Hemel Hempstead, Harvester)
DRIPPS, DONALD A. (1992) "Beyond Rape: An Essay on the Difference Between the Presence of Force and the Absence of Consent" (1992) 92 *Columbia Law Review* 1780
DRYZEK, JOHN S. (1990) *Discursive Democracy. Politics, Policy and Political Science* (Cambridge University Press)
DWORKIN, ANDREA (1981) *Pornography: Men Possessing Women* (London, Women's Press)

—— and MacKinnon, Catharine (1988) *Pornography and Civil Rights: A New Day for Women's Equality* (Organizing against Pornography, Minneapolis)

Dworkin, Ronald (1975) "The original position", in Daniels (ed.) p. 1

—— (1977) *Taking Rights Seriously* (London, Duckworths)

—— (1981) "What is Equality?", Parts I and II (1981) 10 *Philosophy and Public Affairs* pp. 185, 283

—— (1986) *Law's Empire* (London, Fontana)

—— (1989) "Liberal Community" (1989) *California Law Review* 77: 479

—— (1990) "Equality, democracy, and the constitution: We the people in court" (1990) *Alberta Law Review* XXVIII:324

Eaton, Mary (1986) *Justice for Women?* (Milton Keynes, Open University Press)

Eisenstein, Zillah (1988) *The Female Body and the Law* (University of California Press)

Esping-Andersen, Gosta (1990) *The Three Worlds of Welfare Capitalism* (Oxford, Polity Press)

Farmer, Lindsay (1997) *Criminal Law, Tradition and Legal Order* (Cambridge University Press)

Fish, Stanley (1989) *Doing What Comes Naturally* (Durham NC, Duke University Press)

Fitzpatrick, Peter (1987) "Racism and the Innocence of Law" (1987) 14 *Journal of Law and Society* 119

—— (1988) "The Rise and Rise of Informalism", in Matthews (ed.), p. 178

—— (ed.) (1991) *Dangerous Supplements* (London, Pluto Press)

—— (1992a) *The Mythology of Modern Law* (London, Routledge)

—— (1992b) "The Impossibility of Popular Justice", in Santos (ed.) p. 177

—— (1995a) "Being Social in Socio-Legal Studies", (1995) 22 *Journal of Law and Society* 105

Fitzpatrick, Peter (1995b) "The Constitution of the Excluded: Indians and Others" in Ian Loveland (ed.) *A Special Relationship?* (Oxford University Press)

Foucault, Michel (1972) *The Archaeology of Knowledge* (London, Tavistock)

—— (1977) *Discipline and Punish*, transl. A. Sheridan (London, Penguin)

—— (1980) *Power/Knowledge: Selected writings and interviews* (Brighton, Harvester)

—— (1981) *The History of Sexuality* vol. 1 (London, Penguin)

Fraser, Nancy (1989) *Unruly Practices: Power, Discourse and Gender in Contemporary Social Theory* (Oxford, Polity Press)

—— (1997) *Justice Interruptus* (New York, Routledge)

Frazer, Elizabeth and Lacey, Nicola (1993) *The Politics of Community: A feminist critique of the liberal-communitarian debate* (Hemel Hempstead, Harvester)

FRAZER, ELIZABETH and LACEY, NICOLA (1994) "MacIntyre, Feminism and the Concept of Practice" in J. Horton and S. Mendus (eds.) *After MacIntyre* (Oxford, Polity Press) pp. 265–82

—— and —— (1995) "Politics and the Public in Rawls' *Political Liberalism*" (1995) 43 *Political Studies* 233

——, HORNSBY, JENNIFER and LOVIBOND, SABINA (eds.) (1992) *Ethics: A Feminist Reader* (Oxford, Basil Blackwell)

FREDMAN, SANDRA, STANLEY, DEIRDRE and SZYSZCZAK, ERICA (1992) "The Interaction of Race and Gender" in Hepple and Szyszcsak (eds.)

FREEMAN, ALAN (1978) "Legitimising Racial Discrimination through Anti-discrimination Law" (1978) 62 *Minnesota Law Review* 1049

FRIEDMAN, MARILYN (1997) "Autonomy and Social Relationships" in Meyers (ed.) p. 40

FRUG, MARY JO (1992) *Postmodern Legal Feminism* (New York: Routledge)

FUDGE, JUDY (1989) "The Effect of Entrenching a Bill of Rights on Political Discourse", (1989) 17 *International Journal of the Sociology of Law* 445

FUDGE, JUDY and GLASBEEK, HARRY (1992) "The Politics of Rights: A Politics with Little Class" (1992) 1 *Social and Legal Studies* 45

FUSS, DIANA (1989) *Essentially Speaking: Feminism, Nature and Difference* (London and New York, Routledge)

GABEL, PETER and KENNEDY, DUNCAN (1984) "Roll Over Beethoven" (1984) 36 *Stanford Law Review* 1

GARDBAUM, STEPHEN A. (1992) "Law, Politics and the Claims of Community", (1992) 90 *Michigan Law Review* 685

GATENS, MOIRA (1996) *Imaginary Bodies* (London, Routledge)

GENDERS, ELAINE and PLAYER, ELAINE (1989) *Race Relations in Prisons* (Oxford, Clarendon Press)

GIBSON, SUZANNE (1993) "The Discourse of Sex/War" (1993) *Feminist Legal Studies* 179

GILLIGAN, CAROL (1982) *In A Different Voice: Psychological Theory and Women's Development* (Cambridge, Mass, Harvard University Press)

GILROY, PAUL (1987) *There Ain't No Black in the Union Jack* (London, Hutchinson)

GOODRICH, PETER (1986) *Reading the Law* (Oxford, Basil Blackwell)

—— (1993a) "Sleeping with the Enemy": An Essay on the Politics of Critical Legal Studies in America" (1993) 68 *New York University Law Review* 389, reprinted in Goodrich (1997a)

—— (1993b) "Gynaetopia: Feminine Genealogies of Common Law" (1993) *Journal of Law and Society* 276, reprinted in Goodrich (1997a)

—— (1994) "*Jani Anglorum*: signs, symptoms, slips and interpretations in law", in Costas Douzinas, Peter Goodrich and Yifat Hachamovitch, (eds.) *Politics, Postmodernity and Critical Legal Studies*, (London, Routledge) p. 107 reprinted in Goodrich (1997a)

—— (1997b) "Law in the Courts of Love: Andreas Capellanus and the *Iudiciis Amoris*', in Goodrich (1997a)

—— (1997a) *Law in the Courts of Love* (London and New York, Routledge)

GORDON, PAUL (1988) "Black People and the Criminal Law: Rhetoric and Reality", (1988) 16 *International Journal of the Sociology of Law* 295

GORDON, ROBERT W. (1984) "Critical Legal Histories" (1984) 36 *Stanford Law Review* 57

GRAYCAR, REGINA and MORGAN, JENNY (1990) *The Hidden Gender of Law* (The Federation Press, Annandale)

GREGORY, JEANNE (1987) *Sex, Race and the Law* (London, Sage)

GROSZ, ELIZABETH (1994) *Volatile Bodies* (Sydney, Allen and Unwin)

GUTMANN, AMY (ed.) (1988) *Democracy and the Welfare State* (Princeton University Press)

HABERMAS, JÜRGEN (1975) *Legitimation Crisis*, transl. T. McCarthy (London, Heinemann)

—— (1981) *The Theory of Communicative Action*

—— (1984) Volume I: *Reason and the Rationalisation of Society*

—— (1987) Volume II: *Lifeworld and System: A Critique of Functionalist Reason* transl. T. McCarthy (Oxford, Polity Press)

—— (1986) "Law as Medium and Law as Institution", in Teubner (ed.) p. 203

—— (1992) *Faktizität und Geltung* (Frankfurt, Suhrkamp Verlag)

HAKSAR, VINIT (1979) *Equality, Liberty and Perfectionism* (Oxford University Press)

HALL, RUTH and LONGSTAFF, LISA (1997) "Defining Consent" (1997) *New Law Journal* 840

HARDING, SANDRA and MERRILL B. HINTIKKA (1987) *Discovering Reality* (Dordrecht, Kluwer)

HARRINGTON, CHRISTINE (1985) *Shadow Justice: The Ideology and Institutional-isation of Alternatives to Court* (Westport, Greenwood Press)

—— (1992) "Popular Justice, Populist Politics: Law in Community Organizing", in Santos (ed.) p. 177

HARRIS, ANGELA (1990) "Race and Essentialism in Feminist Legal Theory" (1990) 42 *Stanford Law Review* 581

HART, H.L.A. (1961) *Law, Liberty and Morality* (Oxford University Press)

—— (1968) *Punishment and Responsibility* (Oxford, Clarendon Press)

HAYEK, FRIEDRICH (1960) *The Constitution of Liberty* (London, Routledge and Kegan Paul)

—— (1976) *Law, Legislation and Liberty: ii: The Mirage of Social Justice* (London, Routledge and Kegan Paul)

HEPPLE, BOB and SZYSZCZAK, ERIKA (eds.) (1992) *Discrimination: The Limits of Law* (London, Mansell)

HERMAN, DIDI (1994) *Rights of Passage: Struggles for Lesbian and Gay Equality* (University of Toronto Press)

HERNES, HELGA MARIA (1987) *Welfare State and Woman Power* (Oslo, Norwegian University Press)

HILL COLLINS, PATRICIA (1990) *Black Feminist Thought* (London and New York, Routledge)

HILLYARD, PADDY (1993) *Suspect Community: People's Experiences of the Prevention of Terrorism Acts in Britain* (London, Pluto Press)

HONDERICH, TED (1982) "*On Liberty* and Morality-Dependent Harms" (1982) 30 *Political Studies* 504

HUNT, ALAN (1993) *Explorations in Law and Society: Toward a Constitutive Theory of Law* (London, Routledge)

—— and KERRUISH, VALERIE (1992) "Gender Discrimination in Law's Empire", in Hunt (ed.) *Reading Dworking Critically* (New York, Berg Publishers)

HUTCHINSON, ALLAN C. (ed.) (1989) *Critical Legal Studies* (Totowa, N.J., Rowman and Littlefield)

INSTITUTE OF RACE RELATIONS (1979) *Police Against Black People*, London, IRR)

IRIGARAY, LUCE (1985a) *Speculum of the Other Woman* (Ithaca, Cornell University Press)

—— (1985b) *This Sex which Is Not One* (Ithaca, Cornell University Press)

—— (1991) *Marine Lover of Friedrich Nietszche* (Columbia UP)

—— (1992) *J'aime a toi. Esquisse d'une felicité dans l'histoire* (Paris, Grasset) (translated as *I Love to You*, transl. A. Martin, London, Routledge 1996)

—— (1993a) *Je, Tu, Nous: Towards a Culture of Difference*, transl. Alison Martin, London, Routledge)

—— (1993b) *An Ethics of Sexual Difference*, transl. Carolyn Burke and Gillian C. Gill (London, Athlone)

—— (1994) *Thinking the Difference*, transl. Karin Montin (London, Athlone)

JACKSON, EMILY (1992) "Catharine MacKinnon and Feminist Jurisprudence" (1992) 19 *Journal of Law and Society* 195

JAGGAR, ALISON (1983) *Feminist Politics and Human Nature* (Brighton, Harvester)

JAGGAR, ALISON and BORDO, SUSAN R. (1989) *Gender/Body/Knowledge* (New Brunswick, Rutgers University Press)

JEFFREYS, SHEILA (1990) *Anticlimax* (London, Women's Press)

KAHN, PAUL W. (1989) "Community in Contemporary Constitutional Theory" (1989) 99 *Yale Law Journal* 1

KAPPELER, SUZANNE (1986) *The Pornography of Representation* (Oxford, Polity Press)

KELMAN, MARK (1981) "Interpretive construction in the substantive criminal law" 33 *Stanford Law Review*, 591

KELSEN, HANS (1967) *The Pure Theory of Law* (University of California Press)

KENNEDY, DUNCAN (1976) "Form and Substance in Private Law Adjudication" 89 *Harvard Law Review*, 1685

KENNEDY, HELENA (1992) *Eve Was Framed* (London, Chatto and Windus)

KENNEDY, RANDALL (1989) "Racial Critiques of Legal Academia" 102 *Harvard Law Review* 1745

KERRUISH, VALERIE (1992) *Jurisprudence as Ideology* (London, Routledge)

KINGDOM, ELIZABETH (1991) *What's Wrong with Rights? Problems for a Feminist Philosophy of Law* (Edinburgh University Press)

KYMLICKA, WILL (1989) *Liberalism, Community and Culture* (Oxford, Clarendon Press)

LACEY, NICOLA (1985) "The Territory of the Criminal Law" (1985) 5 *Oxford Journal of Legal Studies* 453

—— (1987) "Legislation against Sex Discrimination: Questions from a Feminist Perspective" (1987) 14 *Journal of Law and Society* 411

—— (1988) *State Punishment: Political Principles and Community Values* (London, Routledge)

—— (1989) "Feminist Legal Theory" (1989) 9 *Oxford Journal of Legal Studies* 383

—— (1992) "The Jurisprudence of Discretion: Escaping the Legal Paradigm", in K. Hawkins (ed.), *The Uses of Discretion* (Oxford, Clarendon Press) p. 361

—— (1994a) "Government as Manager, Citizen as Consumer", (1994) 57 *Modern Law Review* 534

—— (1994b) "Making Sense of Criminal Justice", in Lacey (ed.), *Criminal Justice: A Reader* (Oxford UP)

—— (1997) "On the Subject of Sexing the Subject . . .", in Naffine and Owens (eds.) p. 65

LACEY, NICOLA and WELLS, CELIA (1998) *Reconstructing Criminal Law* (London, Butterworths) (second edition)

LACEY, NICOLA and ZEDNER, LUCIA (1995) "Discourses of Community in Criminal Justice" (1995) *Journal of Law and Society* 93

LARRABEE, MARY JEANNE (ed.) (1993) *An Ethic of Care* (New York, Routledge)

LARSON, JANE (1993) " 'Women Understand So Little, They Call My Good Nature Deceit': A Feminist Rethinking of Seduction" 93 *Columbia Law Review* 375

LASH, SCOTT and URRY, JOHN (1994) *Economies of Signs and Space* (London, Sage)

LAWRENCE, CHARLES R. III (1987) "The Id, the Ego and Unequal Protection: Reckoning with Unconscious Racism" 39 *Stanford Law Review* 317

LE GRAND, JULIAN (1982) *The Strategy of Equality* (London, Allen and Unwin)

LEES, SUE (1996) *Carnal Knowledge* (London, Hamish Hamilton)

LEVINAS, EMMANUEL (1969) *Totality and Infinity: An Essay on Exteriority*, transl. Alphonso Lingis (Pittsburgh, Duquesne UP)

LITTLETON, CHRISTINE A. (1987) "Reconstructing Sexual Equality", 75 *California Law Review* 1279

LLOYD, GENEVIEVE (1984) *The Man of Reason* (London: Methuen)

LORDE, AUDRE (1984) *Sister Outsider* (New York, The Crossing Press)

LOVELAND, IAN (ed.) (1995) *Frontiers of Criminality* (London, Sweet and Maxwell)

LOVIBOND, SABINA (1989) "Feminism and Postmodernism" *New Left Review* p. 12

LUSTGARTEN, LAWRENCE (1980) *Legal Control of Racial Discrimination* (London, Macmillan)

—— (1986) "Racial Inequality and the Limits of Law" *Modern Law Review* 68

LYOTARD, J.-F, (1985) *Just Gaming* (Manchester University Press)

—— (1993) "The Other's Rights", in S. Hurley and S. Shute (eds.) *Of Human Rights: The 1993 Amnesty Lectures* (New York, Oxford University Press) p. 135

MCAUSLAN, PATRICK and MCELDOWNEY, JOHN (1986) *Law, Legitimacy and the Constitution* (London, Sweet and Maxwell)

MCBARNET, DOREEN (1981) *Conviction: Law, the State and the Construction of Justice* (London, Macmillan)

MCCOLGAN, AILEEN (1993) "In Defence of Battered Women Who Kill" (1993) 13 *Oxford Journal of Legal Studies* 508

MACCORMICK, NEIL (1993) "Reconstruction after Deconstruction: Closing in on Critique", in Norrie (ed.) p. 142

MACINTYRE, ALASDAIR (1981) *After Virtue* (London, Duckworth) (2nd edn. 1985)

—— (1988) *Whose Justice, Which Rationality?* (London, Duckworth)

—— (1990) *Three Rival Versions of Moral Enquiry* (London, Duckworth)

MACKINNON, CATHARINE A. (1979) *The Sexual Harassment of Working Women* (New Haven, Yale University Press)

—— (1983) "Feminism, Marxism, Method and the State: Towards a Feminist Jurisprudence" 8 *Signs* 635

—— (1987) *Feminism Unmodified* (Cambridge, Mass, Harvard University Press)

—— (1989) *Toward a Feminist Theory of the State* (Cambridge, Harvard University Press)

MACEDO, STEPHEN (1990) *Liberal Virtues* (Oxford, Clarendon Press)

MANSBRIDGE, JANE (1991) "Feminism and Democratic Community", in Chapman and Shapiro (ed.)

MARCUS, SHARON (1992) "Fighting Bodies, Fighting Words: A Theory and Politics of Rape Prevention" in Butler and Scott (eds.) p. 385

MATTHEWS, ROGER (ed.) (1988) *Informal Justice?* (London, Sage)

MERRY, SALLY Engle. (1988) "Legal Pluralism", 22 *Law and Society Review* 869

—— (1992) "Popular Justice and the Ideology of Social Transformation", in Santos (ed.) p. 161

MEYERS, DIANA Tietjens (ed.) (1997) *Feminists Rethink the Self* (Boulder, Colorado, Westview Press)

MICHELMAN, FRANK (1988) "Law's Republic" (1988) 97 *Yale Law Journal* 1493

—— (1990) "Private/Personal but Not Split" 63 *Southern California Law Review* 1783

MILL, JOHN STUART (1859) *On Liberty* (London, Harmondsworth)

MILLER, DAVID (1976) *Social Justice* (Oxford, Clarendon Press)

—— (1990) *Market, State and Community* (Oxford, Clarendon Press)

MILIBAND, RALPH (1969) *The State in Capitalist Society* (London, Weidenfeld and Nicolson)

MINOW, MARTHA (1987) "Justice Engendered" 101 *Harvard Law Review* 10

MINOW, MARTHA and SPELMAN, ELIZABETH (1990) "In Context" 63 *Southern California Law Review* 1597

MITCHELL, JULIET (1974) *Psychoanalysis and Feminism* (London, Allen Lane)

MITCHELL, JULIET and ROSE, JACQUELINE (1982) *Female Sexuality: Jacques Lacan and the Ecole Freudiènne* (New York, W.W. Norton & Co)

MODOOD, TARIQ (1988) "Black and Asian Identity" XIV *New Community* 397

—— (1992) "Colour, Class and Culture", in Hepple and Szyszczak (eds.)

MOI, TORIL (ed.) (1986) *The Kristeva Reader* (New York, Columbia University Press)

MORAN, LESLIE J. (1996) *The (Homo)sexuality of Law* (London, Routledge)

MURPHY, W.T. (1994) "One of Us? Politics, Difference and Affirmative Action", XIII *Current Legal Theory*, Special Issue 2: The Rhetoric of Reconstruction; Architectural Moves Beyond Interpretation, edited by Jan Broekman, David Kennedy and Jacques Lenoble 21–52

MURPHY, TIM (1997) *The Oldest Social Science? Configurations of Law in Modernity* (Oxford, Clarendon Press)

NAFFINE, NGAIRE (1990) *Law and the Sexes* (Sydney, Allen & Unwin)

—— (1994) "Possession: Erotic Love in the Law of Rape" 57 *Modern Law Review* 10

—— (1997) "The Body Bag", in Naffine and Owens (eds.) p. 79

NAFFINE, NGAIRE and OWENS, ROSEMARY (eds.) (1997) *Sexing the Subject of Law* (Sydney, Law Book Company)

NAGEL, THOMAS (1975) "Rawls on Justice", in Daniels (ed.) p. 16

NEDELSKY, JENNIFER (1989) "Reconceiving Autonomy" (1989) 1 *Yale Journal of Law and Feminism* 7

—— (1990) "Law, Boundaries and the Bounded Self" 30 *Representations* 162

—— (1993) "Reconceiving Rights as Relationship" *Review of Constitutional Studies* 1

—— (1995) "Meditations on Embodied Autonomy" 2 *Graven Images* 159

NICHOLSON, LINDA J. (ed.) (1990) *Feminism/Postmodernism* (London, Routledge)

NODDINGS, NEL (1984) *Caring: A feminist approach to ethics and moral education* (Berkeley, University of California Press)

NORRIE, ALAN (ed.) (1993) *Closure and Critique: New Directions in Legal Theory* (Edinburgh University Press)

—— (1993a) *Crime, Reason and History* (London, Weidenfeld and Nicolson)

—— (1993b) "Closure and Critique: Antinomy in Modern Legal Theory" in Norrie (ed.) p. 1

NOZICK, ROBERT (1974) *Anarchy, State and Utopia* (Oxford, Blackwell)

NUSSBAUM, MARTHA (1990) *Love's Knowledge* (Oxford University Press)

O'DONOVAN, KATHERINE (1985) *Sexual Divisions in Law* (London, Weidenfeld and Nicolson)

—— (1991) "Defences for Battered Women Who Kill" 18 *Journal of Law and Society* 219

—— (1997) "With Sense, Consent or Just a Con?" in Naffine and Owens (eds.) p. 47

O'DONOVAN, KATHERINE and SZYSZCZAK, ERIKA (1988) *Equality and Sex Discrimination Law* (Oxford, Blackwell)

OFFE, CLAUS (1984) *Contradictions of the Welfare State* (London, Hutchinson)

OKIN, SUSAN MOLLER (1989) *Justice, Gender and the Family* (New York, Basic Books)

—— (1991) "Gender, the Public and the Private" in David Held (ed.) *Political Theory Today* (Oxford, Polity Press) p. 67

OLSEN, FRANCES (1983) "The Family and the Market", 96 *Harvard Law Review* 1497

—— (1985) "The Myth of State Intervention in the Family" 18 *Michigan Journal of Law Reform* 835

—— (1990) "Feminism and Critical Legal Theory: An American Perspective" (1990) 18 *International Journal of the Sociology of Law* 199

—— (ed.) (1995) *Feminist Legal Theory*, vols I and II (London, Dartmouth)

PANNICK, DAVID (1986) *Sex Discrimination Law* (Oxford, Clarendon Press)

PASSERIN D'ENTREVES, MAURIZIO (1990) "Communitarianism and the Question of Tolerance" (1990) *Journal of Social Philosophy* 77

PATEMAN, CAROLE (1988) *The Sexual Contract* (Oxford, Polity Press)

—— (1989) *The Disorder of Women* (Oxford, Polity Press)

—— (1994) "The Rights of Women and Early Feminism" *Schweizerisches Jahrbuch für Politische Wissenschaft* (Special Issue) *Frauen und Politik* 19

—— (1995) "Democracy, Freedom and Special Rights", University of Wales, Swansea, John C. Rees Memorial Lecture

PETERS, ANTONIE A.G. (1986) "Law as Critical Discussion", in Teubner (ed.) p. 250

PHILLIPS, ANNE (1991) *Engendering Democracy* (Oxford, Polity Press)

PLANT, RAYMOND, LESSER, H. and TAYLOR-GOOBY, P. (1980) *Political Philosophy and Social Welfare* (London, Routledge and Kegan Paul)

POTTAGE, ALAIN (1994) "Recreating Difference" (1994) V *Law and Critique* 131

—— (1995) "A Unique and Different Subject of Law" (1995) 16 *Cardozo Law Review* 1161

POWER, MICHAEL (1994) "The Audit Society", in Hopwood and Miller (eds.), *Accounting as a Social and Institutional Practice* (Cambridge UP), p. 299

RADIN, MARGARET JANE (1990) "The Pragmatist and the Feminist" 63 *Southern California Law Review* 1699

RADIN, MARGARET JANE and MICHELMAN, FRANK (1991) "Pragmatist Poststructuralist Critical Legal Practice" 139 *University of Pennsylvania Law Review* 1019

RAWLS, JOHN (1971) *A Theory of Justice* (Cambridge Mass, Harvard University Press)

—— (1980) "Kantian Constructivism in Moral Theory" (1980) 77 *Journal of Philosophy* 515

—— (1985) "Justice as Fairness: Political not Metaphysical" (1985) 14 *Philosophy and Public Affairs* 223

—— (1993) *Political Liberalism* (New York, Columbia University Press)

RAZ, JOSEPH (1986) *The Morality of Freedom* (Oxford, Clarendon Press)

—— (1995) *Ethics in the Public Domain* (Oxford, Clarendon Press)

RHODE, DEBORAH L. (1990) "Feminist Critical Theories" 42 *Stanford Law Review* 617

RICH, ADRIENNE (1977) *On Lies, Secrets and Silence* (New York, W.W. Norton)

ROBERTS, NICKIE (1986) *The Front Line* (London, Women's Press)

RORTY, RICHARD (1979) *Philosophy and the Mirror of Nature* (Princeton University Press)

—— (1989) *Contingency, Irony and Solidarity* (Cambridge University Press)

—— (1991a) *Objectivity, Relativism and Truth* (Cambridge University Press)

—— (1991b) "Feminism and Pragmatism" 59 *Radical Philosophy* 3

ROSE, NIKOLAS (1987) "Beyond the Public/Private Division: Law, Power and the Family" 14 *Journal of Law and Society* 61

ROSENBLUM, NANCY (ed.) (1989) *Liberalism and the Moral Life* (Cambridge, Harvard University Press)

RUDDICK, SARA (1990) *Maternal Thinking: Towards a politics of peace* (London, Women's Press)

RYAN, ALAN (ed.) (1979) *The Idea of Freedom* (Oxford University Press)

SALECL, RENATA (1994) *The Spoils of Freedom: Psychoanalysis and feminism after the fall of socialism* (London and New York, Routledge

SANDEL, MICHAEL (1982) *Liberalism and the Limits of Justice* (Cambridge University Press)

SANDLAND, RALPH (1995) "Between 'Truth' and 'Difference': Poststructural-ism, Law and the Power of Feminism" III *Feminist Legal Studies* 3

SANTOS, BOAVENTURA DE SOUSA (1982) "Law and Community: The Changing Nature of State Power in Late Capitalism", in Abel (ed.) vol. 1, p. 249

—— (1987) "Law: A Map of Misreading. Toward a Postmodern Con-ception of Law", *Journal of Law and Society* vol. 14 279–302

—— (ed.) (1992) *State Transformation, Legal Pluralism and Community Justice*, vol.1, *Social and Legal Studies*, issue 2

—— (1992a) "State, Law and Community in the World System", in Santos (ed.), p. 131

—— (1995) *Toward a New Common Sense* (London and New York, Routledge)

SARAT, AUSTIN (1990) "Power, Resistance and the Legal Consciousness of the Welfare Poor" (1990) 2 *Yale Journal of Law and the Humanities* 343

SCULL, ANDREW (1983) "Community Corrections: Progress, Panacea or Pretence?, in D. Garland and P. Young (eds.), *The Power to Punish* (London, Heinemann) p. 146

SEGAL, LYNN (1987) *Is the Future Female?* (London, Virago)

—— (1990) *Slow Motion: Changing Masculinities, Changing Men* (London, Virago)

SELZNICK, PHILIP (1987) "The idea of a communitarian morality" (1987) 75 *California Law Review* 445

—— (1989) "Dworkin's unfinished task", (1989) 77 *California Law Review* 505

SHERRY, SUZANNA (1986) "Civic virtue and the feminine voice in constitu-tional adjudication" (1986) 72 *Virginia Law Review* 543

SMART, CAROL (1976) *Women, Crime and Criminology* (London, Routledge Kegan Paul)

—— (1984) *The Ties that Bind* (London, Routledge)

—— (1989) *Feminism and the Power of Law*, London, Routledge)

—— (1990) "Law's Truth, Women's Experience" in Regina Graycar (ed.) *Dissenting Opinions* (Sydney, Allen & Unwin)

—— (1995) *Law, Crime and Sexuality* (London, Sage)

SPELMAN, ELIZABETH (1989) *Inessential Woman* (Boston, Beacon Press)

SPIVAK, GAYATRI (1992) "French Feminism Revisited", in Butler and Scott (eds.) p. 54

STANG DAHL, TOVE (1986) *Women's Law* (Oslo, Norwegian University Press)

SUNSTEIN, CASS (1988) "Beyond the republican revival" 97 *Yale Law Journal* 1539

TAYLOR, CHARLES (1985) *Philosophy and the Human Sciences* (Cambridge University Press)

—— (1989) *Sources of the Self* (Cambridge University Press)

TEMKIN, JENNIFER (1987) *Rape and the Legal Process* (London, Sweet and Maxwell)

TEUBNER, GUNTHER (ed.) (1986) *Dilemmas of Law in the Welfare State* (Berlin, Walter de Gruyter)

—— (1986a) "After Legal Instrumentalism? Strategic Models of Post-Regulatory Law", in Teubner (ed.) p. 299

—— (1993) *Law as an Autopoietic System* (Oxford, Basil Blackwell)

THORNTON, MARGARET (1986) "Feminist Jurisprudence: Illusion or Reality?" 3 *Australian Journal of Law and Society* 5

——(1990) *The Liberal Promise* (Oxford University Press)

TURNER HOSPITAL, JANETTE (1992) *The Last Magician* (London, Virago)

UNGER, ROBERTO M. (1983) "The critical legal studies movement in America" 99 *Harvard Law Review* 561

—— (1987) *Politics: a Work in Constructive Social Theory* (3 volumes) (Cambridge University Press)

URBAN WALKER, MARGARET (1997) "Picking up Pieces: Lives, Stories and Integrity" in Meyers (ed.) p. 62

VOLPP, LETI (1994) "(Mis)identifying Culture: Asian Women and the 'Cultural Defence'" 17 *Harvard Women's Law Journal* 57

WAGNER, PETER (1993) *A Sociology of Modernity: Liberty and Discipline* (London, Routledge)

WALBY SYLVIA (1990) *Theorising Patriarchy* (Oxford, Blackwell)

WALZER, MICHAEL (1983) *Spheres of Justice* (New York, Basic Books)

—— (1987) *Interpretation and Social Criticism* (Cambridge, Harvard University Press)

WATSON, SOPHIE (ed.) (1990) *Playing the State* (London: Verso)

WEAIT, MATTHEW (1996) "Fleshing it Out", in Lionel Bentley and Leo Flynn (eds.) *Law and the Senses* (London, Pluto Press) p. 160

WELLS, CELIA (1982) "Swatting the Subjectivist Bug" *Criminal Law Review* 209

—— (1994) "Battered Woman Syndrome and Defences to Homicide" (1994) 14 *Legal Studies* 266

WEST, CORNEL (1989) *The American Evasion of Philosophy: A Genealogy of Pragmatism* (Madison, University of Wisconsin Press)

WEST, ROBIN (1993) "Legitimating the Illegitimate: A Comment on 'Beyond Rape'" 93 *Columbia Law Review* 1442

WILLIAMS, JOAN C. (1989) "Deconstructing Gender" (1989) 87 *Michigan Law Review* 797

WILLIAMS, PATRICIA J. (1991) *The Alchemy of Race and Rights* (Cambridge, Mass University of Harvard Press,)

—— (1995) *The Rooster's Egg* (Cambridge, Harvard University Press)

WILLIAMS, SUSAN (1990) "Feminism's Search for the Feminine: Essentialism, Utopianism and Community" *Cornell Law Review* 700

WOLFENDEN COMMITTEE (1957) *Report of the Committee on Homosexual Offences and Prostitution* (Cmnd. 247, LONDON, HMSO)

YOUNG, IRIS MARION (1987) "Impartiality and the Civic Public", in Benhabib and Cornell (eds.)

—— (1990a) *Throwing Like a Girl* (Bloomington, Indiana University Press)

—— (1990b) *Justice and the Politics of Difference* (Princeton University Press)

—— (1990c) "The ideal of community and the politics of difference" in L. Nicholson (ed.)

ZEDNER, LUCIA (1995) "Regulating Sexual Offences within the Home" in Loveland (ed.) p. 173

ZIZEK, SLAVOJ (1989) *The Sublime Object of Ideology* (London, Verso)

Index

Abel, 131, 140, 203, 236
academy, 124, 142, 164, 221
accountability of judges, 43
Ackerman, 54
advertising, 87
affective aspects of legal practice, 12
affective aspects of life, 107
affirmative action, 25, 36
Afro-Caribbean perspectives, 29, 31, 33–4, 68
Allen, 203
American philosophical pragmatism, 228
analytical jurisprudence, 3, 13, 169, 224
Anderson, 131, 133
anti-discrimination legislation, 19–45, 230, 239, 242
    feminist critique, 22–32
    implicit validation of discrimination, 25–6
    indirect discrimination, 22
    individual complaint, 23–4
    problems of British legislation, 21
    problems of symmetry, 25
anti-pornography ordinance, *see* pornography
appeal court judges, 162
Ashworth, 104
Asian perspectives, 29, 31–4, 68
Atkins, 61, 189
autonomy, 52, 54–5, 67, 72, 86, 96, 104–6, 112, 115, 117–24, 127, 154, 198, 244
    and relational aspects, 119–22

Barron, 136, 163
Barry, 51, 54, 65, 67
Barber, 65
battered women's syndrome, 96, 202
Bauman, 130, 133, 141, 225, 227
Bell, 19
Benhabib, 65, 125, 128, 139, 154–5, 173, 201, 214, 221, 227
Benn, 71
Berlin, 75, 77, 105, 119
Bernstein, 138, 227
Beveridge Report, 50
body, 201
    male norm, 108
    women's bodies, 109, 136, 197
Bordo, 137
Bottomley, 2, 9
Bourdieu, 109, 174
Box, 139

Boyle, 224
Braidotti, 136, 150
Braithwaite, 141
Brest, 140
Brison, 110, 116, 119–20
Bronnit, 121
Brown, 55, 100, 113–4, 116, 123, 175, 187
Burman, 113
Butler, 100, 108–9, 114–5, 132, 134, 136, 190, 241

Cain, 140, 160, 228
Cameron, 91, 210
Campbell, 39, 51, 57, 139, 243
Canadian Charter of Rights, 92–3
capitalist societies, 74
care in the community, 133
caring model, 201; *see also* ethic of care
Carlen, 203, 230
Carlson, 146
Cartesian, 107, 111
castration, 127, 207
Chambers, 28
Chayes, 37
Cheah, 107
children, 61, 63, 74, 105, 115, 136, 242
    custody, 10, 190, 242
Chodorow, 206
Church, 106, 110, 114–5
citizenship, 50–1, 59, 88, 96, 120, 131, 136, 152, 163, 190, 229, 242
    female conception, 61–2
civic republican thought, 140, 228
class action, 37
closure/critique dichotomy, 167–87
    exploded, 184, 187
closure, 182
    defined, 168
Cohen, 131, 238
Collins, 7, 11, 193, 230, 241
common law, 143
communitarian perspectives, 15, 54–7, 64, 129–47, 183, 228
    conceptual framework, 139
    conservatism, 137–9, 184–5
    dialogic communitarianism, 152
    notions of community, 138
community as metaphor, 146, 148
Conaghan, 2, 9

Connell, 31, 177
conservatism, 137–9, 160, 184–5
constitutional court, 43
construction, 14; *see also* reconstruction
contextualisation, 6, 202–3
    recontextualisation, 6–7, 202–3
contract law, 11, 74
Cornell, 2, 8, 80–1, 94, 99, 111, 117–18, 120,
    123, 141, 146, 149, 151–2, 154–5, 174–5,
    181–3, 187, 190–1, 192, 196, 206–11, 218,
    226, 228, 232, 241, 244
corporeality, 110–24
Cotterrell, 25, 140, 145, 161, 222, 224–5, 232,
    234, 237–8, 245
Coward, 87–8, 91
Crenshaw, 19, 44, 230
criminal law, 11, 98–124, 197–204, 230
    criminal responsibility, 198–9
    defences, 199, 201–2
    philosophical framework, 122
criminal legal subject, 111
critical and ethical *see* ethical issues
critical legal analysis, 145, 200
critical legal scholarship, 8–9
critical legal studies, 4, 8, 130
critical legal theory, 5–7, 11, 13, 27, 126–7, 146,
    161–2, 224
    and socio-legal studies, 163
    conception of, 222
    scepticism about ethics, 224–8
critical methodology, 32–3, 46
critical race theory, 13, 241
critical social theory, 27, 29, 42
critical theory, 205
    and modernist/post-modernist spectrum,
        153
    pluralist approach, 31
critique, 235–49
    and utopia, 225
    defined, 168, 231

Dale, 59
Daly, 199, 203
dangerous supplement, 11, 80, 232
Daniels, 65
Davies, 7, 169
Deleuze, 107
Delgado, 20, 243
democracy, 162–4, 237, 242, 248
d'Entreves, 185
Derrida, 81, 126, 149, 158, 173–4, 176, 208,
    210, 226, 232
dichotomies, 193–4
Diprose, 106, 110, 115
discourse
    discourse ethics, 153–5
    discourse theory, 179
    discursive community, 159
    discursive legitimation, 152, 159

discrimination, 189–92; *see also* anti-discrimina-
    tion legislation, indirect discrimination
Donzelot, 74
Douglas, 123
Douzinas, 141, 146, 151, 155, 161, 228
Dripps, 106
Dryzek, 152–3
Dworkin (A), 87, 89, 91–2, 95, 97, 179, 213,
    228, 235
Dworkin (R), 42, 54–6, 58, 63, 140, 142, 146–7,
    191, 224
    and universalism, 146–7
    on integrity, 10, 146
    theory of justice, 47–50

Eaton, 203, 230
egalitarian ideology, 25
egalitarian pluralism, 43–4
Eisenstein, 107
Eliot, 219
equality, 3, 27, 30, 38, 42, 48, 59–62, 69, 78,
    118, 145, 156, 170, 174–5, 188, 191–2,
    196, 226, 229, 239–42, 248
    equality of opportunity, 22–3
Esping-Anderson, 49, 52
essentialism *see* legal essentialism, woman
ethic of care, 5–6
ethic of rights, 5–6
ethics, 86, 146, 148, 153, 154, 157, 221–33
    and social practices, 230
    critical and ethical, 149–57
    democratic exchange, 153
    post-modernist notion, 226–8

fascism, 154
faith, 155
family, 58, 60, 62–4, 73–6, 81, 85, 138, 186, 223
Farmer, 199
feminism
    epistemological basis, 187
    modernist and post-modernist links, 181–2,
        186–7
    post-structuralist feminisms, 246
feminist jurisprudence *see* feminist legal theory
feminist lawyers, 96
feminist legal scholars, 186
feminist legal theory, 2–3, 7, 11–14, 27, 130,
    167–87
    and interpretivism, 15
    and neutrality, 188–220
    and playing the game, 185
    difference feminism, 3–4, 188–9, 191–3,
        205–6, 211–13, 218, 231–2, 245
    for and against, 168–75
    liberal feminism, 3–4, 188–92, 229, 231
    methodology, 3, 15, 46
    relationship with other forms of critical social
        theory, 13–14
feminist political theory, 62, 71

feminist rhetoric
  as critical tool, 204
feminist social theory, 26–32
Fish, 140
Fitzpatrick, 11, 19, 20, 26, 94, 143, 160, 205,
  221, 224, 232
Foster, 59
Foucault, 7, 98, 107, 110, 176
  on power, 9, 76, 83, 157
Frankfurt School, 11, 130, 228
Fraser, 51, 58–9, 60, 74, 78, 173, 182
Frazer, 15, 42, 47, 55, 65, 91, 105, 119, 130,
  135, 138–9, 152, 185, 191, 193, 213, 225,
  240
Fredman, 19
freedom, 52, 57, 77–8, 81, 194
  positive/negative, 52, 75, 77–8, 119
Freeman, 36, 92
Freud, 107, 207
Friedman, 115, 119, 120
Frug, 6, 12, 192, 201, 230
Fudge, 25, 92–3, 196, 243
Fuss, 173, 182, 206

Gabel, 225, 232
Gardbaum, 146
Gatens, 107
Gaus, 71
gay and lesbian culture, 241
gender see sex/gender
Genders, 23, 31
Gilligan, 5–6, 136, 171, 201
Glasbeek, 92–3
Goodrich, 130, 141–2, 144, 150–1, 159, 208,
  211
Gordon, 20, 23, 224–5, 232
Graycar, 89, 94
Greeks, 50
Gregory, 37
Grosz, 107, 108–9
group rights, 34–45
  cultural rights, 35
  remedial rights, 35–45
Gutmann, 61

Habermas, 11, 58, 74, 130–1, 151, 162,
  227
Haksar, 75
Hall, 121
harassment, 87, 180
Harding, 137
Harrington, 143, 160
Harris, 19, 108, 206
Hart, 77, 198
Hayek, 49
Hegel, 151
Hepple, 21, 41
Herman, 44, 243
hermeneutics, 130

Hernes, 57–60
hierarchy, 194
  hierarchical cultural discourse, 84
  hierarchically dichotomised thinking, 80–1
  hierarchically gendered, 2, 192, 194
  hierarchy of knowledges, 172
Hillyard, 139
Hintikka, 137
Hoggett, 60, 189
holistic approach, 5, 201
Honderich, 105
Hornsby, 240
Hunt, 145, 161, 191
Hutchinson, 224
hysteria, 108

imaginary domain, 117–18, 120–1
inaugural lecture, 98–9
incest, 214
India, 41
indirect discrimination, 36–7, 191
institutional sexism and racism, 23
interpretive communities, 140, 142–3, 158
interpretive method, 15, 183–4
  and conservatism, 184–5
intuitive judgements, 6
Irigaray, 6, 99, 108–10, 150, 154, 156, 188,
  194–5, 206–7, 210, 212–8, 226, 233, 235,
  243–6
Italian Communist Party, 213

Jackson, 100
Jaggar, 65, 68, 72, 73, 85, 137, 193
Jamieson, 113
Japan, 68
Jeffreys, 87, 91
jurisprudence:
  antediluvian, 169
  contemporary, 148
  conventional, 12–13
  traditional, 169–70
  see also analytical jurisprudence, feminist legal
    theory, legal theory
justice, 3, 46–50, 54, 58–9, 63, 65–70, 78,
  145–6, 156–7, 161–3, 190, 196, 226, 247–8
  informal justice, 143, 152, 159–61, 203, 235
  legal and social, 199
  social justice, 49

Kahn, 130, 159
Kant, 115
Kappeler, 87
Kelman, 11, 199, 224
Kelsen, 7, 10
Kennedy, 19, 20, 31, 204, 224–5, 232
Kerruish, 169, 172, 191
Keynes, 237
Kingdom, 196, 243
Kymlicka, 35, 48, 54, 56

Lacan, 99, 111, 118, 132–3, 136, 149, 163, 207–10, 212, 215

Lacey, 2, 15, 19, 42, 47, 52, 55, 65, 93–4, 104–5, 109, 119, 130–1, 138–9, 152, 156, 177, 185, 191, 193, 197–200, 213, 225

language, 150, 152, 178–9, 196, 207, 210–12, 233, 246

Larrabee, 201

Larson, 101

Lash, 130, 139

law, 186, 190, 247–8

  and otherness, 158

  and political action, 44–5

  and politics, 43

  autonomy of law, 7–8, 168–9, 173, 175, 186, 245

  centrality of law, 8–9

  coherence of law, 10–11

  epistemology of law, 8, 125

  equality before the law, 38

  law's community, 125–64

  left-wing scepticism, 44

  legal ideology, 127

  neutrality of law, 5, 7–8, 28, 110, 145, 158, 169, 186

  objectivity of law, 7–8, 28, 125, 145, 158, 169, 186

  power of law, 218

  rationality of law, 12

  substantive law and procedure, 28–9, 37

  system of enacted norms, 9–10

  universality of law, 158

law and society, 8

law in context, 4, 221

law reform, 94, 97; *see also* reformism

Lawrence, 19, 35

law schools, 20, 124, 162, 226

Lees, 101

legal education, 1, 12, 142, 226

legal essentialism, 173

legal paradigm, 164, 193–5

legal pluralism, 161

legal reasoning, 5–6, 144, 168

legal scholarship, 248

legal text, 158–9, 162

legal theory, 2

  most important project, 249

  see also analytical jurisprudence, feminist legal theory, jurisprudence

Le Grand, 59

Levinas, 151, 153–4, 156

liberal-communitarian debate, 129–35

liberal ideolog *see* liberal perspectives

liberal legal scholarship, 4–5, 224

liberal perspectives, 14–15, 22–3, 25, 27–30, 38–9, 42, 46–50, 54–9, 61–7, 72–3, 75, 77–8, 81, 85–6, 88, 104–5, 115, 117–19, 136, 138–40, 144–5, 149, 160–1, 169–71, 174, 183, 188, 190–2, 196, 198–200, 213, 229, 232, 239–40

  and welfare state, 56

  conceptions of the good, 54–5

  discourse of rights, 243–4

  division between individual and society, 55–6

liberation theology, 176

line drawing, 154

litigation strategies, 92–3

Littleton, 30, 157, 196, 240, 241

Lloyd, 79, 193

Longstaff, 121

Lorde, 173, 196

Lovibond, 179, 240

Lustgarten, 19, 34

Lyotard, 163, 174

MacCormick, 168, 225

Macedo, 54

MacIntyre, 64, 129, 183, 185

MacKinnon, 2, 8, 19, 30, 82, 87–9, 91–2, 95, 97, 100, 113, 115, 170–1, 179–80, 213, 235

Malaysia, 41

male/female dichotomies, 79–81

Mansbridge, 65, 137

Marcus, 100, 209

market, 73–4, 131, 136

marriage, 69–70, 74–5

marxist perspective, 8–9, 13, 31, 72, 119, 130, 162, 193, 206, 248

masculinity, 5, 192

Matthews, 140, 203

McAuslan, 76

McBarnett, 230

McColgan, 201

McEldowney, 76

Menski, 41

mens rea, 111–2, 198

Merleau-Ponty, 107

Merry, 140

method in legal theory, 167

Meure, 94, 104, 199

Meyers, 107

Michelman, 81–2, 130, 140, 155

Miliband, 57

Mill, 57, 75, 77, 105, 170

Millar, 28

Miller, 51–4, 57

mind

  primacy over body, 107

  mind/body dualism, 107–10, 111–24

Minow, 201

Mitchell, 206

modernist approach:

  modernity without illusions, 227

  see also post-modernism), 15, 174

Modood, 20, 33

Moi, 99

monetarist economics, 131
Moran, 102, 241
Morgan, 89, 94
multinational corporations, 76
Murphy, 146

Naffine, 2, 74, 102, 104, 107, 115, 192–5, 199, 229
Nagel, 47
nationalism, 133
natural law theory, 170, 176
Nedelsky, 6, 86, 115, 117, 119–20, 123, 154, 157, 193, 196, 240, 243
need, 51–3
neutrality, 28
New College Oxford, 99
Nicholson, 173, 177, 182
Nietzsche, 107, 194, 215
Noddings, 136
Nordic countries, 51–2
normative reconstruction, 221, 239–49
Norrie, 111, 198–200, 205, 225
nostalgia, 228
Nozick, 49
Nussbaum, 183

objectivity, 28
O'Donovan, 2, 19, 25, 30, 57, 72, 83–4, 92, 102, 121, 191–2, 201, 226
Oedipus, 206
Offe, 52
Okin, 46–7, 57, 61–6, 68, 72, 78, 185
Olsen, 2, 11, 57, 72, 75, 80, 84, 137, 191, 194, 232
oppression
    diversity, 31–2, 40–1
Oslo School of Women's Law, 9
otherness, 79–80, 114, 122, 132, 134–5, 143, 147, 149–51, 153–6, 160–1, 163, 194, 205, 207, 209, 216
Owens, 2, 107

Pannick, 37
Pateman, 59–61, 71, 113, 137, 229, 247
penis/phallus distinction, 206–8
personal is political, 72
Peters, 152, 158
Phillips, 41, 65
Plant, 51, 57
Player, 23
pluralism, 31, 161, 184
policing policies, 10
political theory
    feminist critique, 67–70
pornography, 71, 86–97, 213
    and sex discrimination, 91
    anti-pornography ordinance, 89–95, 179, 214, 235, 242
    definition, 89

positivist legal scholarship, 4–5, 7–8
post-enlightenment modernism, 174
post-enlightenment political theory, 83
post-modern approach, 15, 130–1, 174, 181–3, 186
    post-modern jurisprudence, 141, 151
Pottage, 214, 244, 246
Power, 131
power, 76–7, 83–4, 114, 131, 147, 156–8, 162, 196, 200, 203, 210–11, 232, 235, 237, 240–1, 246
    ideological power, 85
    power relations, 69–70, 113, 138
    see also Foucault
precedent, 158
pregnancy, 24, 247
privacy, 81–2, 86
psychoanalysis, 99–100, 111, 132–6, 149, 163, 206–12, 215, 245
public/private distinction, 11, 27, 29–30, 57–60, 62–4, 68–70, 71–97, 137, 209, 232
    normative premises, 57
    regulative inference, 95–7
    spheres, 73, 82–5, 88, 91
    values, 79–82, 84

queer theory, 13

race discrimination, 19–45
racism, 135, 148, 154
Radin, 81–2, 155
rape, 2, 11, 28, 75, 87, 89, 96, 99–102, 105–6, 111–23, 190, 204
    affective dimensions, 115–17
    definition, 106, 121
    marital rape, 69–70, 241–2
    relation to property, 106, 113–14
    trials, 114, 116, 122
Rawls, 47–50, 54–6, 58, 60, 63–6, 78, 129, 183
Raz, 39, 54, 56, 75
Reagan, 51, 131
reasonable person, 8
reconstruction, 11, 221; see also normative reconstruction
redistribution, 49–50, 53, 69
reformism, 89, 234–49
reverse discrimination; see also affirmative action, 41–2
rhetoric, 246–7
    as political action, 211–16, 237
Rhode, 130, 176
Rich, 91
right and good, 130, 227
rights, 3, 27, 67, 119, 145–6, 174, 190–1, 196, 201, 212–18, 226, 229, 235, 239, 241–8
    individualistic character, 27, 39, 247
    liberal rights theory, 27
    original position, 65–6
    political rights, 36

rights (*cont.*):
  reconceived, 243–4
  rhetorical counter-strategies, 219
  right to civil identity, 213
  see also group rights
Roberts, 94
Romans, 50
Rorty, 130, 177, 179, 182, 212, 226
Rose, 76, 206
Rosenblum, 54
Rosenfeld, 146
rotten tomato
  strategy of throwing, 185
Ruddick, 136
rule of law, 25, 27, 188
Ryan, 105

Salecl, 118, 125, 127, 132–3, 135–6, 163
Samson, 106
Sandel, 42, 48, 54–5, 64, 129–30, 183
Sandland, 228, 242
Santos, 126, 140, 148, 158, 160–2, 203, 218,
  224, 236, 238
Sarat, 148
Scott, 190
Scull, 131
Segal, 91, 94
Selznick, 129, 145
sex discrimination, 19–45
sex/gender, 2–3, 5, 7, 9, 13–14, 31, 60–6, 68–9,
  72, 79–80, 85, 98, 107–8, 111–24, 137,
  162, 172, 181, 188, 192, 194, 196–7, 200,
  205, 210–11, 218, 239
  and race, 19–34
  sex/gender distinction, 2, 189–90
  social construct, 109–110
sexism, 19
sexual harassment, 29
sexual integrity, 117–24
sexuality, 10, 63, 98–124
  legal paradigm, 102–3
  values, 104–7
sexual offences, 99–124
Shale, 173
Sherry, 130
signifiers, 132–4, 146, 207
silenced voices, 6, 8, 44, 90, 116, 125, 172, 200,
  208–10
Smart, 2, 7–9, 19, 25, 28, 30, 74, 87, 89, 101,
  114, 157, 167, 171–3, 177–82, 187, 191–2,
  196, 224–6, 229, 242–3
social meaning of law, 9
social theory
  conception of, 222–3
social welfare benefits, 10
socio-legal studies, 4, 157, 159–61, 191, 221
  conception of, 222
  relation with legal theory, 223–4, 237
  relation with sociology of law, 223, 235, 237

sociology of law, 245
  conception of, 222
socio-theoretic understanding, 240–9
South Africa, 41
Southall Black Sisters, 32
Spelman, 201, 206
Spinoza, 107
Spivak, 215
Stang Dahl, 9, 60, 162, 177
Stanley, 19
state, 73–7, 83
stereotypes, 22–3, 32–3, 100, 113–14, 197, 202,
  205, 212, 216, 245
Sunstein, 130, 140
Szyszczak, 19, 21, 25, 30, 41, 92, 191

Taylor, 52, 55, 129, 183, 185, 193, 226
Temkin, 28, 99, 101, 113, 122
Teubner, 8, 160–1, 179, 238
text, 246; *see also* legal text
Thatcher, 51, 61, 131, 133, 237
theory:
  grand and abstract, 172
  grand theory, 176–80, 184, 186
theory and practice, 174
Thornton, 92, 167, 171
tort of sexual deceit, 101
truth, 177–9, 182–4, 186
Turner Hospital, 125–7

Unger, 8, 39–41, 130, 141, 182–3, 225, 232
Urban Walker, 118, 123
Urry, 130, 139
US Constitution, 90
utopian project, 3, 81, 84, 146, 149, 180,
  182, 187, 193, 196, 208, 210, 225–7,
  235–49
  characterisation, 233–4
  link with language, 233

virginity, 213–15
Volpp, 35, 41, 230

Wagner, 130, 182
Walby, 59, 177
Walzer, 50, 64, 67, 129, 183, 185
Warrington, 141, 146, 151, 155, 161, 228
Watson, 59
Weait, 104
welfare state, 46, 50–4, 59–61, 66–70
Wells, 94, 102, 104, 199
West, 113, 120, 130
Western countries, 133
Western metaphysics, 112
Western thought, 193
white male norm, 24–5, 30, 34, 60–1, 113, 123,
  171, 191–2, 230, 240
white male privilege, 27–8
wife battering, 76, 87

Williams, 19, 31, 108, 115, 183, 197, 241, 243, 246
Wolfenden Report, 77–8, 103
woman, 181–2
    essentialist view, 245
    weak essentialist notion, 182
Women Against Rape, 121
Women Law Teachers Group, 1–2

Women's Legal Education and Action Fund, 92
world vision, 248

Young, 58, 69, 74, 79, 81, 86, 96, 107, 139, 157, 214

Zedner, 102, 131
Zizek, 132